AF435665

Incoterms 2020
User's manual

Alfonso Cabrera Cánovas

Collection: Comercio internacional
Director: David Soler

Incoterms 2020. User's manual
1st edition, September 2024

© Alfonso Cabrera Cánovas
© of this edition, ICG Marge, SL
Original title in Spanish: *Manual de uso de las reglas Incoterms 2020*

Publisher: Marge Books
Brutau, 160 – 08203 Sabadell (Barcelona)
Tel. 931 429 486 – marge@margebooks.com
www.margebooks.com

Publisher Manager: Hèctor Soler
Translator: José M. Collazos
Editorial collaborator: Nadia Peiró
Infographic: José Soto
Make-up editor: Mercedes Lara
Printed by: Arteos Digital, S.L. (Barcelona)

ISBN printed edition: 978-84-10238-24-4
ISBN digital PDF edition: 978-84-19109-74-3
ISBN digital ePUB edition: 978-84-10238-43-5

Legal Deposit: B 18199-2024

The paper used in this book has not been bleached with elemental chlorine (CI_2).

*To my wife, Juana Mari,
and my daughter, Virginia,
who make me happy.*

Index

About the author

Alfonso Cabrera Cánovas holds a degree in Economics and Business Studies from the University of Murcia and has been a lecturer in Commercial Organization and Management in the field of vocational training since 1996.

He teaches Administrative Management of International Trade, International Transport of Goods and International Negotiation at the IES Príncipe de Asturias (Lorca, Murcia) as part of the Higher Course in International Trade.

He is a member of the Spanish Committee of the International Chamber of Commerce (ICC), registered in the Register of Customs Agents (aptitude tests in 2017) and holds a Certificate of Professional Competence in the Transport of Goods (2004).

Executive Master in Supply Chain Management taught by ADL (Association for the Development of Logistics), academic year 2013-2014, he is a lecturer in numerous courses, seminars and Masters in different business schools (IOE Group, Iniciativas Empresariales, IEBS, ACEDIS, etc.).

He is author of the following books:

- *El contrato de transporte por carretera (Ley 15/2009)*, Marge Books.
- *Transporte internacional de mercancías*, ICEX.
- *El transporte internacional por carretera*, Marge Books.
- *El Convenio CMR* (co-author together with Francisco Sánchez-Gamborino), Marge Books.
- *Las reglas Incoterms 2010. Manual para usarlas con eficacia*, Marge Books.
- *Normativa del transporte de mercancías por carretera*, Marge Books

alfonsoprofesor@yahoo.es
www.formacionentransporte.es

Foreword

The globalization of the economy and production activities, which has reached significant dimensions, compels many companies to make strategic decisions to optimize their supply, production and distribution processes to reach final markets. These companies also have to manage their international purchasing and selling operations, forced by the opening of markets, competition and the division between producer and consumer economies.

In any case, international trade provides the company with great benefits including the following:

- Increases sales by accessing new international markets.
- Enhances economies through more efficient use of resources.
- Diversifies risk by operating in different markets and countries.
- Reduces exposure to market economic conditions.
- Extends product life cycle.
- Expands market segments and customer profiles as international markets evolve.
- Gains access to a broader network of suppliers and partners.
- Improves competitiveness by optimizing costs through access to purchasing in international markets.

International trade allows companies to compete with foreign companies operating in the domestic market.

However, operating in international markets not only brings benefits but also involves various types of risks, among which the following stand out:

- *Commercial risks:* non-payment or breach of contract.
- *Country risks:* political (war, public sector default, capital controls, etc.) or extraordinary (natural disasters that prevent operations from taking place).
- *Customs risks:* the operation may be hindered or temporarily delayed, or incur higher than expected costs (potentially rendering it unprofitable) due to poor customs procedures that affect nearly all foreign trade operations.
- *Other risks:* transportation (accidents), exchange rate fluctuations, etc.

International trade operations are subject to greater risks and uncertainties than domestic ones due to linguistic and legal differences, the complexity and cost of transportation over long distances, compliance with customs formalities and requirements, and trade dynamics, among other causes.

Given the obstacles that all of this poses to the activities of companies, and in order to facilitate sales in the international arena by applying standardized criteria that offer security and limit disputes, the International Chamber of Commerce (ICC) published the first version of the Incoterms rules in 1936. These are the ICC rules for the use of national and international trade terms. These rules allow the determination of the tasks, costs, and risks that the selling and buying parties must assume based on a sales contract (national or international) and depending on the operations carried out in its execution. In this way, Incoterms rules have the character of *lex mercatoria* (merchant law) and constitute one of the tools used by companies to conduct their business safely and to reduce the risk of disputes and litigation.

The application of an Incoterms rule to the contract of sale determines:

- The main obligations of the selling and purchasing parties in relation to the contract.
- The costs to be borne by each party with respect to transportation and other links in the logistics chain.
- The obligation to perform customs clearance (if the transaction requires it).
- The timing of delivery and transfer of risk from the seller to the buyer.

Consequently, any organization involved in an international trade operation needs to know and correctly apply these rules (which are equally applicable in the national arena), as their ability to do so depends on their capacity to:

- Offer prices adjusted to the costs that it must assume as the selling party (therefore, with a rule that assigns higher costs to this party, a higher price will be proposed).
- Interpret the prices of purchase offers and choose the best one in terms of costs and risks.
- Fulfill the obligations established by the agreed rule and determine those of the other party.
- Determine the time of delivery and transfer of risks of the goods during transportation.
- Negotiate and apply the appropriate rule according to the characteristics of the transaction.
- Identify the aspects not covered by the rule in question and which should be specified in the contract of sale (quality and technical characteristics of the goods, delivery time, means of payment, applicable law in the event of disputes and their resolution by court or arbitration, etc.).

It follows that knowledge of the Incoterms rules is essential for the correct development of commercial activity in the international sphere, as their incorporation into a goods sales contract has implications for almost every aspect of each transaction. Hence, there is a need to use these rules appropriately and effectively to minimize the risks of operations and optimize their costs so that organizations canoperate in international markets under optimal conditions.

Conversely, widespread ignorance of Incoterms rules and the consequences of their improper application can lead companies to use them inadequately for a number of reasons:

- Inertia (by accepting the terms proposed by the other party without assessing their suitability for the organization itself).
- Habit (consistently agreeing to the same rule in all operations).
- Other equally arbitrary criteria that expose companies to increased risks and costs.

These situations often lead to breaches of contract, commercial disputes, duplicate cost payments, legally unfounded claims, customs issues, ineffective combinations with insurance and payment methods, and delivery delays. These issues inevitably harm the company and hinder its international expansion efforts.

This book is a reference guide. The following pages provide an overview of international trade and its recent evolution, as well as its relationship with international transportation. It then presents the essential aspects of international logistics and the main characteristics of each mode of transportation. It also discusses the characteristics and necessity of these regulations, the main innovations of version 2020, their scope, and their relationship with transportation and insurance contracts, as well as with documentary credit.

From a practical and operational perspective, this book provides a thorough analysis of the application of the various Incoterms rules, both multimodal (EXW, FCA, CPT, CIP, DAP, DPU and DDP) and maritime (FAS, FOB, CFR and CIF). The analysis includes a general description of the terms of sale and delivery of the goods, a list of the main obligations and costs to be borne by each party, and basic considerations for their effective implementation. Special attention is paid to various aspects of contracting for transportation and determining the time of delivery, the loading and unloading of the goods, and performing customs clearance. The explanation of each rule is supplemented by illustrations and diagrams showing the allocation of costs and risks between the selling and purchasing companies.

Also included are some inappropriate uses of Incoterms rules for Maritime transport, such as FOB and CIF rules, which are widely used in containerized (multimodal) transport operations. In these cases, the costs and risks are presented, recommending the substitution of maritime transport rules with multimodal ones in container transport operations, in line with the recommendations proposed by the ICC.

Nevertheless, there is no single Incoterms rule suitable for all transactions. In each case, the most appropriate one must be agreed upon according to the circumstances of the sale. For this reason, this book proposes criteria to facilitate the choice of the most appropriate rule and gives precise instructions for its correct and efficient application in the contract of sale.

Finally, to illustrate the theoretical exposition, some practical cases of application of Incoterms rules to different sales transactions are presented. In each of these cases, it is necessary to determine the offered sales prices under different conditions or to choose the optimal purchasing alternative. These cases also illustrate the allocation of risks to the selling or purchasing company in the event of incidents occurring at different points in the logistics chain, depending on the delivery moment stipulated by the agreed Incoterms rule.

In short, this work provides criteria, guidelines, recommendations, examples and practical cases for the appropriate and effective use of Incoterms rules. Its consultation will help to minimize business risks, optimize costs related to the purchase and sale of goods, and thus consolidate operations in international markets. This book is also designed as a handbook for professionals in international and domestic trade. It will be very useful both for companies that manage the purchase and sale of goods and transportation, as well as for all those professionally related to any aspect of these fields, such banking, customs management, consulting, law, teaching, etc.

Incoterms 2020
User's manual

Self-assessment test

Improve your knowledge of the Incoterms 2020 rules.

Learn how to apply them correctly from any device or browser.

Go to **www.margebooks.com** and take the self-assessment tests.

Chapter 1
International trade

1 Introduction to international trade

The history of civilizations can be explained primarily in economic terms. Migrations, conquests, technological developments, and other advances are, strictly speaking, due to the desire to obtain more resources to satisfy the needs of a human group.

From the dawn of humanity, individuals organized in clans discovered that they could increase their wealth and power by establishing relationships of cooperation and exchange with other clans, tribes, and neighboring peoples. Commercial exchange, based first on barter and later on money, has been crucial to the development of civilizations and has shaped social, political, and economic development in every corner of the planet. Trade has allowed countries that engage in it to reap benefits such as access to economies of scale and specialization in production processes, raising people's standards of living and society's overall progress.

Broadly speaking, the stages of economic history have been marked by scientific discoveries, technological advances, and commercial exchanges. These three factors have shaped the characteristics of today's societies, which are largely influenced by international trade, economic globalization, and technological advancements in the digital age.

1.1 Recent developments and current situation

After the Second World War (1939-1945), the victorious economic powers imposed a new world order aimed at maintaining peace in the long term and development based on the mass production, trade and consumption of products. This new order, forged with the support of global institutions (United Nations, World Trade Organization, International Monetary Fund, etc.), coincided with the division of the world into two economic blocs with profound political undertones (the Cold War period between 1945 and 1991). The confrontation between these blocs, led by the United States and the Soviet Union respectively, led in practice to the hegemony of the capitalist system, characterized by private capital accumulation. This socio-economic system is affected by multiple crises, imbalances and social and regional inequalities. Examples include the existing inequalities between the developed countries of the First World and the underdeveloped countries of the Third World, and the crisis suffered since 2008 by the Western economies, especially the European ones, which are still in the process of recovery with many uncertainties about the consolidation of economic growth.

Nevertheless, since the second half of the 20th century, economic development has been undeniable, and the world economy and international trade have experienced the most prosperous and dynamic moment in their history. The technological advances made during this period have had a direct impact on the development of international trade. The advent of the container and the development of transportation increased cargo capacity, speed, and connectivity. But there have been other advances as well, such as the progress of information and communication technologies (the digital era and e-commerce), the opening of international markets, the coordination of customs procedures and the reduction of their restrictions. All this has made it possible to harmonize and streamline banking practices and financial markets, resulting in what has come to be known as "economic globalization".

Since the 1980s, the process of globalization has become much more dynamic with the incorporation of Latin America, Eastern Europe and, above all, Asia, with China and India (the "world's factories") at the forefront, having doubled their exports.

This new situation divides the world into zones of supply, production and consumption. Companies can now consider their location and performance in international markets according to the efficiency they achieve in each one. In other words, they aim for the highest profit margin possible. Companies can strategically study the best options for sourcing, producing, and selling globally because they have the necessary tools, techniques, and resources (transportation, communication, distribution, and means of payment). Today, we work from a holistic perspective: everything is integrated into a global and constantly evolving marketplace.

This change in strategy has given rise to phenomena such as the delocalization of production centers, international competition among logistics chains, corporate integration, extensive outsourcing of processes not central to their operations, the development of e-commerce, the automation of logistical processes, and the widespread application of technology to the logistics chain (transportation, tracking, customs management, warehousing, transmission of information between components, big data, etc.).

1.2   Current trends in international trade

1.2.1   Major trading blocs: free trade vs. protectionism

As part of the evolution described in Section 1.1, and under the accepted premise that international trade is beneficial for all globally, in recent decades (before the 2008 crisis and the arrival of Donald Trump at the White House), there has been a proliferation of commercial approaches among various states, which have contributed to the creation and development of various blocs. These are associations of several countries that aim to increase their economic development and international influence through greater integration of their trade relations.

After the Second World War, economic and trade blocs were created in different parts of the world to counteract the hegemony of the United States. This led to the agreements that laid the groundwork for the European Economic Community, the current European Union, considered the most integrated economic union and the most developed trading bloc in the world, despite the internal political crises it has suffered and the exit of the United Kingdom – Brexit – from the EU.

There are other important trading blocs, each with different levels of integration (trade agreements, customs unions, etc.), such as:

- The United States-Mexico-Canada Contract, better known as USMCA, CUSMA, ACEUM, or TMEC, depending on the signatory country, replaces the previous North American Free Trade Contract (NAFTA), updated under pressure from the U.S. administration upon Donald Trump's presidency.
- The Trans-Pacific Partnership (TPP), was signed in 2015 by Australia, Brunei, Canada, Chile, Japan, Malaysia, Mexico, New Zealand, Peru, Singapore and Vietnam. Although the United States was a signatory at the time, it withdrew in 2017 after Donald Trump came to power.
- The 1991 Southern Cone Common Market (Mercosur), includes Argentina, Brazil, Paraguay, Uruguay, and Venezuela, with associated countries such as Chile, Colombia, Peru, and Ecuador.
- The Association of Southeast Asian Nations (ASEAN), founded in 1967, includes Indonesia, Malaysia, the Philippines, Singapore, Thailand, Brunei, Vietnam, Laos, Burma, and Cambodia.
- The Eurasian Economic Union (EEU), established in 2015, which includes Russia, Kazakhstan, and Belarus.

At present, initiatives to integrate some of these trade blocs into larger ones have been paralyzed due to the "Trump effect". This is the case, for example, of the Free Trade Area of the Americas (FTAA), which seeks to integrate the TMEC countries (formerly NAFTA) with the rest of the American states; or the contract announced in 2013 between the United States and the European Union to create a free trade area that would have brought together almost half of the planet's gross domestic product (GDP) and a third of world trade. This proposal was launched during the Obama era and has also stalled during the Trump era.

Alongside the formation of these trade blocs, large supranational organizations have been created to coordinate policies and promote economic and trade development on a global scale. Examples of these organizations are the Organization for Economic Cooperation and Development (OECD), which integrates more than thirty of the world's leading economies, and the Latin American Integration Association (ALADI), which promotes the creation of a common Latin American market.

As can be seen, world trade is moving towards a dynamic dominated by trade blocs, which can be classified according to the degree of integration and commercial freedom they implement. Thus, it is possible to distinguish between:

- **Free trade zone or area**
  The member countries reduce most of their tariff barriers among them-selves, but each state applies different tariffs and import measures with third countries. This is the case, for example, of the USMCA member countries, which have duty-free trade among themselves but maintain in-dividual trade policies with third countries (in fact, the European Union has trade agreements with Mexico and Canada but not with the United States).

- **Customs Union**
  Member countries do not impose restrictions on trade among themselves, but they do impose a common external tariff on imports from third coun-tries. The European Union is a perfect example of this type of trading bloc.

- **Common market**
  This is a customs union that applies other freedoms, such as the free move-ment of people, services and capital. The European Union is an example of a common market that continues to develop by harmonizing aspects related to security, economy, social development, ecology, etc.

In the context of trade blocs, countries organize themselves to simplify in-tra-member state transactions and normalize practical aspects of their formal-ization and logistics chains across various domains such as transportation (spec-ifications and contracting regulations), customs (procedures, requirements, and documentation), among others.

Following the 2008 financial crisis and the arrival of President Donald Trump in the White House (with his America First policy), there has been a notable resurgence in trade protectionism. This resurgence manifests in various forms, including the ongoing trade war between the United States and China (with cases such as Huawei) and conflicts with the European Union, as well as the Brexit process. This trend represents a counterpoint to the processes of trade rapprochement that have been the paradigm since the middle of the last century.

Nevertheless, there are still ongoing efforts towards commercial integration that provide advantages for all involved parties. For instance, the European Union has signed agreements with countries like South Korea, Canada, Japan, Singapore, Vietnam, and several African nations, and is negotiating another with Mercosur. In practice, the European Union uses various forms of trade rapprochement (contracts, customs unions and the Generalized System of Preferences or GSP with developing countries) to facilitate trade with about two-thirds of the world's countries.

1.2.2   Emerging economies

One of the characteristics of the evolution of world trade since the 1990s has been the emergence of the so-called "emerging economies," with China and India at the head of a group that includes many Asian countries (often referred to as "tiger economies") as well as other global powers from other continents, such as Russia and Brazil.

The development prospects of these countries is largely based on their supply of cheap and highly competitive labor. This labor force, together with public policies favorable to the entry of foreign capital and easily transferable and exportable technologies, has shaped a scenario of economic globalization based on the liberalization of world trade. It is becoming increasingly easy to produce products in these countries at lower economic costs and to sell them more cheaply in consumer markets.

The most representative group of these emerging economies is known as the BRICS group, comprisig Brazil, Russia, India, China and South Africa. However, it is generally observed that the weight of the global economy has shifted towards Asia.

2   Evolution of international transportation

2.1   International trade and transport

Economic growth and the development of international trade would not have been possible without fast, efficient and flexible means of transport.

In fact, "economic growth, in any of its known forms, seems inseparable from an increase in the geographical dimension of the markets for goods and services. Economic growth is nothing other than expanding markets, incorporating new territories, new natural resources or new social groups that were previously tied to the land at the local level, in autonomous or scarcely monetarized subsistence models, into the exchange system. All these incorporations rely on transportation. In reality, economic growth is basically an intensification of transportation. Increased transportation and development are practically the same thing."[1]

In the 21st century, transportation systems make it possible to have all types of products available wherever they are needed in the logistics chain. Whether raw materials (procurement) or finished products ready for sale (distribution).

With economic globalization, international transport is becoming more complex: longer distances and transit times, greater demands in meeting delivery deadlines (the trend is towards tight flow logistics), higher costs, reduced warehousing (zero stock policy), a dramatic increase in e-commerce and its challenges in customer delivery ("last mile"), increasingly complex reverse logistics, the need to implement measures to deal with environmental emergencies, risks that make it advisable to take out insurance, customs procedures, and compliance with international regulations and conventions on vehicles, goods, packaging, safety, etc.

2.2 Recent developments in international transportation

Despite its complexity, the development of international transportation has been spectacular and has evolved since the 1950s mainly in the following directions:

- **Application of economies of scale.** Container ships with a capacity of 24,000 TEU have made economies of scale possible and have facilitated the transport of many cheap products that were previously unprofitable to market[2].

- **Faster and safer.** Transportation companies have increased the speed of their services, both by improving performance and by using more efficient

---

[1] Antonio Esteban, "Transporte contra natura: la inviabilidad ecológica del transporte horizontal", *Boletín CF+S*, Madrid, 2006; 38-39. (Own translation into English.)
[2] TEU (twenty-foot equivalent units) is a unit of measurement for containers that is equivalent to 20 feet (6.10 m). Global capacities of vessels, container terminals, ports or traffic are calculated in this unit.

networks and infrastructure. This applies to all modes of transportation: air, road, sea and rail. Ocean freight, which moves the largest volume of cargo, moves containers from Asia to Europe in 25 to 30 days.

- **Adaptation to shipping requirements.** Different technical applications can be used to transport products that require special care and measures, such as those that needing to maintain the cold chain (fruit, vegetables, fish, frozen goods, etc.) or hazardous goods. For each type of product, specific means and elements have been developed to transport them safely and quickly.

- **Application of information technologies to the logistics chain.** It is now possible to locate and track shipments in real time, provide information to the companies involved in the logistics chain (sender, warehouse operator, carrier, consignee, etc.), confirm final delivery, etc. Transportation must adapt to the digitalization implied by Supply Chain 4.0: robotization and artificial intelligence, market forecasting through big data analysis, e-commerce, mobile applications, etc. The ultimate goal is to have valuable data to anticipate future market needs and plan the supply chain predictively ("Amazon already knows what we are going to order before we feel the need").

- **Moving towards more sustainable and environmentally friendly transportation.** Transport is one of the most polluting sectors and must be transformed to reduce its environmental impact. Many initiatives are already underway: electric vehicles or vehicles powered by other methods such as gas, hydrogen, etc., restrictions on access to cities, limits on driving, eco-design of packaging, reduction in the use of plastic, or the development of new trade routes such as the New Eurasian Silk Road, featuring the train between China and Europe. In any case, many more will have to be implemented (derived from mandatory regulations) to prevent the environmental impact of logistics activities, of which transport is a part, and which will have a significant impact on international transport.

- **Multimodality.** This is the use of different modes of transportation to create efficient logistics chains (co-modality). Its greatest exponent is the creation and rapid expansion of the use of the container, which has been the element that has most revolutionized freight transport since the second half of the 20th century. Its widespread use has given rise to a transport system with its own means (container ships and cranes, stackers, and other handling equipment) and specific infrastructures (container terminals for storage and handling, for example) that offer significant improvements in time and safety.

- **Professionalization and specialization of transportation services.** Supply chains are becoming increasingly complex. Transportation companies have had to specialize in order to offer global services tailored to the needs of each customer and each shipment. Although all modes of transport have evolved and continually offer faster, more reliable, and more flexible services, maritime transport—being the most widely used globally—perhaps best reflects the evolution of international transport. Global data show steady annual growth, especially for dry cargo, including containers. Road transportation also accounts for a large share of traffic, especially in international operations at national and continental levels. In the European Union, approximately half of all shipments are transported by road, while within individual countries, road transport often dominates in comparison to other modes.

2.3 The evolution of international trade and transport and Incoterms rules

The constant growth of global trade and the development of international logistics chains require a unified set of rules to serve as a reference for the parties and agents involved in an international sale and purchase transaction that entail the transportation of goods. This is the role played by the Incoterms of the International Chamber of Commerce (ICC, which have undergone successive revisions since their inception in 1936 to adapt to significant changes in the industry. These adaptations are evident in aspects such as:

- Adaptation to the operational needs of logistics chains based on the connections between terminals of all types and the use of multimodal systems, such as the container. Thus, rules have been developed for multimodal and maritime transport, detailing the most common phases and costs (such as loading containers and handling at terminals).

- Cost allocation specifications so that each of the parties (seller and buyer) involved in the sales transaction can clearly understand the segment of the logistics chain for which they are responsible for the costs (including information on handling operations in multimodal transport).
- Clarification of Customs Clearance Obligations. Customs requirements are increasingly focused on technical and security aspects rather than tax and fiscal issues. The Incoterms have had to be adapted and the obligations and responsibilities of each party with respect to these formalities and their documentation have been detailed.
- Incorporation of Electronic Documents, allows for greater speed in transportation and agility in the processing of the related documentary elements.

To conclude, the Incoterms rules discussed in this book are designed to adapt to the reality of international sales transactions and their evolution, trying to clarify the obligations and risks attributable to the seller and the buyer by including them in the distribution of costs. This is a fundamental aspect that aims to provide greater security and lower risks for organizations that engage in international trade operations.

Chapter 2
International trade logistics

The logistics function takes on a special importance in an internationalized environment, with a high level of market openness and a globalized economy. Companies compete in a global market, and the optimization of logistics management is one of the key aspects to position themselves in it and to achieve the established goals.

Business logistics is the set of activities that optimizes:

a) the flow of products, from the purchase from suppliers to the delivery of the finished products,
b) the reverse flows that derive from it,
c) the information flows generated by this process, which ensure customer satisfaction at the minimum cost.

If we analyze this process from the point of view of a manufacturing company, the logistics function can be chronologically divided into three phases: procurement (purchasing), production and distribution (sales). At the international level, these phases are translated into a series of activities that are more or less affected by the Incoterms rules. Among them, we can distinguish the following types.

- **Market analysis and information**
  This issue encompasses numerous activities that provide the company with information about the global environment in which it operates. In this way, it can anticipate and ensure its survival and expansion. All these activities are included in the company's market information system, which should serve to:

  - Gather basic market information to feed back into the business process: forecast demand, anticipate market developments and trends, etc.
  - Analyze expectations in potential markets: market niches, competitive developments, product redesign and adaptation to different markets, etc.
  - Identify risks from market evolutions, in which the company already operates: rising prices of raw materials and other inputs, significant economic indicators, implementation of restrictive regulations requiring changes to aspects of the product, etc.

  The sources of information for this system can be very diverse: direct information (sales performance), information about the competition (competitive intelligence),[1] etc. In addition, the digital age and the availability of big data allow organizations to access continuously updated data in order to adapt to an environment that is changing more than ever before.
  This type of analysis allows the company's management to propose the most appropriate Incoterms rule for a sales transaction depending on the characteristics of the market and the company's position in the transaction (as the seller at the origin or the buyer at the destination).

- **Purchasing or supply management**
  This function defines the purchasing policy of the supplier companies. It involves the selection of suppliers and, therefore, the markets from which purchases are managed (the optimal Incoterms rule must be chosen for each case), as well as the periodicity and characteristics of the orders

---

[1] There are competitive intelligence services on the market that provide information on the performance of competitors in international markets.

(regular and small, large and sporadic, urgent, etc.). These decisions must be made for each range or type of product and its origin in the different markets from which the company obtains resources for its production process.

- **Wrapping, packing and preparation of goods**
  A distinction should be made between:

  - *Container.* Receptacle that contains, protects, and attractively presents the product for sale to the ultimate consumer. The term "primary package" refers to a package that directly contains the product (e.g., a can of tomato sauce) and "secondary package" refers to a package that protects and groups primary packages into units for sale (e.g., a package that groups six cans of tomato sauce).
  - *Packaging.* Process consisting of the application of techniques to identify, protect and handle packaging throughout the product's logistics chain. Some examples of packaging are palletizing techniques and the use of boxes, bags, containers, etc. Its purpose is to protect the product and facilitate its handling, so it must be adapted to the product's logistics chain. Packaging must be designed to meet international marking and labeling standards, allow customs inspection, and minimize the risks of handling the goods.

Although there is a wide range of packaging types (boxes, bags, bottles, pallets, etc.) made of very different materials (cardboard, wood, glass, plastic, etc.), the choice of one or another depends on the legislation of the destination countries. Optimizing and, if necessary, redesigning containers and packaging is the key to making the most of the capacity of the means of transport and storage, as well as ensuring safe delivery.

On the one hand, the Incoterms 2020 regulations stipulate that the selling company is obliged to package the goods in a manner suitable for transportation, adhering to any specific requirements notified by the buyer. This is a fundamental aspect for the success of any sale and purchase of goods and for the quality of the logistics chain. In fact, providing inadequate packaging constitutes a breach of the seller's obligations.

On the other hand, the rules governing transportation contracts usually exempt the transport company from losses and damage caused to the goods by inadequate packaging. It places the responsibility on the person who packed and prepared the goods for transport, whether it is the selling company or other links in the logistics chain, such as warehousing, transport or consolidation. In addition, strict regulations on packaging and packaging related to the transportation of goods must be taken into account):

a) Compliance with customs regulations (especially for imports: international regulations concerning the phytosanitary treatment of wooden pallets, etc.).

b) Compliance with the distribution and sale of products in the target markets (regulations regarding the labeling of each product, marking and identification requirements on containers and packaging, recycling of materials, regulations regarding perishable or dangerous goods, etc.).

- **Production plant location**
  Strategic planning includes important aspects such as the design of the production process, the location of manufacturing facilities, and managing warehouse networks and inventories. The aim is to ensure the availability of resources needed for the production process. The location of the production plants determines the origin and destination points of the transportation of goods, as a result of sales and purchases and possible exchanges between different facilities.

- **Information availability**
  One of the most crucial functions that significantly advances the management and optimization of international logistics is the availability of information. Information and communication technologies (ICT), the internet, and specific management systems for areas such as warehouses and shipment tracking allow for global logistics chain control and information sharing with preceding and subsequent chain links, optimizing management until the final consumer sale.

  Incoterms rules give the same validity to electronic documents as to those issued on paper, provided that this has been agreed in the contract of sale. Certain applications, such as those derived from the traceability of shipments, can also be used to determine the point at which an incident occurs; for example, if the cold chain is broken during transport, the vehicle's thermograph provides reliable evidence.

- **Customs management and documentation**
  Customs procedures are increasingly crucial due to heightened security requirements (environmental and national heritage protection, food safety and traceability, control of illegal arms and drug trafficking, etc.), necessitating more extensive documentation, inspections, and controls. Planning for the impact of customs on international trade, through its instruments (tariffs and taxes, determination and certification of origin, customs value, customs regimes, etc.), is essential for successful operations.

  In most cases, each country or economic-fiscal region determines, through its own legislation, the requirements for the export and import of each product. Both the seller and the buyer must provide each other with all necessary assistance to ensure compliance with the requirements of the relevant customs office in accordance with the agreed Incoterms rule.

  According to Incoterms, the seller is responsible for export clearance and the buyer is responsible for import clearance. The reason for this is obvious: each has a better knowledge of the regulations in his own country and can easily comply with them. There are only two exceptions:

  a) Under EXW terms: the purchasing party clears for export.
  b) Under DDP terms: the selling party clears for import.

- **Payment methods**
  Means of payment are closely related to the supply chain. Although the Incoterms do not explicitly regulate payment methods, in certain cases (such as documentary credits), it is more appropriate to apply specific Incoterms rules. This is because the proof of delivery or transport document required in a documentary payment method will depend on the Incoterms rule agreed upon in the sales contract.

- **Transportation and insurance**
  The Inconterms Rules are very important in these two aspects, since a large part of their action is focused on the obligations and costs related to the transportation and insurance of the goods that must be assumed by the seller and buyer parties in a sales contract.

2   International logistics: trends and outsourcing

2.1   Trends in international logistics

Since the middle of the 20th century, the development and implementation of logistics systems and optimization techniques have become a strategic factor in the development of markets, companies and the economy in general. Logistics is so important that it can be defined as the efficient management of a company.

The main trends in logistics are focused on the coordination and creation of efficient chains and the exploitation of the potential of the Internet and e-commerce.

In the 21st century, competition in international markets is between logistics chains. The management of any company knows that it must cooperate with the other links in the chain. Whether the company is involved in sourcing, manufacturing, distribution, or logistics, the goal is to optimize the entire chain to provide the best product at the lowest price and with the flexibility demanded by the market. This description can be expressed by the concept of "tight flow", where inventory is minimized and market demand is prioritized, as an evolution from the push to the pull system.

From an integrated logistics perspective, this collaboration between organizations in the same logistics chain must also exist between those involved in the same supply chain.

Collaboration between organizations can reach different levels of integration. From a strategic point of view, various logistics optimization techniques and methods can be employed, such as just-in-time delivery, inventory minimization, warehouse management and transportation systems, etc. Integrated logistics systems in the apparel industry, for example, have achieved tremendous efficiencies, encompassing design, manufacturing, and distribution. The same applies to the automotive industry with its "supplier park", where the transfer of information via electronic data interchange (EDI) and the Internet and the use of ICT are key.

The customer demands not only the delivery of products in the best conditions of quality and price, but also additional information such as shipment status, delivery time, and confirmation. This has forced transport and logistics operators to broaden their range of services adding more value by incorporating services that go beyond the traditional physical transfer of goods from one point to another.

This type of application and the rise of e-commerce offer new opportunities for companies looking to expand into international markets. In business-to-business (B2B) exchanges, integration between importers and distributors is encouraged. This allows all parties involved to know the actual inventory levels at all times and to place their orders according to demand. In e-commerce, the possibilities are endless and the prospects point to a radical change in the marketing models for products in certain related sectors (fashion and accessories, household appliances, leisure and entertainment, etc.).

2.2 Logistics outsourcing

The tasks that make up the logistics function can be performed with the company's own resources or outsourced to a specialized external actor. Every organization has outsourced some of its logistics functions and activities.

There is a wide variety of operating companies offering a wide range of logistics services and adapting to the needs of the corporation to which they provide these services, even integrating to some extent into its structure.

Outsourcing reduces fixed costs by converting them into variable costs, generates financing through the sale of assets, and allows the organization to focus its efforts on its core business. However, it also means a loss of autonomy, as a key aspect such as logistics is placed in the hands of another company. It is not always easy to find the right logistics provider and manage a mutually beneficial relationship.

3 Freight transportation

In international logistics, functions often need to be performed that are generally not feasible with the organization's own resources, such as maritime, air, or rail transport. In this context, the transport company, in its various forms (road haulier, freight forwarder, logistics operator, transport agency, etc.), is fundamental to the development of freight trading operations.

The most appropriate mode of transportation must always be chosen according to the origin and destination points, the requirements of the shipment, the type of cargo, and the value of the goods in relation to the cost of transportation.

The modal split varies depending on whether the goods are being exported, imported, transported within the same economic-fiscal region, or transported nationally, as discussed in Chapter 1.

In a national or international sales transaction, the seller and the buyer assume different obligations regarding the transportation of the goods according to the agreed Incoterms rule. For this reason, it is essential that you are familiar with the basic aspects involved:

a) *commercial* (transport providers and service modalities)
b) *technical* (infrastructure, type of vehicles, loading capacity and presentation of goods); and
c) *legal* (regulatory framework of the contract of carriage for each mode of transportation).

Each Incoterms rule determines the effective moment of delivery (transfer of risk). When the seller transfers to the buyer the responsibility for any loss or damage caused to the goods during transportation. Therefore, although the transport contract is independent from the contract of sale and the agreed Incoterms rule, both parties must coordinate closely, to avoid costs and risks and effectively apply the agreed rule.

3.1   Road transportation[2]

Road transportation is characterized by its independence (it is the only one that offers a door-to-door service), flexibility (it adapts to the requirements of each shipment) and autonomy (it does not require additional infrastructure to develop its services).

This mode of transportation allows almost any shipment to be transported without breakage, quickly, and at a direct cost that is absorbed by the market.

For distances greater than 1,000 or 1,500 km, there are more efficient modes. Nevertheless, autonomy and door-to-door service have made Road transportation the most widely used mode in national and continental exchanges, despite

---

[2] For further information on road transportation, we suggest consulting the book El transporte internacional por carretera, by Alfonso Cabrera Cánovas, Marge Books, Barcelona 2011 (Biblioteca de Logística).

restrictive rules such as driving time limits, fuel taxes, highway tolls, pollution and access restrictions to urban centers, etc.

Road transportation is also present in every logistics chain and facilitates intermodality, since pick-ups and deliveries (for example, of a container transported by sea) are often carried out in combination with this mode.

3.1.1 Commercialization

Companies providing Road transportation services are usually regulated by national legislation and its complementary regulations, and are basically:

- *Road haulage companies.* Companies with their own fleet dedicated to the provision of Road transportation services.
- *Transport operating companies.* These can be divided into transport agencies, freight forwarders, and logistics companies that act as warehouse-distributors.

The contracting of transport based on the agreed Incoterms depends on several factors:

- Scope of activity (national or international).
- Complexity and specialization of the operation (e.g. freight forwarders or carriers are involved in international operations).
- Type of services required (for example, a logistics provider can perform more functions and add more value than just transportation).

These Road transportation providers offer different types of services, which can be divided into two categories:[3]

- *Full truck (FTL),* when a specific vehicle is assigned to a shipment.
- *Less-than-truckload (LTL) or consolidation,* when different shipments share the same vehicle.

----

[3] These two categories are usually identified internationally with the following acronyms and meanings: FTL or full truck load and LTL or less than truck load.

LTL can be further subdivided into different types of traffic: full pallets, parcels (all types of packages) and courier services (documents and parcels up to 2 kg). These main types of service are adapted to the needs of the shipment and offer express transport, delivery commitments within a specific time frame, maintenance of the cold chain, etc.

3.1.2   Vehicles and cargo types

There is a wide variety of vehicle types, both in terms of loading capacity (van, rigid truck, trailer, etc.) and shipping capability (refrigerated vehicle, flatbed, container carrier, hopper, etc.).

The largest trucks have a loading capacity of between 22 and 28 tons, depending on the type of vehicle (the implementation of "megatrucks" with greater capacities is underway). The higher the tare weight, the lower the loading capacity. The weight limit for circulation varies according to the legislation of each country, which may also differentiate between different types of roads, and is between 35 and 40 tons, including the weight of the vehicle and the load. The loading capacity on pallets is 26 isopallets (33 or 34 europallets) for trailers, while the loading volume of vehicle boxes ranges from 85 m3 (refrigerated truck) to 102 m3 (truck covered with tarpaulin up to 13.6 m internal length).

Loads transported by road can be of any type: bulk raw materials, finished products ready for sale, waste intended for recycling processes, etc. However, of all the load unitization systems, palletizing is the one that has gained the widest acceptance among most production sectors.

Since the introduction of the pallet as a load unit in the transport process, its combination with road semi-trailers offers enormous benefits. Palletizing offers safety, speed, automation and cost savings, especially when containers and packaging are adapted to pallet dimensions.

The main classification of pallet types is based on their size and load capacity. There are isopallets or universal pallets (1,200 × 1,000 mm), europallets or European pallets (1,200 × 800 mm) and other sizes (800 × 600 mm, 600 × 400 mm, etc.). For the availability of pallets for continuous service, there are basically two modalities: pallet exchange pools (EPAL) and pallet rental pools (CHEP, LPR, etc.).

Most pallets are made of wood. When they are used in international trade, they are subject to the International Standard for Phytosanitary Measures No.

15 (ISPM 15), drawn up by the Food and Agriculture Organization (FAO) of the United Nations. This standard regulates the use of wood packaging in foreign trade to reduce the risk of introducing and spreading forest pests and diseases. This standard requires a fumigation certificate to be presented at the destination customs as a condition for completing the import clearance, a requirement that both the seller and the buyer must consider to provide this documentation with the shipment and avoid delays at the import customs and associated costs.

Since import clearance is usually the responsibility of the purchasing company, it should inform the selling party of this customs requirement, if applicable, so that they can provide the necessary documentation, or an alternative packaging system to the pallet should be agreed upon in the sales contract.

3.1.3 International regulation of the contract of carriage

- **The 1956 CMR Convention**[4]
  The Convention of 19 May 1956 on the Contract for the International road transport of goods, better known as the CMR Convention (from the French **Convention relative au contrat de transport international de Marchandise par Route**), applies in Europe and its area of influence in North Africa, the Middle East and the Far East. Its main guidelines are as follows:

  - **Mandatory Application**: It applies to paid international transportation (i.e. when a carrier is hired).

---

[4] At the time of this edition (2024), the contract has been signed by 56 countries: Albania, Armenia, Austria, Azerbaijan, Belarus, Belgium, Bosnia-Herzegovina, Bulgaria, Croatia, Cyprus, Denmark, Estonia, Finland, France, Georgia, Germany, Greece, Hungary, Iran, Ireland, Italy, Jordan, Kazakhstan, Kyrgyzstan, Latvia, Lebanon, Lithuania, Luxembourg, Macedonia, Malta, Moldova, Mongolia, Montenegro, Morocco, Netherlands, Norway, Pakistan, Poland, Portugal, Romania, Russia, Serbia, Slovakia, Slovenia, Spain, Sweden, Switzerland, Syria, Tajikistan, Tunisia, Turkmenistan, Turkey, Ukraine, United Kingdom and Uzbekistan. Therefore, the 27 states of the European Union, other countries of the European continent that do not belong to the EU and countries of other continents (North Africa, and Middle and Far East).

For further information on the CMR Convention, we suggest consulting the following book El Convenio CMR, by Francisco Sánchez-Gamborino and Alfonso Cabrera Cánovas, Marge Books, Barcelona 2012 (Biblioteca de Logística).

- **Liability**: The carrier is liable for its actions and those of any professionals it subcontracts (a common practice with freight forwarders).
- **Responsibility for Goods**: The carrier is liable, unless exempted, for the total or partial loss of goods, damages that reduce their value, and delays in delivery.
- **Compensation Limit**: The carrier's indemnity is set at 8.33 Special Drawing Rights (SDR) per kilogram of gross weight in case of loss and damage, and at the transport cost in case of delay.
- **Claims**: Claims against the carrier must be made at the time of delivery (in case of apparent loss or damage) or within 7 days of delivery (in case of non-apparent loss or damage). In case of delay, the claim must be formalized within 21 days of delivery.
- **Prescription Period**: The period of limitation for filling claims is one year.
- **Jurisdiction**: The competent jurisdiction is agreed upon by the parties involved in the contract of carriage, the shipper and the carrier, or, failing that, the courts of origin, destination or domicile of the latter. It is also possible to agree to submit to transport arbitration.
- When the carrier takes over the goods, the CMR consignment note is formalized. The CMR consignment note certifies the receipt of the goods by the carrier and the existence and terms of the contract of carriage. This document consists of three originals signed by the sender and the carrier. Original No. 1 is kept by the sender and the others travel with the goods to the final destination, where original No. 2 is handed over. Original number 3 is for the transport company, which usually sends a copy with the invoice to prove that the service has been provided and to request payment.

- **Regulation of International Road transportation Contract in the United States**

  On the American continent, there is no convention that regulates and harmonizes the international Road transportation contract in a way similar to the CMR in Europe. Nor is there one among the Latin American countries. Nevertheless, several initiatives have been promoted that have failed to achieve such harmonization, both for lack of sufficient ratifications and for lack of coordination and integration with each country's specific regulations on the subject.

Among these initiatives, we can cite the Agreement on International Land Transportation (ATIT), promoted by the Latin American Integration Association (ALADI), and the Inter-American Convention on International Road Transport of Goods, developed by the Organization of American States (OAS). The main aspects of the latter are as follows:

- It applies to the international carriage of goods by road between signatory countries, but does not preclude the application of other bilateral or multilateral conventions or other extended practices.
- The contract of carriage is formalized in the bill of lading issued by the carrier (the Convention uses the term "carrier") and contains the conditions of carriage.
- It is a negotiable document unless expressly stated otherwise.
- The parties to the contract are responsible for the accuracy of the information contained in the bill of lading, and reservations may be made in this respect.
- The carrier is liable for loss, damage, breakdown or delay, except in certain situations (causes of exoneration).
- The carrier's liability shall not exceed the actual value of the goods at the place and time of delivery or at the place and time when delivery should have been made, or the declared value in the bill of lading, whichever is greater. Such liability shall extend to all acts or omissions of its agents, employees and servants or of third parties entrusted with all or part of the service. An increase or limitation of the carrier's indemnity may be agreed in writing, specifying an amount per unit or weight of cargo. In cases of fraud, these limits do not apply. As for the competent jurisdiction, the defendant may be sued in the courts of his domicile or of the place of departure or of delivery at the destination of the shipment. Disputes may also be settled by arbitration.

3.2 Maritime transport

It is the mode of transportation that moves the most goods internationally. Its main advantages are its large cargo capacity, its adaptability to different types of goods, its competitive price, and its low environmental impact compared to other modes.

However, shipping is the slowest mode of transportation, depends on port infrastructure, and requires other modes of transportation for pickup and delivery. In addition, the legal regulation governing its transport contract tends to favor shipping companies.

3.2.1   Commercialization

Maritime transport of goods operates under two operating regimes: the liner system and the charter system. In the liner regime, there are pre-determined routes, frequencies and rates. This is the regime under which containers are transported, since the goods of many shipping companies share the means of transportation, the ship.

The transportation of containers or general cargo in liner shipping is one of the fastest-growing traffic types and is primarily marketed through two channels: by contracting the service directly with the shipping companies through their shipping agencies or commercial departments, and through freight forwarders or cargo agents. The latter do not own vessels, but reserve and rent cargo space through contracts or service contracts with shipping companies, which they then offer to their clients (selling or purchasing companies). In general, freight forwarders offer a more global and flexible service, better adapted to shippers' needs than that offered directly by shipping lines. In this way, they represent a fundamental element by providing, in addition to the contracting of Maritime transport, the development of ancillary services such as the consolidation or deconsolidation of cargo units, temporary storage, customs clearance, transport at origin or destination, document management of the operation, insurance of the goods, etc.

There are freight forwarders with global coverage and local or national coverage. All of them offer the possibility of providing international services through the network of correspondents in which they are integrated. Typically, the selling or purchasing company works with two or three freight forwarders.

The Company contracts the transportation according to the agreed Incoterms rule and the agencies select the best offers and services from the shipping lines. The company always tries to maintain a dominant position over the agencies in order to obtain transportation at the lowest cost and under the best possible conditions.

The range of services offered is wide. In the case of container transportation, there are two basic modalities:

a) *Full container load (FCL):* the goods are cubic or heavy enough to be transported in a full container.

b) *Less than container load (LCL):* the goods share the container with other goods. In this way, the consolidator, usually a freight forwarder, optimizes the use of the container by transporting several shipments from different shipping companies in the same FCL container.

In any case, if more than half of a container is occupied, it is better to contract for exclusive use on FCL terms. This avoids delivery delays, higher costs associated with consolidation and deconsolidation operations, and the risk of handling. The decision depends on the value of the goods and the cost comparison between the two options. However, the FCL option offers more security. The selling company loads, stows, and seals the container, and the contents are not handled until they reach their destination. One of the keys to cost optimization is to analyze ocean freight quotes, break them down into their components, and allocate them to the selling or purchasing party according to the agreed-upon Incoterms rule. These quotes are not standardized, as each shipping line or freight forwarder breaks down and names its components in one way or another. This detail makes it difficult to determine what each component and cost item covers, and which party (seller or buyer) is responsible for it according to the agreed Incoterms rule.

A door-to-door quotation (from the seller's warehouse to the buyer's warehouse) can be broken down into three groups of costs: pre-shipment (often referred to as "FOB charges"), freight and surcharges (transportation between ports), and landed costs (similar to pre-shipment, but in the country of destination). Chapter 7 provides guidance on how to allocate the most typical components of these quotations according to the various Incoterms rules.

There are no pre-established regular services and contracts (per voyage or per time) are negotiated in all their terms (charter party or charter policy) according to the market situation. This type of service is used to transport bulk cargoes (oil, gas, minerals, etc.) and is marketed by chartering brokers.

3.2.2 Infrastructure, vehicles and cargo types

Maritime transport takes place between ports, which are configured as a network of logistics hubs and modal interchange platforms, where land connections by road and rail are key.

Ports are organized into specialized terminals according to the cargo they handle: they can be container, breakbulk (coils, sheets, pallets, etc.), roll-on/roll-off (trailers or semi-trailers, trucks, wagons, etc.) or bulk (oil, minerals, gas, etc.) terminals. Specialized vessels operate at each terminal depending on the cargo.

In this mode, the main traffic by number of operations is container traffic carried out by container ships. Goods are loaded into large containers (usually steel) in the form of a box, which allows multimodal transportation (transfer between modes: for example, from truck to rail or ship) without handling the contents, i.e. without cargo breakage.

Containers can be basically classified according to two variables: their suitability for the type of goods (dry or general cargo, refrigerated, open top, flatbed, etc.) and their dimensions (although there are numerous sizes, the most common are the 20-foot and 40-foot containers, which are the "large capacity" variant, whose greater height provides more volume).

3.2.3   International regulation of the contract of carriage

The so-called Hague-Visby Rules[5] are the main legal framework for the contract of international maritime carriage under the bill of lading regime (for inland transport or national cabotage, each country's own legislation must be applied). There are other conventions applicable to international transport, such as the 1978 Hamburg Rules (United Nations Convention on the Carriage of Goods by Sea, in force since 1992, but of limited application) and the 2008 Rotterdam Rules (not yet in force at the time of writing, as they require twenty signatory countries and only five have ratified them).[6]

This legal framework is very protective of the interests of the carrier, as can be seen from an analysis of the main aspects of the Hague-Visby Rules:

[5] The Hague-Visby Rules of 1968 are an update of the International Convention for the Application of Certain Rules Relating to Bills of Lading or Brussels Convention of 1924, to which the Protocol on Special Drawing Rights was added in 1979.

[6] United Nations Convention on Contracts for the International Carriage of Goods Wholly or Partly by Sea, adopted in 2009 by the United Nations Commission on International Trade Law (UNCITRAL or UNCITRAL) in Vienna (Austria), which describes the rights and obligations of all parties subject to a door-to-door contract of carriage involving an international sea leg.

- The carrier is liable from hook to hook (from the crane at the port of origin to the crane at the port of destination).
- The carrier can benefit from an extensive list of exemptions from liability.
- The carrier's compensation limit is set at 666.67 SDRs per package or 2 SDRs per kilogram of gross weight (whichever is greater).[7]
- Claims against the carrier must be made at the time of delivery (in the case of apparent loss or damage) or within three days of delivery (in the case of non-apparent loss or damage).
- The statute of limitations for claims in case of loss or damage is one year.

3.2.4   Bill of lading

The contract of carriage by sea is formalized by a bill of lading (BL). This document, of particular significance in international trade, performs the functions of any other bill of lading: it serves as an acknowledgement of receipt of the goods by the carrier and as proof of the contract and its terms. It is also a form of security. Its legitimate holder is the only one who, upon presentation of the original, can demand delivery of the goods at the destination from the carrier. It can be issued to the carrier, nominative or to order (i.e. negotiable and endorsable) and its assignment allows the transfer of ownership of the goods. Combined with a means of payment such as a letter of credit (governed by UCP 600 rules), it allows the goods to be transferred from the seller to the buyer with certain guarantees for both parties.

In this way, the seller is paid upon presentation of the BL and other documentation to the bank, and the buyer has access to the goods at the destination. The seller must ensure that the document complies with the formal requirements of the credit terms (maximum duration of the shipment, ports, freight paid or due, information in the Consignee box, form of issue with regard to the possibility of endorsement, etc.).

---

[7] The package limit is calculated using the so-called "container rule". According to this rule, used in the groupage of goods in containers, a package is considered to be any unit shown on the bill of lading as being loaded in the container (bags, pallets, boxes, etc.); otherwise, the entire container is considered to be a single package.

If a company does not want to use the Bill of Lading function, it can request the issuance of a BL that does not contain the Bill of Lading, called a Sea Waybill (also known as an Express Bill of Lading, Liner Bill of Lading, Straight Bill of Lading, or Non-Negotiable Bill of Lading). This document tells the consignee that he can claim delivery of the goods from the shipping company by simply identifying himself at the destination.

3.3   Air transport

It is the fastest and most agile mode of transportation and the one that offers the greatest global coverage, but it is expensive and has significant limitations in terms of weight, size, and safety measures.

3.3.1   Commercialization

There are two types of air cargo transportation: regular and charter services. Regular airlines offer scheduled routes, so the itineraries, schedules, prices and conditions are known in advance. International airlines, most of which are members of the International Air Transport Association (IATA), allocate cargo and documents at intermediate airports through contracts.

The selling or purchasing company that needs to contract air transport usually does so through an IATA cargo agency. This is usually a freight forwarder with the training and requirements mandated by this association and authorized to issue transportation contracts on behalf of the airlines.

Nowadays, there are services adapted to the needs of companies, such as courier services offered by international operators specializing in express air transport.

Air cargo rates represent the cost of transportation between airports and are periodically published by IATA in its TACT rules (The Air Cargo Tariff and Rules). These rates, which are increasingly competitive and tailored to shipment needs, are classified as follows:

a) *normal by weight* (the greater the total weight of the shipment, the less you pay per kilogram),
b) *specific* (for some goods)
c) *per air container* (Unit Load Device or ULD).

Each shipment has a corresponding airfare based on its tariff weight. The tariff weight is the greater of its scale weight and its volume weight. The most commonly used equivalency is the volume in cubic centimeters divided by 6,000. To this rate, origin and destination costs are added, as well as surcharges corresponding to the total cost of transportation, which are allocated to the seller or buyer according to the agreed Incoterms rule. In addition, air freight charter services cover specific or temporary needs that are managed and contracted according to the needs of the shipment and the market supply.

3.3.2 Infrastructure, vehicles and cargo types

Airport infrastructures act as intermodal logistics platforms. They usually combine air and land (mainly road) transportation. Airports with significant cargo traffic have terminals and cargo centers where pre- and post-flight operations are carried out (storage, consolidation into pallets and air containers, customs clearance and inspections, etc.).

There are many types of aircraft with more or less cargo capacity. Freighters and combination aircraft (the latter carrying both passengers and cargo) are the most common. Cargo is usually transported in the aircraft's cargo holds, consolidated in unitized load devices (ULDs). This allows for more efficient, faster and safer cargo handling. The types of ULDs are also varied: net pallets, closed igloo pallets, etc.

3.3.3 International regulation of contract of carriages

The Montreal Convention[8] governs the contract for international air cargo transport. Its main provisions concerning the air carrier's liability are as follows:

- The carrier's liability extends to the entire air transport operation.
- The carrier is presumed liable for loss of or damage to the cargo, as well as for delay in delivery.

....

[8] International Convention on Civil Aviation for the Unification of Certain Rules for International Carriage by Air. The 1999 Montreal Convention is an update of the 1929 Warsaw Convention and entered into force in November 2003.

- The limit of the carrier's compensation is set at 22 SDRs per kilogram of gross cargo lost, damaged or delayed. When the Convention was published, the limit was set at 17 SDRs, but an updating mechanism was included if the average value of the goods transported increased. It was first increased from 17 to 19 SDRs and to 22 SDRs per kilo as of December 28, 2019.
- Claims against the carrier must be made at the time of delivery (in the case of apparent loss or damage) or within 14 days of delivery (in the case of non-apparent loss or damage). In the event of delay, the reservation must be made within 21 days of delivery at destination.
- The statute of limitations for the exercise of possible actions is two years.

The contract of transportation by air is formalized in the Air Waybill (AWB), which performs the functions of a bill of lading. It is issued on a form standardized by IATA.

3.4   Rail transport

This mode of transportation offers a high load capacity, a high level of safety, and a competitive and stable price. It is also the most environmentally friendly. However, it is relatively slow and requires large investments in infrastructure and international standardization (track gauge, driving standards, safety, intermodality, etc.).

3.4.1   Commercialization

Railway transportation is carried out on a regular or optional basis. In the regular regime there are fixed routes, services, schedules, stations and conditions for periodic transportation.

It can be contracted through combined transport operators (freight forwarders specializing in this type of transport), railway operators or road transportation operators, who group cargoes that can then be transported in semi-trailers or swap bodies using adapted railway wagons.

There is a growing flow of container traffic between seaports and inland through rail terminals and dry ports, as well as the possibility of connecting with international destinations. Container rates depend on the type of container, its weight, the route and the additional services required (loading, unloading, handling, etc.).

In the optional regime, entire trains can be contracted depending on the requirements of the shipment. The railroad has specialized in the transportation of certain types of goods, such as vehicles, raw materials and bulk goods, which are handled under this formula, also known as "customer train" or "single customer".

3.4.2   Infrastructure, vehicles and cargo types

The railway network connects freight stations or terminals, which serve as intermodal logistics platforms. At these stations, goods or their transport units (containers, semi-trailers or swap bodies) are handled during loading, unloading, consolidation, etc.

Trains consist of locomotives (electric or diesel) and freight cars. The latter can be of different types depending on their adaptation to the goods to be transported: container platform, semi-trailer, closed car, hopper car, etc.

3.4.3   International regulation of the contract of carriage

International rail transport contracts are governed by the COTIF-CIM Convention, as last amended by the Vilnius Protocol of 1999. The carrier's liability is governed by the following general principles:

- The carrier is liable for loss of or damage to the goods and for delay in delivery, although their liability may be excluded for certain reasons.
- The limit of the carrier's compensation is set at 17 SDRs per kilogram of gross weight for lost or damaged goods. In case of delay, the limit is set at four times the price of transportation.
- Claims agains the carrier must be made at the time of delivery (in the case of apparent loss or damage) or within seven days of delivery (in the case of non-apparent loss or damage). In the event of delay, the reservation must be made within 60 days of delivery at destination.
- The statute of limitations for filing claims is one year.

The international railway consignment note or the CIM consignment note proves the existence of the contract and its conditions, as well as the receipt of the goods by the carrier.

3.5 Multimodal transportation

More than a mode of transport, it is a form of contracting where a multimodal transport operator, usually a freight forwarder or another transport operator, issues, as the sole carrier to the shipper, a contract that covers a service using multiple modes of transport (road, sea, air or rail). The goods are transported in intermodal transport units, such as containers, swap bodies or semi-trailers, without breaking the load.

Multimodality is a growing trend that makes it possible to create multimodal transport chains in which each mode offers its advantages (speed, cost, etc.) and promotes the creation of efficient and competitive logistics chains (co-modality).

3.5.1 International regulation of multimodal transportation contracts

At the international level, there is no specific and global legal framework for multimodal transportation contracts. The model consignment note used may refer to the general terms and conditions of freight forwarders or other associations. In some cases, this situation can lead to legal uncertainty. There are two most widely used conventions that can be used as a regulatory framework: the 1980 Geneva Convention and the UNCTAD (United Nations Conference on Trade and Development)/ICC (International Chamber of Commerce) Rules on Multimodal Transport Documents.

The most widely used multimodal bill of lading model is the FIATA Negotiable Bill of Lading for Multimodal Transportation (FIATA FBL), which refers to the UNCTAD/ITC Rules in its standard format. Its general principles concerning the liability regime of the multimodal transport operator are as follows

- The carrier's liability limit, if no sea transport has been involved, is set at 8.33 SDR per gross kilogram. Otherwise, the limit is the greater of 666.67 SDR per package (using the container rule) or unit, or 2 SDR per gross kilogram.

- Claims against the carrier must be made at the time of delivery (in the case of apparent loss or damage) or within six days of delivery (in the case of non-apparent loss or damage).
- The statute of limitations for any action is nine months.

Chapter 3

Incoterms and the Supply Chain

1 The need and functions of the Incoterms rules

Incoterm rules are a key tool for managing the purchase and sale of goods, whether on a domestic or international scale. These rules are paramount for ensuring that parties to a contract of sale delineate their respective obligations comprehensively.

In this sense, the contract reflects aspects such as packaging and loading of the goods, transportation, delivery performance (something very important and specifically provided for by the Incoterms rules), customs clearance, transport insurance and the documentation required in each operation, as well as a documentary means of payment. All these aspects, moreover, have a decisive influence on the rule agreed in each purchase and sale operation.

International purchase and sale transactions are inherently more complex than national or domestic transactions due to several factors:

- *The regulation of sales and purchases across different countries poses various challenges due to local customs, practices, and regulatory differences.* For instance, an Egyptian company may have different obligations compared to companies in Colombia, Brazil or Russia. Moreover, each country has distinct commercial customs and practices, such as varying negotiation styles, levels of trust, and initial margins in bargaining. Without standardized international terms, such as Incoterms rules, discrepancies in understanding and fulfilling contractual obligations can lead to disputes and controversies. Providing a common framework is one of the main objectives of the Incoterms rules.

- *Longer transportation times and a more complex supply chain.* It is therefore advisable to take out insurance to mitigate the risks associated with transportation and its related functions, such as storage and handling.

- *The obligation, in some cases, to undertake export and import customs clearance, along with providing all requisite documentation and paying associated taxes.* Except for national operations or within the same customs territory (as in the case of intra-European Community trade within the territory of the Community Customs Union), customs procedures involve risks and formalities that can complicate, condition or impede the development of foreign trade operations, both because of their fiscal effects and because of the restrictions stemming from customs control and security measures.

- *The need to adapt the product to the regulatory requirements* (imposed by technical barriers, which are by far the most difficult to surmount) *and commercial requirements of the destination market* (packaging, packing or distribution conditions, e.g. marking, recycling, traceability, safety, etc.).

- *A high level of mistrust between buyers and sellers regarding the fulfillment of each party's primary obligations in a sale or purchase: delivery of the agreed-upon product and payment of the price.* This mistrust increases when dealing with new customers, suppliers, or markets. There are various procedures, resources and means to reduce or cover the risks of non-compliance. For example, specific payment instruments such as letters of credit and export credit insurances can be used to prevent non-payment.

- *The influence of international relations* (trade geopolitics) on the application of greater or lesser restrictions on trade relations (depending on the existence or not of trade agreements or greater or lesser "political affinity"), linguistic and cultural differences, and others.

An analysis of all these factors reveals the need to standardize terms of sale and purchase as much as possible to streamline operational procedures, accelerate transactions, and foster a common understanding between parties by standardizing commercial practices. This is the purpose for which the Incoterms were created.

Thus, the inclusion of an Incoterms rule in a contract of sale clearly allocates a large part of the obligations and responsibilities for both the seller and buyer parties in relation to the main aspects of transaction management. These include the transportation contract, delivery of goods and the transfer of risk (from seller to buyer) for loss or damage during transportation. Additionally, it addresses customs clearance for export and import (including transit countries), requirements for transportation insurance (if mandated and its conditions), documentation related to proof of delivery, and other associated obligations.

Knowledge and effective application of these rules are essential for companies to improve the risk/reward ratio of any purchase and sale transaction and to strengthen the commercial relationships that enable their international expansion.

The correct use of Incoterms will enable companies to acquire key skills for strategically planning their internationalization and, in particular, for managing foreign trade in the following areas:

- **Proposing pricing options based on agreed Incoterms rules**

  The selling company has to make an estimate according to each Incoterms rule, which allows it to offer different price options. For instance, consider a scenario where a company based in Seville, Spain, is tasked with providing a price quote for shipping goods via container to San Luis Potosi, Mexico. An EXW quotation (not recommended for containers and international operations for reasons to be discussed later) includes costs like manufacturing, packing, packaging, markup, and additional expenses such as issuing the certificate of origin. However, if the agreed rule is DDP, the selling company must include in its quotation the costs covered by EXW, along with those required to deliver the goods to the buyer's warehouse, including import duties and taxes. This approach ensures that the buyer only needs to unload the goods from the container upon arrival.

  Between these two "extreme" rules there are nine other options (eleven rules in total), and the costs to be assumed are different for each of them, ranging from EXW to DDP, so that a higher cost Incoterms rule for the selling company must correspond to a higher price proposal.

- **Correct interpretation of the prices and terms and conditions of purchase in the offer**

  The amount of an offer, along with the associated Incoterms rules, determine the obligations and costs of the seller. This transparency enables the buyer to assess the detailed obligations and costs he will have to assume until the goods are placed in his warehouse. This makes it possible to compare different pricing options from different suppliers in the same country and even offers from different countries (for different Incoterms rules).

Consider a company based in Santiago, Chile, negotiating the purchase of a containerized shipment of goods from China on FOB Shanghai port terms. To evaluate the attractiveness of the offer, the importing company needs to perform a cost study that takes into account the cost of ocean transportation from China (including freight and surcharges), expenses at the Chilean port of entry, customs clearance fees (and taxes), and overland transportation to its warehouse in Santiago de Chile. This cost analysis can be compared to quotes from other suppliers with different Incoterms rules. Let's assume that an Indian supplier offers the Chilean company a similar product under CFR terms at the port of Valparaiso. In this case, to make the comparison, the purchasing company must take into account that it will have to bear the cost of the import port, customs clearance (and taxes) and overland transportation to its warehouse in Santiago de Chile (in CFR terms, the ocean transportation is paid by the selling party and is already included in the price of its invoice).

The process involves aligning various offers under different Incoterms rules, while accounting for the costs that the buyer will incur in each scenario. By systematically adding these costs to each offer, a "selection price" can be derived. This selection price serves as a basis for comparing the offers. Detailed instructions for this process are provided in the case studies section. Although the comparison of costs is not the only factor in determining the best offer (other aspects such as product quality, delivery time, payment terms, and reliability of each supplier, may be decisive), it will undoubtedly have an important weight in the supplier selection process.

- **Fulfilling the relevant obligations related to the sale**
  Each Incoterms rule sets out the obligations of the selling and purchasing parties with respect to certain key elements of the sale. It is imperative for both parties to adhere to these terms, conducting their contracts, communications, contracts, and documentation in accordance with the specified rules, and ensuring compliance from the other party.

For example, a Portuguese company that has sold a product under DAP Rabat conditions must assume the costs and obligations until the goods are placed in the buyer's warehouse in Rabat. Conversely, the buyer assumes responsibilities such as import clearance at Moroccan customs. Thus, if the importer does not properly manage the customs clearance and the seller incurs additional costs, the seller can recover these costs from the buyer according to the agreed Incoterms rule.

- **Determination of the time of delivery and transfer of risk**
One of the most important aspects of the Incoterms is the determination of the time and method of goods delivery, along with the subsequent transfer of risk encompassing possible damage to the goods during transportation, from the seller to the buyer.

  For example, a company in Zaragoza (Spain) sells a container of goods to an American company under CPT conditions at the port of New Orleans. In this case, delivery and risk transfer occur when the goods are loaded into the container in Zaragoza. In the event of loss, the buyer is responsible for the loss or damage from that point on. On the other hand, if the same sale is made on DAP Jackson terms (the city north of New Orleans where the importer is located), the seller does not deliver the goods (and therefore assumes the risk) until the container containing the goods arrives at the importer's facilities in the city of Jackson. Consequently, any loss up to that point must be borne by the exporting company.

  When one party bears the risk and experiences the consequences of the loss, it entails bearing the resulting economic burden and, therefore, liable for the loss incurred:

  a) The seller must either replace the goods or fulfill the buyer's requirements as agreed upon in the contract of sale. However, the seller cannot demand payment from the buyer under any circumstance.
  b) The buyer pays the seller for the goods.

  In both cases, the party who suffers the economic loss may consider the possibility of claiming compensation from the transport insurance (if there is one and the loss was covered by it) or from the transport operator (depending on what was agreed in the transport contract and the relevant legal framework).

- **Negotiation and adoption of the appropriate Incoterms rule depending on the characteristics of the operation**
  There is no one-size-fits-all rule that is optimal for all operations. Instead, the choice of Incoterms rule should be carefully considered in conjunction with other factors such as the company's internationalization strategy, market entry approach (direct sale, distributor, agent, etc.), and the negotiating power of the counterparty. In general, each company should try to apply the rules that allow it to control the logistics chain and minimize costs and risks. This approach ensures customer (or supplier) satisfaction, fostering customer loyalty, a key aspect for international expansion.

2   Characterization of Incoterms rules

2.1   History and nature of Incoterms rules

At the beginning of the 20th century, the International Chamber of Commerce (ICC), an organization that promotes the development of international economic relations, created the Incoterms (acronym for *International Commercial Terms)* to provide a standard that would contribute to standardization, legal certainty and understanding in the international sale and purchase of goods. Until then, the heterogeneity of the commercial rules and customs governing sales and purchases in each country had led to legal uncertainty, disputes and problems of all kinds, which were a burden on the development of international trade.

In an attempt to standardize contractual practices, the ICC commissioned several studies which resulted in the first version of the Incoterms, published in 1936. Since then, subsequent versions followed in 1945, 1953, 1967, 1976, 1976, 1980, 1990, 1990, 2000, 2010 and the latest version, which came into effect on January 1, 2020. These successive iterations reflect ongoing efforts to adapt Incoterms to evolving global trade practices, technological advancements (the advent of the container in 1956, intermodality, etc, and regulatory changes.

Incoterms rules are identified by three-letter abbreviations (see Table 3.1) that summarize their meaning in English (e.g., EXW corresponds to the ex works rule). In the course of their evolution, "variants" of these rules have emerged, intended for specific uses that do not enjoy standardized regulation, such as EXF *(ex factory),* EXW loaded, EX cellar, FOR *(free on rail),* FOT *(free*

Incoterms rules 2020	
Usual acronyms	**Meaning**
EXW	*Ex works*
FCA	*Free carrier*
FAS	*Free alongside ship*
FOB	*Free on board*
CFR	*Cost and freight*
CIF	*Cost, insurance and freight*
CPT	*Carriage paid to*
CIP	*Carriage and insurance paid to*
DAP	*Delivered at place*
DPU	*Delivered at place unloaded*
DDP	*Delivered duty paid*

Table 3.1. Incoterms rules are commonly used by their acronyms,
which correspond to the name of each rule in English.

on truck), PAF *(packed at factory)*, DIS *(delivery into store)* or FIS *(free into storage)*. The rules published in 2020 do not prohibit the use of the latter, but they discourage it because it is a source of uncertainty for both parties. If they are still used, it is necessary to specify their meaning in the contract of sale.

Although the new versions do not repeal the previous ones, it is advisable for companies to use the rules contained in the latest version and to make this explicit by using the phrase "Incoterms 2020" at the end of the text. As an example, consider a correctly worded clause:[1]

FCA Avda. Libertad, 737, Viña del Mar, Valparaíso. Chile. Incoterms 2020.

[1] In order to make the reading of this work more dynamic, most of the examples cited in the text do not represent the exact wording, unless, as in this case, it is stated otherwise.

Within the framework of the so-called new *lex mercatoria,* the Incoterms have the character of rules or usages of trade between companies, which the ICC itself has granted to itself to regulate its commercial transactions. Because of the Chamber's status as a non-governmental organization, the Incoterms rules do not constitute a source of law, as they do not emanate from the legislature, nor are they ratified and incorporated into national legal systems through publication in official journals.

However, these rules acquire contractual character and force to the extent that the parties voluntarily incorporate them in their contracts of sale, and are also recognized, as follows, in Article 9 of the Vienna Convention:[2]

- The parties shall be bound by any usage that they may have agreed upon and by any practice that they may have in place among themselves.
- Unless otherwise agreed, the parties are presumed to have impliedly incorporated into the contract or its formation any usage that they were or ought to have been aware and which is widely recognized in international trade and regularly observed by parties in contracts of a similar nature within the relevant trade.

It is very convenient to know the content of the Vienna Convention, because it is the only legal system of international reach, albeit not universally adopted (though predominantly so), regulating the contract of international sale of goods. If the seller and the buyer are domiciled in countries that are signatories to the Convention (currently 93) and have not expressly excluded it in their contract of sale, the Convention applies to everything that is not agreed in the contract.

The Convention thus establishes the primacy of the usages (understood as rules) to which the parties have adhered to over the provisions outlined within this legal framework. The Convention, as stipulated in its 6th article, has a dispositive nature, that is to say, it applies unless expressly specified otherwise by the parties. This principle aligns with the prevailing notion in international commercial law, which advocates for the freedom of contract between parties. Thus, it is possible to modify and specify certain provisions of the Vienna Con-

---

[2] United Nations Convention on Contracts for the International Sale of Goods (CISG) or Vienna Convention of 1980. Full text and ratification status available on the website www.uncitral.org.

vention, such as those pertaining to the transfer of risk, through the utilization of an Incoterms rule.

However, the Incoterms cannot supersede the rules and regulations in force in a given country. The mandatory applicable law takes precedence over the contracts between the parties. For example, a selling company may not be able to clear imports into a country because the legal system of that country does not allow it. In such cases, the strict application of an Incoterms rule like DDP (where the seller is responsible for clearing imports into the buyer's country) may become unfeasible.

2.2   New features in the Incoterms 2020 rules

The most relevant new features of the Incoterms 2020 rules are the following:

- **Update of the DAT rule and its reformulation to DPU**
  The DAT rule has been replaced with DPU, providing greater versatility. Unlike DAT, DPU no longer necessitates that the specified point designated by the Incoterms rule be a terminal; it can now include locations such as the buyer's warehouse or another agreed-upon site. We will discuss this in detail when we deal with this rule.

- **The wording of the Incoterms 2020 publication is improved and clarified compared to previous versions**
  Efforts have been made to better explain the terms and their proper use, as well as the relationship and implications of the contract of sale with other types of contracts; explanatory notes have been added to each rule; and emphasis has been placed on some key aspects, such as delivery and passing of risk, to clarify when these occur.

- **Attempt to combine the use of FCA and container transport with the requirement that the seller obtain a shipped BL**
  Although it will be discussed in detail in the analysis of this Incoterms rule, an attempt has been made to include an option in the obligations of the parties to enable it to be combined with the seller obtaining a shipped BL (BL on board). Therefore, the feasibility of this option will need to be carefully evaluated to determine its practical applicability.

- **Modification of the insurance coverage in the CIP rule**
  Under this rule, if agreed upon, the selling party must take out insurance with coverage equivalent to at least ICC "A" cover. Previously, the required coverage was ICC "C," but now it has been elevated to ICC "A" cover, reflecting a higher standard of protection. However, it is important to note that certain risks may still be excluded under ICC "A" cover.
  The CIF rule, which also includes an insurance requirement, CIF, retains the lower ICC "C" coverage mandate (more appropriate for bulk and commodities), although the parties may voluntarily agree to higher coverage (recommended when using this rule with container shipments).

- **Allowing the parties to use their own transportation means is explicitly included**
  While we believe this flexibility was implicitly understood in previous versions of the Incoterms, the 2020 update expressly mentions this possibility. For instance, under the DAP for road transportation, the selling company may choose not to hire a carrier, but to perform the transport to the place of destination using its own fleet of vehicles and personnel. In any case, the Incoterms 2020 rules explicitly mention this possibility.

- **Clarification of the costs to be borne by each party**
  The obligations A9/B9 of each Incoterms rule contain a list of costs to be borne by the selling and purchasing companies, respectively. While this obligation existed in previous versions under the same name, the 2020 edition introduces a more explicit breakdown of costs assigned to each party within every term. This clarification is significant as one of the primary functions of Incoterms is to allocate and apportion the costs of the logistics chain between the selling and purchasing parties.

- **Comparison of the obligations of each party according to each of the ten obligations or articles of the Incoterms rules**
  The Incoterms 2020 version offers a valuable resource at the end of its text: a cross-referenced table outlining the obligations of each party (seller or buyer) according to each of the ten obligations or articles specified in the rules. This table provides a clear comparison, illustrating how each party's obligations are modified —either extended or reduced— in relation to the performance of each obligation.

It is important to bear in mind that the new version of Incoterms is an excellent opportunity to learn about the updates and ensure their correct usage. In my long professional career as a teacher and consultant to companies in foreign trade, I have observed that while the rules may be "known", their practical application often falls short. Certain aspects may be overlooked, or actions may deviate from what is outlined in the official publication.

On the other hand, in many cases, the people responsible for negotiating and applying an Incoterms rule in a contract of sale (commercial area) are different from those who have to put it into practice (logistics area). It is often the case that the commercial eagerness to conclude a contract of sale leads to the acceptance of a rule that is difficult to implement in reality. Let's take the case of an export from Europe or South America to an inland location in an African country with a poor transport infrastructure and a customs office that is notoriously insecure in the application of its procedures. Now, the commercial department may have accepted, for example, the buyer's warehouse DDP rule, but when it comes to carrying out the operation, the logistics department may encounter innumerable problems in fulfilling its obligations.

These practical considerations highlight the importance of thoroughly understanding the implications of each Incoterms rule and ensuring alignment between commercial negotiations and operational feasibility. A new version seems to be an excellent opportunity to update them together and to establish communication channels that allow them to be better applied according to the characteristics of each operation.

2.3 Scope of Incoterms rules

In general terms, the Incoterms are rules that are primarily designed to facilitate international commercial transactions. They address several key aspects of these transactions, including:

- The main obligations of the selling and purchasing parties with respect to the contract of sale.
- The costs attributable to each party in relation to transportation and the rest of the logistics chain.

- The obligation to carry out customs clearance.
- The time of delivery and the transfer of risks from the seller to the buyer.

Table 3.2 schematically summarizes the obligations of the purchasing and selling parties under the agreed Incoterms. However, these rules do not in themselves constitute a contract of sale, as some important aspects of the commercial transaction are outside their scope.

2.3.1 Incoterms regulated issues

Since the 1990 version, the wording of the Incoterms rules has been structured according to the obligations of the seller and the buyer, as summarized in Table 3.3.

It should be noted that in the 2020 version, the ten obligations that make up the Incoterms rules have been restructured. Some obligations now feature entirely new definitions, which have occasionally encompassed elements previously expressed across multiple obligations in earlier versions.

The obligations to which the parties are subject are listed below.

1 General obligations of the seller and the buyer (A1 and B1)

The selling company must deliver the goods and the commercial invoice as agreed in the contract of sale, as well as any other document or proof of conformity, such as packing list, certificate of inspection or certificate of origin, specified in the contract. For its part, the purchasing company must pay the agreed price for the goods as stipulated in the contract of sale. It should be noted that the Incoterms rules do not determine the means of payment (we will discuss the relationship and influence of documentary means of payment in due course). Therefore, this first obligation reaffirms the most basic duties of any sale and purchase: the seller delivers a good and the buyer must pay for it.

The transfer of ownership is not determined, it depends on the terms or laws applicable to the contract of sale. In general, if the conditions for the transfer of title are not specified in the contract and a dispute arises, the law of the place where the goods are located (*lex fori* or "law of the forum") will be applied. Even the 1980 Vienna Convention on the International Sale of Goods did not establish a definitive criterion for the transfer of title at that time.

Incoterms rules 2020 – Allocation of efforts and costs												
	EXW	FCA local seller	FCA another location	FAS	FOB	CFR	CIF	CPT	CIP	DAP	DPU	DDP
Packaging	●	●	●	●	●	●	●	●	●	●	●	●
Other export costs: documents, certifications, etc.	●	●	●	●	●	●	●	●	●	●	●	●
Loading of the goods on the initial transport vehicle	○	●	●	●	●	●	●	●	●	●	●	●
Export clearance	○	●	●	●	●	●	●	●	●	●	●	●
Initial transportation	○	○	●	●	●	●	●	●	●	●	●	●
Transportation to terminal	○	○	●	●	●	●	●	●	●	●	●	●
Costs at origin terminal: THC, fees and others	○	○	○	●	●	●	●	●	●	●	●	●
Cargo on board	○	○	○	○	●	●	●	●	●	●	●	●
Main transport	○	○	○	○	○	●	●	●	●	●	●	●
Transport insurance	◉	◉	◉	◉	◉	◉	◉	◉	◉	○	○	○
Terminal download	○	○	○	○	○	○	○	○	○	●	●	●
Costs at destination terminal: THC, fees and others	○	○	○	○	○	○	○	○	○	●	●	●
Import clearance	○	○	○	○	○	○	○	○	○	○	○	●
Transportation from terminal to destination	○	○	○	○	○	○	○	○	○	●	●	●
Unloading of goods from the final transport vehicle	○	○	○	○	○	○	○	○	○	○	●	○

● Cost to be borne by the selling company.
○ Cost to be borne by the purchasing company.
◉ ○ Insurance is not compulsory as a condition of an Incoterms rule, but it is indicated which party, seller or buyer, should consider taking out insurance as it bears most of the transport risks. In general, it is convenient for the buyer from EXW to CPT, while it will be convenient for the seller from DAP to DDP.

Table 3.2. List of the steps and costs assumed by the seller and the buyer according to the different Incoterms rules agreed upon for an international sale and purchase transaction.

Obligations of the selling company	Obligations of the purchasing company
A1. General obligations	B1. General obligations
A2. Delivery	B2. Reception
A3. Risk transfer	B3. Risk transfer
A4. Transportation	B4. Transportation
A5. Insurance	B5. Insurance
A6. Delivery/transport document	B6. Delivery/transport document
A7. Export/import clearance	B7. Export/import clearance
A8. Checking/packing/marking	B8. Checking/packing/marking
A9. Cost sharing	B9. Cost sharing
A10. Notifications	B10. Notifications

Table 3.3. Obligations of the selling and purchasing companies regulated by the Incoterms rules.

It is generally recognized that any document or procedure stipulated within the obligations of both parties may be presented in electronic format, provided mutual contract or customary practice permits. It is important to acknowledge the growing trend towards the adoption of electronic documentation over traditional paper-based processes, a trend expected to continue expanding in the foreseeable future.

2 Delivery and receipt of the goods (obligations A2 and B2)

This deals with the reciprocal obligations of the seller to deliver the goods and the buyer to receive them (and is closely related to the point of transfer of risk in the carriage of the goods discussed in the following obligations A3 and B3).

A2 determines the place and manner of delivery (placing the goods at a place, handing them over to a carrier, making them available to the buyer for unloading, etc.) so that the seller is deemed to have delivered the goods to the buyer. Note that the main obligation of the seller in a contract of sale is to deliver the goods, so it is essential to fulfill this obligation in the manner prescribed by the Incoterms rules.

B2 specifies the buyer's obligation to take delivery of the goods in a manner related to the form of delivery indicated in A2 for the seller (this may consist of hiring and positioning a vessel at a port, sending a truck to pick up the goods at the seller's warehouse, receiving the goods sent by the seller at its facilities at the place of destination, etc.) once the buyer has been notified of the seller's obligation to take delivery of the goods.

3 Passing of risk (obligations A3 and B3)

Specifying at what point in the logistics chain the risk of damage to the goods in transit is transferred is a key aspect of the Incoterms rules. Each rule specifies where and when the risk passes from the seller to the buyer, which coincides with the point of delivery/receipt of the A2/B2 obligations. However, the point of delivery/transfer of risk does not always coincide with the place to which the seller must pay for transportation, as is the case with the Group C rules, where the seller must pay for transportation to the country of destination, but delivers (for risk transfer purposes) in the country of origin.

The ability to determine the place of delivery and the transfer of risk in each rule is paramount. When a loss occurs, it is necessary to compare the place where the loss occurred with the place of delivery and transfer of risk indicated by the rule applied in the sale and purchase. Two possibilities result from this comparison:

a) Loss before delivery/transfer of risk. The seller has failed to deliver (this is his main obligation under the contract of sale) and must replace the goods or act as specified in the contract of sale. In any case, the buyer is not obliged to pay because the goods have not been delivered.

b) Loss after delivery/transfer of risk. The seller has delivered (fulfilled its main obligation) and, therefore, the buyer must pay the purchase price.

In both cases, other *a posteriori* effects are derived, such as determining who can claim against the transport operator, in the event that it is responsible for the loss or damage of the goods, to receive compensation for it, or the part that can be claimed from the transport insurance contracted to cover the risks of the operation.

4 Transport (obligations A4 and B4)

These obligations specify which party is responsible for arranging or conducting the transportation of the goods, whether through contracting with a third-party carrier or utilizing their own means of transportation. It specifies the obligations and implications of each party with respect to the contracting of transportation in its various stages (from the warehouse to the port where the shipment is carried out on board, from the port of shipment to the port or terminal in the country of destination, etc.) within the logistics chain that will develop the operation. Transportation can also be facilitated using the seller's own transportation assets, such as a fleet of trucks.

5 Insurance (obligations A5 and B5)

It indicates whether the parties have an obligation to take out insurance to cover the risks of the goods during transportation. This obligation is specified in two ways:

a) *Taking out insurance.* Only the CIP and CIF rules state that the seller is obliged, as a condition of the contract of sale, to take out insurance to cover the risks borne by the buyer in connection with the carriage of the goods. Each of these rules specifies some aspects that such insurance contracts must comply with, such as coverage, insured value, etc. In the Incoterms 2020 rules, the minimum coverage in the CIP has been modified (extending it from ICC "C" to ICC "A").

b) *Insurance information.* Both parties are obligated to provide each other with the information required for insurance purposes. This would be the case, for example, in a transaction under FCA conditions at the seller's warehouse, where the buyer requests information from the seller (weight, packaging, exact location of the goods, etc.) in order to take out insurance to cover the risks of transporting the goods from the seller's warehouse, where the transfer of risks occurs under this rule.

6 Delivery/transport document (obligations A6 and B6)

It details the aspects that must be satisfied by the document proving delivery of the goods. Depending on the seller's involvement in the contract of carriage (and the form of delivery detailed in A2), each rule specifies what such proof must be:

a) A transport document (a contract of carriage meeting certain requirements such as carriage paid, etc., when it is the seller who contracts for carriage, e.g., in DAP).

b) A simple document proving delivery to the transport operator contracted by the buyer (when it is the buyer who contracts the transport, e.g. in FCA seller's warehouse).

7 Export/import clearance (obligations A7 and B7)

It refers to which party must perform export or import customs clearance, if required.

In all Incoterms, export clearance is performed by the seller and import clearance is performed by the buyer (who is more familiar with its legislation, customs procedures and fiscal implications), except for EXW (where export clearance is performed by the buyer) and DDP (where import clearance is performed by the seller).

It also indicates the obligation of each party to assist the other (at the latter's request and expense) by providing any documents or information necessary to manage the customs clearance. This would be the case, for example, of a buyer company that has informed the seller (and has agreed with the seller in the contract of sale) that it needs to obtain and present a certificate of preferential origin (e.g. a EUR1 to obtain a tariff reduction on importation at destination, assuming, of course, that it meets the requirements for requesting the issuance of such a certificate). In this case, the seller would be obliged to obtain such a certificate and pass on its cost to the buyer by including it in the invoiced price. It is very important to take into account the documents to be presented to customs. These must be consulted beforehand (with the customs representative or in databases such as TARIC or Market Access Database, for example, for transactions to or from the European Union) to confirm the viability of the transaction (there are products that are subject to significant restrictions in their marketing) and the fiscal aspects (duties and other taxes). These and other sources of customs information are discussed in detail below.

8 Checking, packing, and marking (obligations A8 and B8)

The selling party has the obligation (and bears the corresponding costs) to check that the goods comply with the requirements as to quality, dimensions, weights, etc., at the time of delivery. In addition, he must mark and package the goods in a manner suitable for transportation or, more specifically, comply with the marking and packaging requirements specified in the contract of sale. If the marking and packaging requirements have not been specified in the contract, this obligation is formulated in a very general way (even, in certain rules, the seller may not know the means of transport to be contracted by the buyer), so it is advisable that the specific aspects of packaging and packing are expressly agreed in the contract of sale.

9 Cost sharing (obligations A9 and B9)

The division of costs between the seller and the buyer is established in relation to aspects specified in other obligations of the Incoterms. These are mainly costs up to the point of delivery, transportation, loading or unloading, insurance and customs formalities and the assistance provided between the parties for their development.

10 Reporting (obligations A10 and B10)

Adequate transmission of information between the parties is essential for the proper and efficient management of the sale and purchase from the point of delivery of the goods and their transportation (and to resolve some of the incidents that may arise during its development). This transmission of information, in the form of notifications to the other party, refers to aspects such as: notification that the goods have been delivered, notification that the designated carrier has not accepted the goods, the name of the carrier, the mode of transport, the time chosen within the agreed delivery period, etc.

2.3.2 Issues not covered by Incoterms rules

As stated above, the Incoterms do not constitute a contract of sale in themselves, since certain essential aspects of the commercial transaction are outside their scope, although they may be affected by them. For this reason, the conditions governing these aspects must be negotiated, agreed and expressed in the contract of sale in order to prevent the lack of contract in these areas from creating legal and commercial uncertainty between the parties. Among the aspects not regulated by the Incoterms are the following:

- **Transfer of ownership of the goods and the law and jurisdiction competent to resolve breaches of the contract of sale**
  The expressions used in the wording of the Incoterms rules, such as "delivery" or "placing at the disposal" of the company concerned, do not in any way imply the transfer of ownership of the goods. This is governed by what is agreed in the contract of sale (which may contain clauses directly affecting the goods, such as retention of title) or, failing that, by the law applicable under the conventions ratified by the countries of origin and destination. It is important to note that the Vienna Convention of 1980, which typically governs international contract of sales, does not explicitly define the conditions under which ownership of the goods is considered transferred.

  Something similar occurs with the rules applicable to breaches of the contract of sale. Since the Vienna Convention has been ratified by most of the major countries in international trade and applies (by default, i.e., unless expressly excluded) to transactions between companies domiciled in those countries, it will usually be the legal framework that regulates what is not expressly specified in the contract of sale (i.e., calculation of damages for breach of contract). However, the Vienna Convention's provisions are definitive and take precedence over any contracts made by the parties. While the parties may include a clause in the contract of sale designating a different applicable law, such contracts are less common.

  If the transaction involves companies from countries that are not signatories to the Vienna Convention, the applicability of the Convention may be determined by private international law, a legal field dedicated to resolving international jurisdiction conflicts. For instance, within the European Union, Regulation (EC) No. 593/2008, known as "Rome I," governs the law applicable to contractual obligations. Under Rome I, for sales and purchases, the applicable law is typically that of the country where the selling party is based, thereby potentially subjecting the transaction to the Vienna Convention. In the case of an import from a country that is not a signatory to this Convention, such as Morocco, Moroccan law will apply, in accordance with the universal principle of Rome I.

  It does not seem reasonable to leave such an important aspect as the legal framework applicable to the contract depending on the countries with which it is traded, which is why it is advisable to expressly agree on it in the contract of sale. Certainly, for the sake of legal standardization, the most sensible thing to do is to agree in all contracts to submit to the Vienna Convention.

The same is true with respect to the means of dispute resolution and competent jurisdiction (judicial channels and venue). In general, when negotiating a purchase and sale transaction, it is not expected that a breach will occur, but for this reason the contract should include a clause specifying how the parties will resolve their disputes in the event of a breach.

In the first instance, it is always advisable to try to resolve breaches by negotiation. Preserving the business relationship often outweighs the additional costs that might arise from the breach, but sometimes this proves impossible. In this case, the parties may have agreed on amicable means of conciliation or commercial mediation (a third party tries to get the parties to reach an contract before going to court or arbitration), but when the time comes, one or both parties may not abide by them.

Courts (the default option) are binding unless the parties have agreed to submit to international commercial arbitration through a clause in the purchase contract. The advantages of arbitration over litigation include:

a) *Greater effectiveness.* An arbitral award is effective if it was issued in a signatory country and in accordance with the rules of the 1958 New York Convention (Convention on the Recognition and Enforcement of Foreign Arbitral Awards), and the country where it is to be enforced is also a signatory to the said Convention. It should be noted that the Convention has been signed by 161 countries (virtually all major ones), so the effectiveness of an arbitral award in terms of enforcement is high. This is a great advantage in comparison with the judicial process, since an award issued by the courts of one country faces many difficulties in being enforced in another (a recognition procedure must be carried out, which sometimes ends up rendering the award ineffective).[3]

b) *Promptness.* Arbitral awards are typically rendered within six months from the acceptance of arbitration.

---

[3] For example, in the European Union, this recognition is automatic for judgments issued by the courts of its member countries, as established by Regulation 1215/2012 of 12 December, in force since 10/01/2015, on jurisdiction and the recognition and enforcement of judgments in civil and commercial matters, known as the Brussels Convention.

c) *Foreseeable costs.* Unlike litigation, where costs can escalate unpredictably, arbitration allows parties to anticipate expenses in advance. While this doesn't inherently make arbitration more or less economical, arbitration institutions such as chambers of commerce typically provide transparent cost structures on their websites.

d) *Neutrality of arbitrators.* In court proceedings it is possible to "suspect" that the judge of the "national" company will protect its interests against the claim of the foreign company.

e) *Specialization of arbitrators.* Highly specialized arbitrators (i.e., experts) may be appointed on a subject matter basis, depending on what is being adjudicated.

f) *Legal certainty.* Once the arbitral award has been issued, the process is over as no appeal is allowed. This stands in contrast to the judicial process, where appeals can prolong proceedings and escalate costs until a final judgment is reached. Thus, while this point can be an advantage, it also means that there is no recourse if parties are dissatisfied with the outcome.

Therefore, parties have the option to resort to either litigation or arbitration, with the latter requiring a specific clause designating the chosen arbitration court. In the absence of such an contract, the means of resolution are the courts, so it would be necessary to determine the competent courts if they have not been specified in the contract of sale (as it would be advisable). In fact, the place of delivery determined by the Incoterms rule agreed in the transaction indirectly determines the competent courts if they have not been expressly agreed in the contract of sale. For example, in the case of a sale between a Spanish company and a Colombian company, if FCA Madrid has been agreed, delivery must take place in Spain and the competent courts are Spanish, whereas if DAP Bogota has been agreed, the competent courts are Colombian.

In any case, in view of the above, it is recommended that the parties expressly agree in the contract of sale on the applicable law, the means of settling disputes and the competent courts or arbitration tribunals.

- **Means and term of payment**
  Although the Incoterms do not regulate the means and terms of payment, they may be more or less dependent on the circumstances of the transac-

tion. It is therefore advisable to adopt the appropriate rule for each transaction. This issue is discussed in detail in Section 6 of this chapter, which deals with documentary credits, and in the corresponding analyses of the Incoterms rules (see Chapters 4 and 5).

- **Quality and technical characteristics of the goods for sale, as well as their delivery time**

  The Incoterms only indicate in A1 the obligation of the seller to deliver the goods and the commercial invoice in accordance with the contract of sale and any other evidence of conformity that the seller may require. It is therefore important that the contract specifies the goods and the characteristics they must meet: quality, technical requirements, caliber, size, brands, warranty, shelf life, etc. It is also very important to specify the packaging to be used (type, materials, strength, marking, labeling, etc.).
  In accordance with the tight flow logistics that often characterize foreign trade operations today, it is also important to specify the delivery time of the goods. Usually, it is specified that it should take place before a certain date, in an interval or within a maximum period after a certain event, such as the date of opening of a documentary credit, etc.

- **Trade in services**

  Incoterms rules exclusively apply to the sale and purchase of tangible goods, meaning that trade in services falls outside their scope.

3   Incoterms rules and transport contract

Incoterms rules apply to the contract of sale and not to the contract of carriage, despite the logical implications for the latter, such as management, contracting and assumption of costs and risks of carriage. These contracts are governed by the rules applicable to the mode of transport and its scope (see Chapter 2), irrespective of the agreed Incoterms rules. The contract of carriage is therefore governed by the terms and conditions agreed between the shipper and the carrier, regardless of whether the shipper is the seller or the buyer in the sale and purchase.

However, the important consequences for the transport resulting from the application of one or the other rule have made it common practice to ask carriers to quote for their services on the basis of a particular Incoterms rule.

Another not less common practice is to express the Incoterms rules in the bills of lading as an indication of which party (seller or buyer, consignor or consignee) is to bear the cost of carriage. Although these indications cannot be imposed on the regulatory framework of the contract of carriage, they may prove useful in resolving disputes concerning the obligation to pay for the service, as well as liability in the event of loss of or damage to the goods or delay in delivery, unless the applicable regulations and the contract of carriage provide otherwise.

In fact, depending on the Incoterms rule agreed in the contract of sale, the time of delivery and transfer of risk determines which party can claim against the carrier in the event of damage. If the seller is responsible, any loss incurred by them due to the obligation to replace the goods or arrange for alternative transportation grants them the right to claim against the carrier. This claim is based on the provisions outlined in the contract of carriage and the agreed conditions therein. Conversely, if the damage occurs subsequent to delivery and the transfer of risk to the buyer, the buyer, who is obligated to accept the damaged goods and proceed with payment for the purchase, retains the right to seek compensation from the carrier to recoup their losses. This entitlement is contingent upon the provisions delineated in the contract of carriage.

As we can see, the direct relationship between the Incoterms and the contract of carriage should lead the parties, in order to save costs and gain legal certainty, to reconcile both aspects by contracting and managing the carriage strictly to the extent required by the Incoterms.

4 Incoterms rules and transport insurance

Incoterms do not make it compulsory to take out transport insurance to cover the risks that the goods may suffer (loss, damage, delays in delivery, etc.), except for CIP and CIF terms (which require the seller to take out transport insurance to cover the buyer's risks under certain conditions). Nonetheless, as we shall see, it is strongly advisable to obtain insurance.. It is worth noting that, typically, the selling company is obliged to provide the buyer, at the latter's request and expense, with the information necessary to take out insurance, and vice versa. It is up to the seller or the buyer to decide:

- **Not to take out transport insurance**
  In the event of loss or damage during the transportation of goods for which one of the parties has assumed the risk, that party may, where appropriate, bring an action against the carrier. If the carrier is found to be liable for the damage (there are grounds for exonerating the carrier from liability, which are specified in the regulations governing each contract, depending on the mode of transport), he must compensate the party concerned on the basis of the applicable liability regime.

  In instances where the carrier is found liable for the damage, they are typically obligated to compensate the affected party based on the applicable liability regime. While carriers often maintain liability insurance to cover such scenarios, it is crucial to understand that these policies may not perfectly align with the liability assigned to carriers by the relevant legal framework. For example, the CMR Convention makes the carrier liable for late delivery, but generally the insurance policies taken out by the carrier do not cover this breach, so the insurance would not compensate in the event of delay.

- **Taking out transport insurance**
  In the event of a loss on the leg of the journey where one of the parties assumes the risk (an indispensable condition for having an insurable interest), the latter may, where appropriate, claim compensation from the insurer for the loss of its property, under the conditions laid down in the insurance policy. In such a case, it is common for the insurer to subsequently pursue a recovery action against the carrier responsible for the damage, which is normally covered by its own insurance. It is very common for the carrier (e.g. freight forwarder) to offer the shipper (the seller or buyer) the possibility of insuring the shipment.

Although not required to do so, it is advisable for parties entering into a contract of sale to consider the advisability of obtaining insurance coverage to mitigate the risks associated with the agreed Incoterms rule, which dictates the place of delivery and the transfer of risk. Various scenarios may arise:

- The damage is due to a cause for which the carrier cannot be held responsible under the terms of the contract of carriage: for example, force majeure such as natural disasters, etc. In this case, if the risk is covered by insurance, compensation may be claimed from the insurer.
- The value of the goods exceeds the limit of indemnity of the carrier as stipulated in the contract of carriage (see chapter 2). In this case, it is possible to specify in the insurance both the insured value - with an amount equal to the value of the goods - and the limit of indemnity, if it is a carrier's insurance, in order to recover the full amount of the damage suffered in the event of a claim.
- The carrier refuses to respond to the claim or the claim cannot be executed for various reasons (the carrier does not consider itself liable, declares itself insolvent, its insurance does not cover the damage and it cannot pay the compensation, etc.) or it tries to expedite the claim through the insurer (collect the compensation from the insurer and it is the insurer that claims from the carrier).

Although closely related, the carrier's insurance contract and the contract of carriage are independent. Therefore, a carrier may not refuse to respond to a claim on the grounds that his insurance does not cover the risk causing the damage, as long as the carrier's liability regime (regulated by the relevant legislation) applies in such a situation. For example, in road transportation, the carrier is liable for the economic damage caused by the delay in delivery up to the amount of the transportation price, but his insurance does not usually cover the delay as a risk. In this case, it is possible to make a claim, and the carrier cannot refuse to respond on the grounds that his insurance does not cover such a risk, unless they can invoke an excuse contained in the regulation governing the contract of carriage.

5 Incoterms rules and customs clearance

The relationship between customs clearance and the Incoterms rules is embodied in Commitments A7/B7 (Export/Import Clearance) which, in two subsections, indicate which party (seller or buyer) must manage and bear the costs of customs clearance and the assistance that both parties must provide to each other in this regard.

Customs clearance is the key to a company's foreign trade operations with third countries. Customs has two basic functions: control/security (compliance with safety, health, cultural heritage, environmental, trademark, etc. requirements) and collection (collection of taxes - tariffs, VAT and others such as excise, anti-dumping, etc., which are normally applied only to imports).

Customs procedures affect the development of the sale and purchase operation, since if the documentary requirements are not met, the goods to be sold or purchased may be detained at the customs offices of export or import.

Generally, Incoterms rules indicate that the seller clears for export (except in EXW) and the buyer clears for import (except in DDP), but import customs may require documentation that must be formalized and certified in the exporting country (license, certificate of preferential origin such as a EUR-1, etc.). Therefore, the correct management of customs procedures depends to a large extent on the importing and exporting companies having analyzed the customs implications before the operation is carried out. The following issues are important:

- Tariff classification of the goods (TARIC code in the European case) and the requirements for their export/import, as well as the associated costs and taxes.
- Determining if the origin of the goods is preferential (allows for lower tariffs normally as a result of a trade contract or preferential tariff treatment, such as for GSP countries) or nonpreferential, and the type of certificate of origin or other proof (authorized or registered exporter's declaration, REX system) required to optimize the operation (reduce taxes to be paid, if possible).
- Knowing the trade barriers that are imposed on the export or import of a good and the best way to make it possible, if necessary, to carry out the operation despite them (obtaining certificates, licenses, etc.).
- Other aspects related to customs clearance such as the customs value (taxable base of the tariff that coincides, in most countries, with the value of the goods under CIF or CIP conditions), customs procedures, the customs declaration (DUA or single administrative document in the European case, customs declaration or *pedimento* in Mexico), etc.

First of all, comprehensive knowledge of export and import customs procedures is paramount to understanding the documentation requirements and their fiscal impact on planned operations, since there might be restrictions hindering development or import taxes rendering the operation unprofitable.

For all these reasons, it is essential for the company to consult reliable sources of information on customs procedures. Nowadays, the Internet has become the main source of information, so in addition to directly consulting the other party involved in the transaction (supplier or customer), companies should also reach out to freight forwarders, the customs agents (customs brokers) and customs agencies. Here are some websites that might be helpful in this regard:

- **TARIC consultations**[4]
  They allow to know the trade barriers that the EU imposes on the import of products from third countries. By entering the TARIC code of the product (there is an advanced search option) and its country of origin (which may be different from the country of origin), you can obtain information on the trade barriers imposed by the European Union on its import (tariffs, restrictions, certifications, etc.). Information is also provided on any restrictions on the export of products from the European Union to third countries, such as required certifications.

- **Trade Helpdesk**[5]
  This is a free portal of the European Commission that provides information on how to import products into the European Union, so it is particularly useful for European importers and exporters from third countries whose destination is the EU. By entering the country of origin of the import (only those with which the EU has a trade contract or GSP countries appear), the country of destination (among those that make up the EU, as it offers, in a tab, information on the national VAT, which is different in each country) and the TARIC code of the product, the following information is offered:

  - *Product requirements:* specific requirements applicable to the goods indicating their legislation, technical standards, labeling, phytosanitary controls, etc.

....

[4] TARIC is available at: http://ec.europa.eu/taxation_customs/dds2/taric/taric_consultation.jsp?Lang=es.
[5] Trade Helpdesk is available at: https://trade.ec.europa.eu/tradehelp/es.

- *EU import duties:* tariffs applicable to imports, especially those reduced for goods originating in the country indicated in the search criteria as a result of trade agreements in force.
- *Internal taxes:* VAT and, where applicable, other taxes applicable to the product (excise duties, etc.).
- *Rules of origin:* the rule that must be complied with in order for the product to be considered as originating in the country specified in the search criteria (this rule appears in the protocol of the trade contract between the EU and this country).
- *Statistics:* concerning the trade of that product between the country of reference and the EU.

- **Market Access Database**[6]

  It provides information on the trade barriers that EU products face when imported into third countries. To find the information related to the operation, go to the Procedures and Formalities tab and enter the tariff classification of the goods (six digits, which is the world's common tariff classification under the Harmonized System) and the country of destination, and you will receive information on the taxation (customs and other taxes) and barriers (formalities, certifications, etc.) that will be applied to the European product when it is cleared for import in the destination country.

With regard to the documents to be presented at customs clearance, it is normal for the exporting company to present at least the invoice, the list of packages and the certificate of origin (which is required at import clearance), but it should be ascertained whether, depending on the goods or the country of origin or destination, it is necessary or convenient (to reduce import taxes) to present some type of specific document, such as a certificate of preferential origin, a certificate resulting from a technical barrier, a license, the consular invoice, the transport contract, etc.

Customs regulations and procedures are as numerous and diverse as the countries or customs unions, and they are constantly changing, reflecting the commercial relations between countries (contracts and conflicts). This presents

---

[6] Market Access Database is available at: http://madb.europa.eu/mkaccdb2/datasetPreviewFormIFpubli. htm?datacat_id=IF&from=publi.

a significant challenge for companies, as it leads to a high degree of legal uncertainty.

The importing company (which knows best the requirements of its customs) must consult the specific documents required and communicate them to the exporter so that the latter can, as far as possible, manage their processing and pass on the cost of this in the agreed price. Similarly, the importer must provide the seller with all the information necessary for export clearance.

6   Incoterms rules and documentary credit

Means of payment can be divided into simple and documentary. The latter require the presentation of certain documents as a condition for the selling company to collect the transaction. The most commonly used is the documentary credit or letter of credit.

A documentary letter of credit is an contract whereby a bank (the letter writer), at the request and in accordance with the instructions of its client (the ordering, purchasing or importing company), undertakes to make payment for the goods to a third party (the beneficiary, selling or exporting company), provided that the latter complies with the agreed terms and conditions and delivers the required documents in the agreed form and within the agreed period. As these are usually international transactions, the issuing bank requires another entity (the intermediary bank) to perform certain functions in the exporting country (verification of documents, notifications, etc.).

Thus, a documentary credit transaction usually involves four parties: the originator (buyer's company), the issuing bank (buyer's bank), the beneficiary company (seller) and, if applicable, the intermediary bank (seller's bank).

The purpose of a documentary letter of credit is to provide a documentary guarantee that the seller will fulfill his obligations under a contract of sale (evidenced solely by the documents he presents) and will collect the transaction, and that the buyer, in exchange for payment, will receive the documents proving that the seller has fulfilled his obligations and that he can take possession of the goods at the destination. For this reason, it is a means of payment used when there is insufficient trust between the two organizations (first transactions, new companies, uncertain markets, etc.).

As parties gain confidence, documentary credit can be replaced by other more flexible and less costly means, such as documentary remittances or forms of payment based on documentary evidence managed by the parties themselves (cash against documents or CAD) Another increasingly popular option, particularly with Asian suppliers, is staged payments, typically consisting of three stages: an initial advance payment, followed by the presentation of documents verifying the delivery and receipt of goods at the destination.

Like the Incoterms, the documentary credit has the nature of a new *lex mercatoria* and is an contract or contract (in this case a banking one) not included in the legal systems. It is regulated by the Uniform Customs and Practice for Documentary Credits (published by the ICC since 1933), the latest version of which, from 2013, is known as UCP 600, in force since 2007. This standard expresses the independence of the documentary credit with respect to the sale and purchase, so that the intervening banks are not affected or bound by such a contract (despite the fact that the credit refers to it). As a result, it is crucial for the parties to align the delivery obligations outlined in the contract of sale with the documentation required for the documentary credit.

It is essential to comply with the UCP 600 rules regarding the requirements (formal and content) of the transport documents (places or ports of origin and destination, signature of the transport company, etc.), invoices, certificates of origin, amounts, endorsements, etc.).

The phases that make up the documentary credit and its relationship with the Incoterms rules are as follows:

- **Contract of the sale and payment by documentary credit**

  This first phase is closely related to the agreed Incoterms rule, since the documentation presented by the seller must coincide with that which proves the fulfillment of his obligations (usually the delivery of the goods, to which can be added others such as the contract of transport, documentation for customs, documentation relating to quality, etc.). In this way, the seller's obligations under the sale contract are matched with the documentary obligations of the letter of credit, so that the seller can obtain payment in exchange for the fulfillment of his obligations under the sale contract (delivery of the goods).

  In practice, it is most convenient to use a documentary credit under Incoterms Group C (and even F) rules, but it is neither usual nor advisable to use this means of payment under EXW conditions (unless the documentation required in the credit is that which the selling company can obtain by simply placing the goods at the disposal of the buyer) or when rules D apply (in which case documentation of delivery at destination should be required, which in practice would distort the usual mechanics of a documentary credit).

Chapters 4 and 5 specify the documents required in a documentary credit to prove delivery or carriage, within the framework of the application of each of the Incoterms rules. In addition, certain documents may be required or requested by the purchasing company, primarily for two reasons:

- **Customs clearance.** In addition to the essential documents (invoice and packing list), the purchasing company may require other documents in order to comply with customs regulations or to obtain a tariff reduction: certificates of origin, certificates of fumigation of pallets, certificates of any technical requirements, etc. In this respect, the requirements of the importing customs office, whose formalities are normally assumed by the buyer, are decisive.
- **Transaction security.** In order to reinforce the buyer's assurance that the goods received at the destination are as agreed in the contract of sale, it is customary to require a quality certificate or technical inspection, which may be contracted with a certifying company or issued by a third party or even by the buyer's own agent at the point of origin.

- **Opening of the credit**
  The buyer requests the opening of the documentary credit from the issuing bank and informs them of the conditions agreed with the seller. The issuing bank, through the intermediary bank (which can also confirm the transaction and be obliged to pay the issuing bank on equal terms), relays these terms to the seller for confirmation, usually facilitated through SWIFT[7] messaging. In addition to ensuring that it is in a position to meet the documentary requirements, the selling company must check in particular:

---

[7] Issued in accordance with the standards of the Society for Worldwide Interbank Financial Telecommunications (SWIFT) and based on a bank identification code for international money transfers.

- That the Incoterms rule, as a determinant of the terms of delivery, is correctly worded and agreed.
- That they will not have problems in complying with the due dates, the shipping time and the presentation of the documents.
- Loading and unloading locations, partial shipments and transshipments (if applicable), etc.
- Other aspects, such as description of goods, amounts, insurance requirements (if applicable), etc.

- **Preparation of the goods, delivery or transportation, presentation of the documents and collection or payment against delivery of the documents to the purchasing company**

  The selling party prepares the goods and delivers them to the transportation company (which may or may not provide transportation, depending on the agreed rule). It must then have the complete and compliant documentation (in form and time) required for the documentary credit and ensure that it meets the requirements of the UCP 600 rules.

  In this regard, it is essential to pay attention to the formal aspects in order to avoid discrepancies and problems in the credit. For example, if a Bill of Lading (BL) is to be presented, it is very common and advisable to request a copy or proforma of this document from the shipping company or freight forwarder (whoever is going to issue it) and to verify that all the data comply with the requirements of the credit (issued to order or nominative, indication of freight paid or due, etc.) before authorizing the issuance of the originals.

  Once these documents have been obtained, the selling company submits them to the intermediary bank. There, depending on the type of credit, the documents are verified and forwarded to the issuing bank. Two parallel processes take place at this stage: the one that follows the goods, evidenced by the delivery documents, and the financial one, in which, after both banks have checked the documents and verified their validity, the selling company generates a collection right against the debiting of the buyer's account and the delivery of the documents to the buyer by the issuing bank.

  The documentary letter of credit ends with the buyer's access to the goods, which he has been able to receive on the basis of the documentation obtained from the issuing bank.

This is the most common type of documentary credit, which can be in the form of a confirmed letter of credit, a sight letter of credit, a deferred letter of credit, or any other type of letter of credit. Consequently, there exists a direct correlation between the chosen Incoterms rule and the utilization of documentary credits structured in accordance with the terms and conditions that align with this rule. Such alignment ensures the fulfillment of the objectives outlined in the contract of sale.

Chapter 4
How to use Incoterms 2020 multimodal rules

The multimodal Incoterms, suitable for any mode or modes of transportation other than port-to-port maritime transport, are as follows:

- EXW (ex works)
- FCA (free carrier)
- CPT (carriage paid to)
- CIP (carriage and insurance paid to)
- DAP (delivered at place)
- DPU (delivered at place unloaded)
- DDP (delivered duty paid)

These rules can be applied to any combination of modes of transportation:

- Container transportation with sea phase and its pre-carriage by road or rail.
- Road transportation by full truck or groupage.
- Rail transport and its pre- and post-carriage by road.
- Air transport and its pre- and post-carriage by road.
- Air transport and its previous and subsequent transport by road.

According to the classification proposed in the version of Incoterms published in 2000, the multimodal regulations are divided into four groups:

- **Group E (EXW).** Delivery takes place when the seller places the goods at the disposal of the buyer on his own premises without loading them onto the vehicle sent by the buyer. The seller does not arrange transportation.

- **Group F (FCA).** The seller must deliver the goods onto the vehicle contracted by the buyer. If the place of delivery is different from the seller's premises, the seller must cover the transport costs to the agreed place of delivery.

- **Group C: (CPT and CIP).** The seller contracts the main transport to the location specified by the Incoterms rule, but delivers and transfers the risk to the buyer at the place of origin, when the goods are handed over to the contracted carrier (if there are several, when they are handed over to the first).

- **Group D (DAP, DPU and DDP).** The seller contracts the main transportation to the location specified by the Incoterms rule and delivers and transfers the risk to the buyer at the place of destination. Under DAP conditions, the goods are delivered to the designated place without unloading from the arriving vehicle. Under DPU conditions, the goods are delivered in the same way as DAP, but with the added obligation and cost for the seller to unload them at the named place, and they are considered delivered when this has been done. DDP is the same as DAP (Delivered Without Unloading), but with the addition that the seller is responsible for import clearance.

As far as customs clearance is concerned, export clearance is always the responsibility of the selling company (except under EXW conditions), and import clearance must be handled by the buyer (except under DDP conditions). This chapter provides a detailed analysis and overview of the multimodal Incoterms rules. Examples of drafting are included, as well as the main obligations, the distribution of costs and certain considerations regarding the peculiarities of each rule and the specific characteristics of the operation. The following aspects, among others, are dealt with:

- Relationship with the contract of carriage and its insurance.
- Loading and unloading of goods.

- Customs clearance.
- Control of the logistics chain and level of service offered by the selling company.
- Documentation and proof of delivery.
- Transportation documentation and its relationship with the documentary means of payment.

1   EXW (ex works)

1.1   Overview and delivery

The seller delivers the goods by making them available to the buyer at the seller's premises or at another designated place (e.g., the warehouses of the seller's logistics provider) without loading them onto a vehicle or clearing them for export (if applicable). Such party shall notify the buyer of such delivery and upon such notification the goods shall be deemed to have been delivered.

Upon delivery, the risk in the goods passes to the buyer, so that under EXW conditions it is particularly important to clearly specify the place and time of delivery and to notify the buyer within that time.

This arrangement is the one with the least obligations for the selling company, since its responsibility is limited to having the goods properly packed, conditioned and marked for transport at its own premises. Together with the goods, the selling company must provide the minimum documentation required by the buyer and that may be required by customs, of which it must have already been informed by the buyer in charge of customs clearance.

The purchasing company must hire or manage transport on their own[1] including the loading operations at the place of origin, since the seller is not obliged by this rule to load the goods onto the transport vehicle presented by the carrier contracted by the buyer. This initial transport, as well as the rest of the operations that make up the logistical chain to the destination, are managed and assumed by the buyer company, which also bears the risks of the entire logistical chain.

----

[1] The purchasing company may have a fleet of vehicles with which to carry out complementary private transportation from the seller's warehouse.

> *General formulation*
>
> EXW (designated place of delivery). Incoterms 2020.
>
> *Writing examples*
>
> - EXW parcela 10, pol. industrial Alcobendas, Madrid. España. Incoterms 2020.
> - EXW nave 3, parque industrial Finsa, Cuautlancingo, Puebla. México. Incoterms 2020.
> - EXW nave 6, parque industrial Los Libertadores, Colina, Santiago de Chile. Chile. Incoterms 2020.

For all these reasons, it is highly recommended for the selling company to specify a delivery time for the goods (prepared and documented). According to this specification, the purchasing company, which has already been informed, will proceed to collect the goods by means of the transport company it has contracted or by its own means.

1.2 Main obligations and costs

- **Obligations of the selling company**
  1. To deliver the goods agreed upon in the purchase contract (after checking and verifying their quality) within the agreed timeframe, to pack them properly for transportation and adequately mark the packaging (it is highly desirable that these two aspects are specified in the purchase contract).
  2. Provide the commercial invoice and other documents agreed in the contract of sale (as proof of conformity) and assist in obtaining, at the buyer's expense and risk, any other documents required for customs clearance (export, transit and import), such as licenses, certifications or inspections.
  3. Notify the Buyer of the delivery so that they can proceed to receive the goods.

- **Obligations of the purchasing company**
  1. Pay the price of the goods specified in the contract of sale. The Incoterms rule does not specify or regulate this.

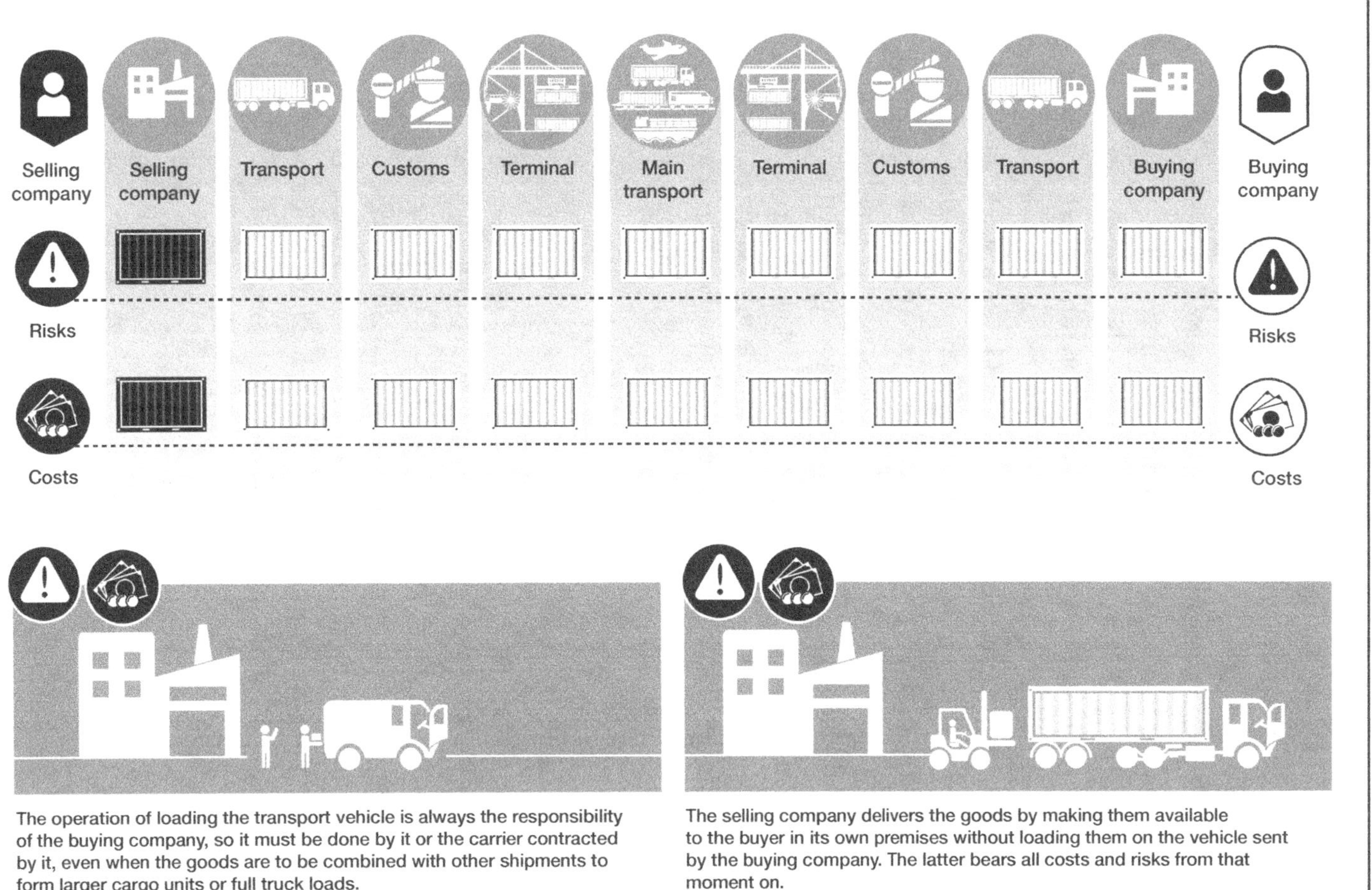

The operation of loading the transport vehicle is always the responsibility of the buying company, so it must be done by it or the carrier contracted by it, even when the goods are to be combined with other shipments to form larger cargo units or full truck loads.

The selling company delivers the goods by making them available to the buyer in its own premises without loading them on the vehicle sent by the buying company. The latter bears all costs and risks from that moment on.

2. Notify the Seller of the time of receipt (within the agreed period) and the exact place of collection, if this has been agreed in the contract of sale. If not, the seller may choose the place of delivery.
3. Receiving the goods delivered by the seller.
4. Organize, manage and pay for the rest of the operations in the logistics chain: loading the goods onto the first vehicle, transport to the destination (with a contracted carrier or by its own means), reimburse the selling company of the costs of obtaining the documents required for customs clearance, formalities and procedures for export or import customs clearance (including taxes) and, where applicable, in transit countries, and unloading at the destination. Customs clearance includes costs and licenses, security clearance (e.g., Verified Gross Container Weight or VGM, Verified Gross Mass, etc.) and inspections, such as red channel after customs declaration and specific phytosanitary, sanitary, pharmacological, safety, etc. inspections.
5. If the buyer is late in accepting the goods delivered by the seller within the agreed period, the buyer shall also bear the costs and risks arising from such a situation from the end of the agreed period.

1.3   Considerations for effective use of the rule

EXW is one of the most widely used Incoterms, although it is often misused. As mentioned in the introduction, its use should be limited to domestic transactions or transactions within the same economic-fiscal region that do not require customs clearance. In most cases, it is only suitable for use in the transportation of parcels and small consignments, where loading of the goods is carried out by the carrier at the premises of the selling company. The following are some considerations for effective use of the EXW rule.

1.3.1   Export clearance and related documentation

Applying this rule to transactions other than those described above may create the following problems:

- ***For the purchasing company.*** It must make sure that it can carry out the export clearance directly or indirectly (through a customs agent), since the latter, depending on the rules governing it, may require a condition that the company cannot meet (remember that Incoterms rules cannot contradict legal norms or laws) and that prevents the application of such a rule.

- ***To the selling company.*** In the case of a company domiciled in the European Union (although this risk exists worldwide), the exporter loses control over the actual exit of the goods from the UCC (Union Customs Code), which is evidenced by the SAD with which the export was cleared. This SAD would allow the seller to justify the export invoice without VAT in the event of a possible tax audit, which can take place up to four years after the export (three years for customs duties and the fourth for VAT). In addition to confirming with the SAD that the goods have been exported (they have left the UCC), it is important that the data contained in the SAD are correct (amount, currency, consignee, etc.) and that they match the documents in the seller's possession in the event of a possible tax inspection by the tax authorities. Of course, this company can obtain the SAD, even if it did not manage it, from the records of the Customs and Excise Department, but this does not necessarily mean that the data in the declaration are correct (if it did not manage the export clearance and therefore could not verify that the SAD was correctly formalized). This can even facilitate fraudulent actions, such as the buyer company not exporting the goods and competing with the seller in its own market (under unfair conditions because it has not paid the VAT that the seller's "domestic" customers pay), since the seller loses control of the goods once they have left its premises. These problems are eliminated when the exporter takes over the management of export clearance, since they control its documentation (SAD and related documents).

1.3.2 Loading of the goods by the transportation company

This rule should not be applied to full loads, whether transported by road or by other means, but only to parcels or similar shipments where it is customary for the road carrier to load the goods onto the vehicle, and which is usually regulated in each country.

Sometimes, even though the EXW rule has been agreed, the seller loads the goods onto the vehicle for a first road transport in a box truck or container. This situation occurs when this company has sufficient resources to perform the loading. However, any incident that occurs in the development of these operations raises a dispute for which it may end up being responsible for having carried out an operation that corresponds to the buyer through the carrier contracted by them.

The first operator to pick up the goods at the seller's premises is usually a road haulier to whom the buyer does not usually specify that they must carry out the loading at the point of origin. This can lead to numerous problems or uncertainties from the point of view of the selling company and the carrier in relation to the regulations governing the road transport contract or other legislation in force.

With regard to these regulations, in the case of international road transportation, the regulatory conventions in Europe (CMR Convention) and in Latin America and the Caribbean (Inter-American Convention on Contracts for the or others) do not specify anything about the party obliged to load the goods.

Under EXW conditions, loading is at the risk and expense of the buyer, but if loading is performed by the seller and the goods are damaged, it is necessary to determine who is responsible for the consequences. The EXW rule provides that the responsibility must be assumed by the buyer; however, if the damage was caused by the seller's personnel, the seller may be reasonably obligated to replace the damaged goods.

Similarly, discrepancies may arise if the goods, upon arrival at their destination, show damage that can be attributed to the loading and stowage carried out by the seller. In this sense, the carrier is obliged to check the goods and, if necessary, to indicate in the bill of lading any damage or defect found. Therefore, they should not allow damaged goods to be loaded, for their safety (legal and physical, in relation to the minimum conditions for transport) and because they will be held responsible at the destination if they do not have a reservation on the waybill. However, if they have such reservations, it implies that the goods were loaded in poor condition by the seller, which will cause a conflict between the seller and their customer. In addition, a bill of lading with reservations is not accepted in a documentary credit.

Therefore, under EXW conditions, the purchasing company must first of all agree with the carrier (in the loading order or in the continuous service contract) that it will carry out the loading work at origin, which does not exclude other inconveniences that must be assessed:

- The transport company must be provided with the means to carry out these tasks safely, as it does not usually have its own means (docks, pallet trucks, personal protective equipment, etc.).
- This is a risky activity for the carrier. Regarding the outcome of these operations, it is advisable to consider taking out insurance to cover potential damage to the goods during their execution. Both the seller and the carrier are subject to occupational risk regulations (information obligations, training and equipment to work safely on the seller's premises, etc.).

Faced with these problems of inadequate use of EXW in full truckload operations (not parcels) and in cases where export clearance is required, companies are advised to replace EXW with FCA at the seller's warehouse (as indicated below). In fact, even when EXW has been formally agreed upon in the contractual documents, operations are often managed under FCA terms, particularly concerning the loading process at origin, which is typically handled by the seller's personnel and resources. This change ensures that what is agreed in the contract of sale is reflected as accurately as possible in the operations carried out by the seller and the buyer, and consequently, the carrier.

Given this complex scenario, we can conclude that there are three options for full loads:

a) Take all the precautions mentioned above: include loading at the place of origin in the transport service contract, provide the carrier with the necessary means, ensure risks are covered by the carrier, comply with the regulations on occupational risks, etc.

b) Replace the EXW conditions with FCA at the seller's premises, which means that the seller loads the vehicle (which is already done in many cases) and, if necessary, handles the export customs clearance, thus eliminating the above-mentioned disadvantages.

c) Although not advisable, since these are unregulated variations of the Incoterms, agreements like EXW loaded or ex cellar for warehouse deliveries can be made, where the seller is responsible for loading the goods, with the seller's obligations, costs, and risks clearly outlined in the sales contract.

1.3.3   Other considerations for the use of EXW

- **Minimal control of the logistics chain and packaging risks**
  Although the selling company knows the requirements of the logistics chain for its goods and could select the right carrier, under EXW conditions it loses control of the chain from its own warehouse and cannot use its knowledge of the product to optimize it. In addition, they are unaware of the stages of transportation and, unless the purchasing company informs them in detail, they may not even provide the right packaging and packing, which could result in the goods arriving damaged and disputes may arise as a result.

- **The selling company provides the minimum level of service and loses competitiveness**
  Under EXW conditions, it is the purchasing company that must carry out all the operations in the logistics chain, which may mean that the seller's offer loses competitiveness against other alternatives (from other suppliers) able to deliver their products by applying an Incoterms rule of greater scope in relation to the purchasing company.

- **Transport insurance**
  This Incoterms rule does not imply any obligation to take out transport insurance. However, since the purchasing company assumes the risks from the moment it receives the goods at the place of origin, it must consider the advisability of taking out insurance to cover these risks, including those relating to loading operations at the place of origin. In this sense, the selling company is obliged to provide the buyer, upon request, with the information necessary to insure the goods.

  Another consequence of the inappropriate use of this rule is that if the seller delivers the goods after notifying the buyer, but the buyer delays in receiving them and an incident occurs causing loss or damage to the goods, there will be reasonable doubt as to whether insurance purchased by the buyer (since they have the interest in insuring it, given that the seller has already delivered) would cover it, as it would occur in premises not owned by them and before the buyer's carrier has effectively taken charge of the goods.

- **Documentation and proof of delivery**

  EXW terms do not impose any documentation requirements on the seller, rather, they require the buyer to provide proof of collection of the goods. This is usually done at the seller's premises on the first road leg. In the case of international door-to-door transportation, a consignment note is usually formalized, combining the functions of proof of contract and receipt of goods by the carrier. In the case of other multimodal transports, the first carrier usually performs a national transport to the corresponding terminal (port, airport or railway station). This is formalized in a national bill of lading or waybill, which has no specific format but performs the same functions as the international bill of lading.

- **Transport documentation and documentary means of payment**

  Under EXW conditions, the document that should be required from the seller, in accordance with its delivery obligation, would be a notice of availability of the goods for collection by the buyer's contracted carrier. This document should be issued by the seller itself and would therefore provide a minimum of security to the buyer. This Incoterms rule is therefore hardly compatible with documentary credit. In practice, it is common to require a copy of the relevant bill of lading from the shipper or carrier, which is formalized when the goods are delivered to the carrier designated by the buyer. This document can be used, for example, with documentary credits as indicated in the UCP 600 rules. However, if the carrier does not show up to collect the goods, the seller has fulfilled its delivery obligation, but has not received the document enabling it to collect by documentary credit.

  Therefore, in general, it is not advisable to apply the EXW rule with this method of payment, nor to agree on a contract of carriage, such as a Bill of Lading (originals of the BL), since the seller has not contracted the carriage and is not sure that he will be provided with the originals necessary to request the collection of the transaction. In order to obtain with certainty a consigned Bill of Lading, a document that is usually required in the documentary credit, it is preferable to agree on more extensive Incoterms rules, such as those of Group C, under which the selling company contracts the transport, and the shipping company or freight forwarder will deliver the originals of the Bill of Lading with total security.

1.4   Conclusions

The application of the EXW rule should be limited to domestic sales transactions or transactions within the same economic and tax region and to packages. For all other transactions, it is customary to agree on this rule when companies start their international operations, as this way the selling party assumes less involvement and risk. Subsequently, when the operation is simple or experience is gained, it is advisable to apply more extensive Incoterms rules.

EXW terms are also suitable when the buyer has the capacity to manage the logistic chain under better conditions than the seller (since it obtains cheaper freight rates, although this is also applicable to FCA without the negative aspects mentioned above) and in operations between companies of the same business group, which resolves and coordinates all the above-mentioned disputes internally. In all other cases, it is advisable to consider replacing the EXW rule with FCA seller's premises.

2   FCA (free carrier)

2.1   Overview and delivery

Under FCA conditions, the selling company must deliver the goods cleared for export (i.e., it will take care of this clearance when it is due) to the carrier (trucking company, freight forwarder, international logistics operator, etc.) that will perform the main transportation and that has been hired by the buyer.

When applying this rule, it is essential to determine the exact place of delivery, which can be agreed in two ways:

- **FCA seller's premises**
  Delivery takes place when the seller loads the goods onto the vehicle of the carrier chosen by the buyer (usually a trucking company), at which time the risk passes to the buyer.

General formulation

FCA (designated place of delivery). Incoterms 2020.

Writing examples

- FCA parcela 10, pol. industrial Alcobendas, Madrid. España. Incoterms 2020.
- FCA nave 3, parque industrial Finsa, Cuautlancingo, Puebla. México. Incoterms 2020.
- FCA nave 6, parque industrial Los Libertadores, Colina, Santiago de Chile. Chile. Incoterms 2020.

- **FCA another location**
  Delivery takes place when the seller places the goods at the disposal of the carrier on a vehicle, ready for unloading, at the place indicated. This implies that the seller, by contract or by his own means, must provide initial transportation to that place.

General formulation

FCA (designated place of delivery). Incoterms 2020.

Writing examples

- FCA Terminal Marítima Valenciana, Valencia. España. Incoterms 2020.
- FCA almacén transitario Transur, Paterna, Valencia. España. Incoterms 2020.
- FCA almacén agente de carga, San Rafael Poniente, Puebla. México. Incoterms 2020.
- FCA almacén operador logístico, avda. Américo Vespucio, s/n, Renca, Santiago de Chile. Chile. Incoterms 2020.

2.2   Main obligations and costs

- **Obligations of the selling company**
  1. To deliver the goods agreed upon in the purchase contract (after checking and verifying their quality) within the agreed term, to pack them properly for transportation and to mark the packaging properly (it is very advisable to specify these two aspects in the purchase contract).
  2. Provide the commercial invoice and other documents stipulated in the contract of sale (as a proof of conformity).
  3. Notify the buyer that the delivery has been made or, if applicable, that the carrier designated by the buyer has not taken charge of it.
  4. Load the goods onto the vehicle hired by the buyer.
  5. In the case of agreeing to FCA another location (different from the seller's premises), to arrange and pay for the transport of the goods to that place (or to manage it with its own means), without including the unloading there.
  6. To carry out the export customs clearance (if required by the operation) and the related formalities and costs: licenses, security clearance and inspections (orange or red channels after presentation of the SAD, specific inspections due to the goods, such as phytosanitary, sanitary, pharmacological, safety, etc.). It must also provide the buyer with assistance and information to obtain (at the buyer's expense) the documents that may be required to manage the import clearance (and, where appropriate, in transit countries), such as licenses, certifications or inspections.

FCA seller's premises (free carrier)

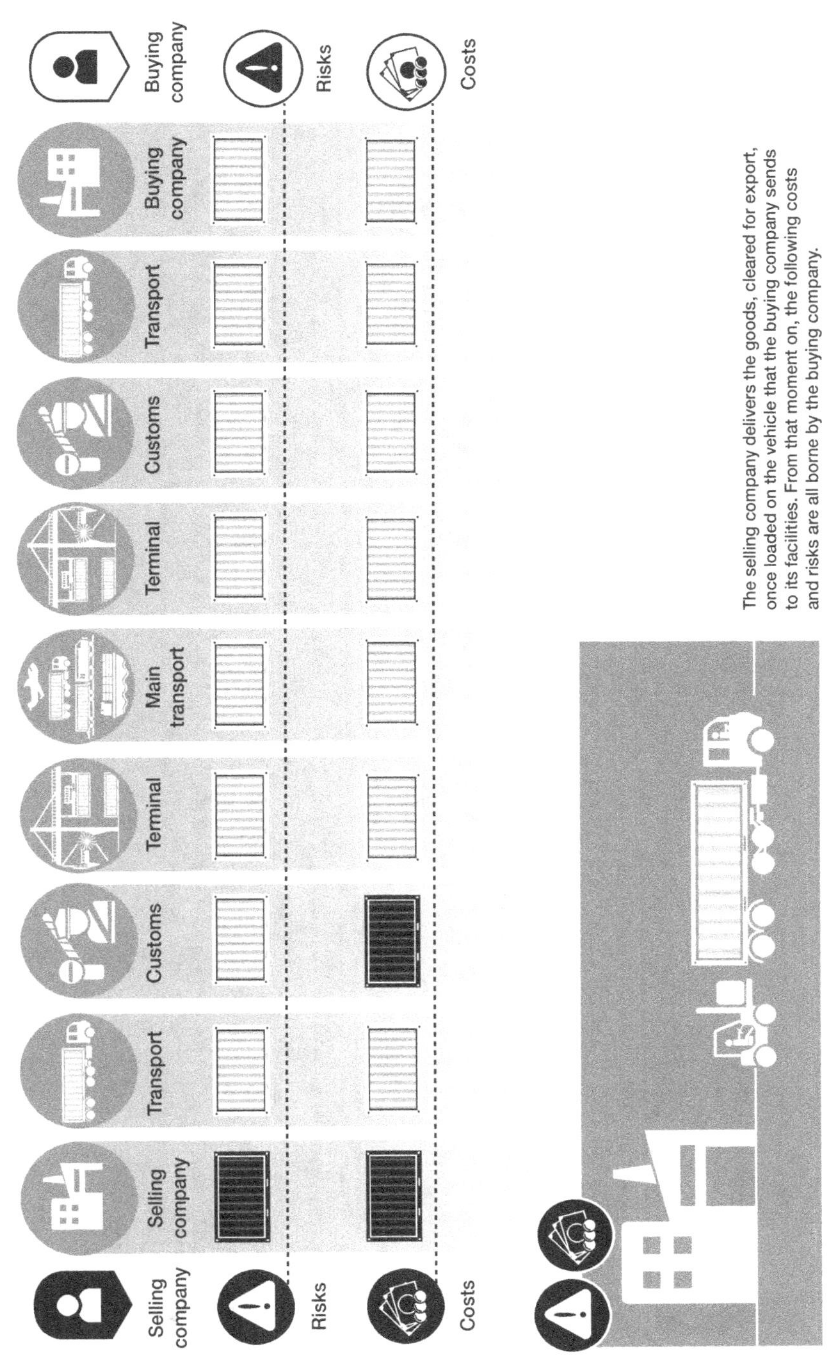

The selling company delivers the goods, cleared for export, once loaded on the vehicle that the buying company sends to its facilities. From that moment on, the following costs and risks are all borne by the buying company.

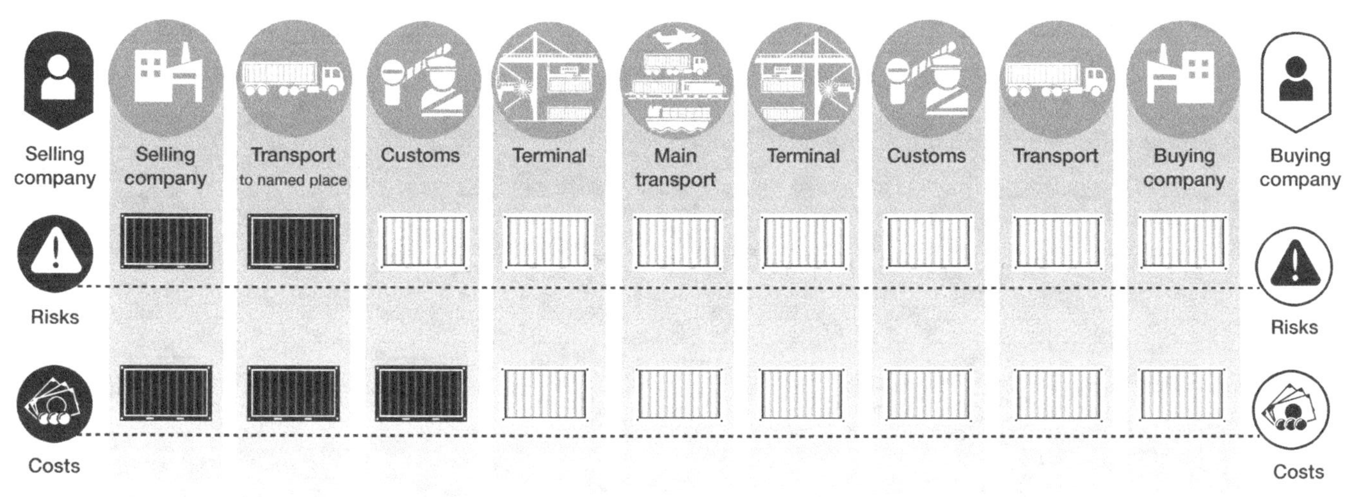

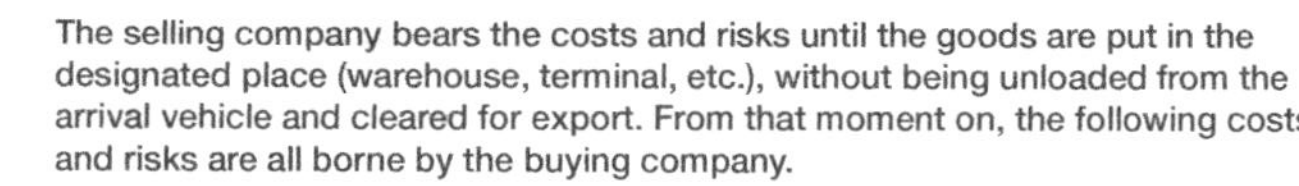

The selling company bears the costs and risks until the goods are put in the designated place (warehouse, terminal, etc.), without being unloaded from the arrival vehicle and cleared for export. From that moment on, the following costs and risks are all borne by the buying company.

The selling company delivers the goods to the agreed place (without unloading them from the vehicle with which they are transported) and cleared for export. From that moment on, the following costs and risks are all borne by the buying company.

- **Obligations of the purchasing company**
  1. To pay the price of the goods as agreed in the contract of sale (it should be noted that the means of payment is not specified in the Incoterms rule).
  2. Receive the goods loaded on the vehicle at the seller's premises or elsewhere (in the latter case, unloading is at the seller's risk).
  3. Organize, manage and pay for the remaining operations in the logistics chain after delivery of the goods (except for export clearance, if applicable): transport from the seller's premises (if applicable), unloading, other initial transport and operations (storage, consolidation, etc.) to the terminal, costs at the terminal of origin (THC, ISPS, others), main transport, costs at the terminal of destination, import clearance in the country of destination (and, if applicable, in transit countries), final transport and unloading.
  4. Notify the selling company to which carrier the goods will be delivered, the time of receipt within the period agreed in the contract of sale, the mode of transportation to be used and the specific point where the goods will be received (if there are several possible, e.g. several warehouses in the same city).
  5. If the purchasing company fails to comply with this point 4, or if its carrier fails to accept the goods, the purchasing company shall bear all risks of loss or damage to the goods from the date or time agreed in the contract of sale for delivery.

2.3   Considerations for effective use of the rule

The use of the FCA rule is becoming increasingly common, partly because it better reflects the practices and obligations related to the loading of goods and often replaces the EXW rule, and partly because of the recommendation to use FCA instead of FOB in multimodal container transportation.

2.3.1   Use of FCA with respect to EXW in cargo loading

Under FCA terms, the loading of the goods onto the first vehicle is done at the risk and expense of the selling company, which avoids many of the problems that can arise when the goods are loaded by the carrier hired by the buyer under EXW terms.

In view of these considerations, most of the international sale and purchase transactions that do not require customs clearance and are agreed on EXW terms are actually carried out (considering that the loading is done by the seller's personnel) according to the criteria of the seller's FCA facilities, and it is therefore advisable to replace one rule with another.

2.3.2   Use of FCA vs. EXW for transportation of goods

Different situations can be considered:

- **Door-to-door full truckload trucking**
  There is no distinction between the stages of transportation, and the purchasing company must hire the carrier to pick up the goods at the seller's warehouse. In this case, the use of FCA fits perfectly with the "carriage due" formula contained in many road consignment notes, the copy of which is kept by the selling company as proof of delivery of the goods. In fact, we believe that the two most suitable rules for this type of transport are FCA seller's warehouse and DAP buyer's warehouse (in which case "carriage paid" would be indicated), since in both cases the full costs and risks of the transport are assigned to the seller (DAP) or to the buyer (FCA), thus facilitating the allocation of the risk and the party entitled to claim subsequently, if necessary, from the carrier or any insurance (in neither case is it compulsory to take out insurance).

- **Multimodal transport with initial road phase to terminal (port, airport or railway station)**
  In these cases, a distinction can be made between a first transport and a main transport.

  - *First Transport.* Depending on the location specified in the FCA rule, it can be performed by the seller (FCA other location) or by the buyer (FCA seller's premises). In the first case, the seller can contract the transport (usually national road transport) or carry it out with their own means if they have their own fleet. In the case of contracted transport, it is customary that, in the case of a full load, loading is carried out by the seller's personnel and means and that unloading at the place of delivery is carried out at the buyer's risk and expense. Copies of the bill of lading signed by the consignee (acting for the buyer) and by the carrier (usually required by the seller as a condition of payment for the service) will serve as proof of delivery and receipt. In the case of parcels or a similar mode of transport, loading and unloading are normally carried out by the carrier (in accordance with the provisions of the contract of carriage).

The FCA other place option is suitable when the buyer wishes to receive the goods at the carrier's premises (freight forwarder or logistics operator in charge of the main transport), at a warehouse where the shipment is to be consolidated for subsequent international transport (for groupage or LCL container loads) or at a specific point at the beginning of the logistics chain, e.g. at a terminal (port, airport or railway station) in the case of full containers (FCL) loaded at the seller's warehouse.

In the latter case and in multimodal containerized transport, the seller must assume the costs and bear the risks of the first journey by road to the port terminal, railway station or airport terminal or cargo center.[2] Once there, and without the need to unload the truck, the goods are delivered and the selling company transfers the risks to the buyer, so that all subsequent costs are already borne by the buyer.

In the case of multimodal door-to-door or door-to-port container transportation (i.e., where the entire container is loaded and sealed at the seller's premises and only opened at the destination, either at the buyer's warehouse or at the port of destination), it should be noted that this initial transportation is usually relatively expensive compared to general transportation. Therefore, it is possible to transport the goods, for example, by truck to the forwarder's warehouse near the port, where the goods are unloaded and loaded into the container, which can result in significant savings (although there may be a loss of security due to the inclusion of a handling operation). This implies that in the event

---

[2] In multimodal ground-air transport, the difference is that on the first leg the goods are transported not in containers but in trucks or vans (loose packages or palletized goods), and at the terminal or air freight center they are consolidated and prepared for transportation in unit loads (air containers of various types: closed, pallets with netting, etc.).

that the selling company wishes to take advantage of the option of loading the container at its facilities, but the agreed rule is FCA elsewhere, it must ask the buyer for the details of the forwarding agency involved in the port of origin to contact it so that it can calculate the previous transport between its facilities and the port, as this must be taken into account as a cost to be borne by the seller to calculate the selling price.

— *Main transport.* Although it must be contracted by the purchasing company, the Incoterms offer the possibility in FCA conditions (as well as in FAS and FOB for maritime transport) that the seller may contract it at the risk and expense of the buyer, if the latter requests it and if it is customary (in any case, the seller may refuse this possibility). However, it is not advisable to make use of this possibility, because if the seller, who is not bound by the Incoterms, contracts the transport, they assume the position of shipper in the transport contract with the resulting obligations. This could affect the seller as they might be asked to pay for transport they are not obliged to contract and have not included in the sales price, since it was contracted as freight collect for the buyer to pay.

- **Rail transport by full train or customer train (optional)[3]**
  The FCA rule at the seller's facilities is perfectly suited to rail transport of bulk or full loads contracted on an optional basis or customer train, since in many cases the companies have their own railway sidings to which the train contracted by the buyer has access and where the seller loads it with their own means.

2.3.3 Use of FCA with respect to EXW in export clearance

The management of this process by the selling company, which is usually not excessively costly, offers advantages over the drawbacks of EXW terms (where it is the responsibility of the buyer). These include the following:

....

[3] Rail transport service of large volumes of goods, generally by leasing complete vehicles, without having to serve a specific geographic area or be subject to fixed frequencies or rates, since prices are subject to market fluctuations.

- Export clearance is a procedure that the exporting company is in a better position to carry out satisfactorily due to its legislative, administrative, linguistic, etc. knowledge of the country of origin.
- The exporting company ensures that it obtains the customs export document for tax purposes, which constitutes proof of the actual departure of the goods from the customs territory of export (which supports the VAT-free invoicing of the export).

2.3.4 Implications of using FCA versus FOB

- **Use of FCA in place of FOB with containers**
  The Incoterms expressly discourage container transport under FOB, CFR and CIF conditions. This is one of the most striking features of the latest versions (2000, 2010 and 2020), as these rules are often used for this type of transport. In particular, it is recommended that the FOB rule be replaced by the FCA rule for the cost and risk reasons summarized below and explained in detail in the discussion of the Incoterms rules for ocean freight (see Chapter 5).

  - *Cost reasons.* Under FOB terms, the selling company must bear the costs until the container is loaded on board the container ship at the port of shipment. It should be noted that port costs, which represent an increasing percentage of the total cost of a multimodal container shipment, are highly dependent on the primary mode of transportation contracted by the purchasing company.

    Thus, depending on the shipping line and the freight forwarder (all contracted by the purchasing company), the selling company has to bear costs over which it has no bargaining power (although it must of course have consulted first in order to be able to offer a price). In addition, if there are delays in loading the container on board the ship due to the buyer's poor choice of carrier, the seller will have to bear these costs (delays and stays in port, etc.), since it bears them in full until the container is loaded on board the ship.

    Although these additional costs can be claimed from the purchasing company (since they are due to a breach of contract by the latter), in practice the carrier usually charges them to the seller, making it difficult for the seller to subsequently claim them from the buyer, as they were not included in the initial price and often lead to commercial disputes.

– *Risk reasons.* Under FOB terms, the seller does not deliver or transfer risk to the buyer until the container is loaded on board the vessel at the port of export. However, at the time of loading (and thus transfer of risk), the condition of the goods is not inspected.

Let us assume that the damage to the goods occurred at an unlocated point in the logistics chain (e.g., defective handling of the container by machinery at the origin or destination port). If FCA is agreed at the seller's warehouse, the seller controls and can check the condition of the goods at the time of delivery (when the goods are loaded into the container), but if FOB is agreed and the damage is found when the goods arrive at the buyer's warehouse at the destination, a dispute is likely to arise, since the former will argue (to their advantage) that the origin of the damage was before the FOB point and the latter will argue the opposite. In contrast, FCA clarifies the allocation of risk, since container transport must be considered as a global phase from origin to destination, in which facts such as loading at the port of shipment are not relevant for determining the risk of loss.

Thus, to eliminate these factors of uncertainty, the Incoterms recommend replacing FOB with FCA. This way, the seller's control over delivery, whether at his premises or elsewhere, does not depend on when the goods are loaded on board the vessel, but on when the goods are handed over to the carrier (usually a freight forwarder) designated by the buyer.

2.3.5   Other considerations for the use of FCA

- **Less control of the logistics chain by the selling company and risks in packing and packaging**
  Under FCA conditions, the seller loses control of the logistics chain when delivering the goods (at their premises or elsewhere) to the carrier contracted by the buyer. Therefore, the seller cannot use their product knowledge to choose the means of transport or benefit from the advantages of contracting the main transport (better prices when contracting large

volumes, negotiation of conditions, choice of carriers and routes, etc. Additionally, being unaware of the main stages of the logistic chain, it may not use the right packaging and packing, which may cause damage to the goods. From the point of view of the buyer company, the FCA rule allows them to control the logistics chain from the seller's country (their facilities or a terminal) through the carrier operating there and contracted by them, which brings significant advantages:

— They obtain competitive transport conditions and costs as their contracting volume increases.
— They choose the transport operator on the basis of parameters such as quality of service, regularity, price, etc., as well as the other elements of the logistics chain.
— They increase their security with regard to the delivery conditions of the suppliers, which are not affected by any inefficient management these may carry out.

The next alternative to the FCA rule is to agree on the CPT port of destination, a practice that can involve high costs (if not previously agreed), so that the purchasing company can dispose of the goods and the goods are freed from the shipping company (especially in cases of groupage, LCL) contracted by the selling company (these same costs at the port of destination are significantly reduced if the main transport has been contracted by the buyer).

- **The selling company offers a low level of service and loses competitiveness.**
  The fact that the buyer assumes virtually the entire logistics chain (except for export clearance and, if applicable, initial transportation) may mean that the seller's offer is less competitive than alternatives offered by other companies that are able to deliver their products under more extensive conditions, i.e. closer to the buyer; for example, under CPT conditions or in the buyer's DAP warehouse.

- **Transport insurance**
  This rule does not require insurance, although both companies, especially the buyer, must consider the convenience of taking out a policy to cover

the risks (the seller, until the moment of delivery, and the buyer, from then on).

- **Documentation and proof of delivery**

  The selling company can fulfill its obligation to prove delivery in three different ways, the third of which is a novelty of the Incoterms 2020 that we do not find convenient and will explain in the next point:

  - The usual proof that the goods have been delivered. In this case, both the copies that the transporters give to the sender/shipper as receipt and proof of the contract and the corresponding copy of the bill of lading or the delivery note with the carrier's signature, among others, are valid.[4] In a containerized multimodal transport, other options may be used, such as a Forwarding Agents Certificate of Receipt (FIATA FCR) issued by a forwarding agent. This document, although not a contract of carriage, proves the receipt of the goods by the forwarder for subsequent transport under the conditions included in the document itself.
  - Assisting the buyer in obtaining a transport document (without the "on-board" notation). This corresponds to what happens in the case of multimodal container transport, for which a multimodal BL or a negotiable FIATA bill of lading for multimodal transport (FBL) is issued, which the selling company must try to obtain from the carrier, even if the latter has been instructed by the buyer (for example, because the FBL covers the transport from the selling company's premises and, by agreeing a terminal FCA, this first transport must be assumed by the seller, which makes payment for this service conditional on obtaining the original of this document).
  - If the buyer has instructed the carrier to deliver to the seller a transport document marked "on board", the latter will deliver this document to the buyer. This last possibility deserves a more detailed explanation in the following point.

---

[4] Providing the purchasing company with the usual proof does not imply that the seller must physically send such document (the original copy kept by it), but it can send it to it, for example, scanned, so as to prove its existence. The seller must keep it, since for the seller it serves as the carrier's receipt, and therefore proves that it has fulfilled the delivery in the contract of sale and that there is a contract of carriage (even if this contract has been made by the buyer).

- **FCA and its combination with *Shipped BL* in Incoterms 2020 rules**
  Taking into account what has been said about FCA, it is surprising that the 2020 version of the Incoterms Rules attempts to reconcile the use of FCA with documentary credits which require a BL on board as proof of delivery. The International Chamber of Commerce, in FCA Explanatory Note 6, states that it is common for documentary credits to require a shipped BL (bill of lading issued by a shipping line stating that the container has been loaded on board); It is issued by the latter only when the goods have been shipped) and that, therefore, in order to reconcile this situation in FCA sales and purchases, the parties may stipulate in their contract that the buyer (who orders the maritime transport) instructs the shipping company to provide the seller with the originals of the shipped BL so that the seller can present them in the documentary credit and thus subsequently reach the buyer (who needs them at the port of destination to request delivery from the shipping company).

  It seems to be a cumbersome and risky procedure involving third parties (the shipping company, outside the contract of sale and operating according to the rules and customs of contracts of carriage by sea) and arising from an initial irregularity such as the requirement as proof of delivery of a shipped BL when the delivery in FCA is prior. This irregularity seems to derive from the custom of some banks to "suggest" that, among the credit documents, a shipped BL is required, which may be explained by the fact that, as long as the bank has the BL, it "retains control" over the disposition of the goods until the final delivery to the buyer (once the amount of the credit is debited, which in turn guarantees payment to the seller).

  Another explanation may be the force of habit of always agreeing to require this document in a documentary credit, and doing so in transactions agreed in FCA would result in the irregular procedure indicated for the credit to work.

  All this would be resolved if the document or proof of delivery/transport that the seller receives when delivering the goods is requested in the letter of credit (this principle is general to all Incoterms rules). In FCA, this is usually Copy 1 of the original waybill, a receipt from the carrier, delivery at the terminal, etc. Under such a synchronization, the seller presents this document (once the goods have been delivered) and, having fulfilled their principal obligation under the contract of sale, has the right to payment in the documentary credit (issued under a separate contract from the contract of sale, but which should be synchronized as much as possible).

However, if the seller's FCA facilities are combined with a transaction where the letter of credit requires the seller to produce a shipped BL, it is possible that having delivered the goods, cannot prove it by not being able to present this document and does not have the right to payment. This situation would arise if a loss occurs between the seller's warehouse and the time of shipment on board at the port of export (for example, during the road trip or during the stay and handling of the container at the port). In such cases, if the goods are not shipped, the shipped BL will never be issued and the seller will not be able to collect the documentary credit.

In addition to the existence or not of the document, it must be taken into account that the BL, if it exists, must comply with a series of requirements, such as its form of issue (nominative or to order, indications that the freight is paid or due, etc.), which creates a second uncertainty, since in FCA, the seller being a warehouse where the carrier has to collect goods, it is not clear that it has the capacity to control that the BL is issued in the correct form in the documentary credit.

- **Transport documentation and documentary means of payment**

  If documentary means of payment are agreed, their combination with FCA must address a number of practical aspects related to the documentation required in multimodal containerized transportation with a maritime phase (some of which have already been discussed above). As already mentioned, the FCA rule is the alternative proposed in the Incoterms rules to the use of FOB in multimodal container transportation. However, many companies continue to use FOB for various reasons (see chapter 5). For example, under these conditions, the seller ensures, as a condition for payment of all costs to the carrier until the container is shipped, that the full set of originals of the BL is received (normally, with the on-board condition, which is usually required in documentary credits to allow the buyer to access the goods at the destination). As the seller loses involvement in the management and costs in the country of shipment by applying the FCA rule, they also logically lose the certainty of obtaining the full set of originals of the BL (despite the "formula" proposed by the ICC and discussed above). Therefore, when using documentary means of payment, it is advisable to request documents other than the delivered BL that correspond to the document obtained at the time of delivery by the selling company, since it has control over the goods until that time. If the agreed terms are FCA seller's premises, the appropriate document is either the shipper's copy of the bill of lading covering the road transport of the container from the seller's premises to the port terminal, or the collection slip or a Forwarder's Receipt Certificate (FCR). Any required BL must be multimodal (covering transportation from the seller's premises) and received for shipment (does not prove loading on board the vessel, i.e., not on board).

If the FCA container terminal rule is agreed, it is correct to require in the letter of credit that the seller submit a copy of the same bill of lading, but with the signature certifying the delivery of the container at the terminal to the appropriate carrier (shipping line or freight forwarder of the buyer), a FIATA FCR or a BL received for shipment. Thus, the seller can condition the payment of the initial transport on obtaining this document for presentation to the bank. On the other hand, it is not advisable to combine the FCA rule with a consigned BL, as this requires the selling company to obtain a document issued after delivery and over which it has no control. If, despite the inadvisability of this choice, it is desired to force the situation, it is advisable at least to agree on the FCA rule for container terminals and to make the payment of the first road transport conditional on the selling company's obtaining the BL, although this does not avoid the dysfunction of this document being obtained, if necessary, by the seller long after the latter has complied with the delivery provided for in the rule (on arrival at the terminal) and with the risks mentioned above.

In cases where the credit requires an inland bill of lading or a pick-up bill of lading instead of a BL, the purchasing company seems to lose documentary evidence and security with respect to the usual practice of requiring a shipped BL (proving that the goods are transported by sea to them as the consignee, with the corresponding endorsement of the BL, if any). However, this is not the case, as it should be noted that the forwarding agent in the country of origin is already contracted by the purchasing company and that the documentation recommended here provides the same guarantee, as it proves the delivery to this forwarder, who must deliver the goods at the destination, based on the instructions and the transportation contract agreed with it.

In another scenario, with greater trust between the parties (where a documentary credit is likely not used), the replacement of an on-board BL for collection could be negotiated. In cases where, despite agreeing FCA, a shipped BL is required a priori to collect, its substitution could be negotiated, be it multimodal waybill or sea waybill (BL without the merger of value title) and also be issued in electronic format (called express release or telex release). This option offers the advantages of speed, security, and economy. By issuing the sea waybill in this manner, the consignee, with mere identification at the destination, can claim the goods. If we assume that the goods are already under the consignee's control from the warehouse of the selling company, this option logically smooths the process and facilitates the logistical management of the operation without compromising security in payment, as long as the obtainment of the sea waybill is guaranteed.

This option is highly recommended because it makes the maritime logistics chain cheaper (the cost of issuing the BL is saved) and faster, since it is no longer necessary to issue the BL on paper at the port of origin and present the originals at the port of destination to claim delivery of the goods from the shipping company. This other form of management is ideal for transactions between companies of the same group (about 20-25% of the total) or in cases where the trust between the parties is high or even the goods have been paid in advance. In all these cases, the BL implies an additional cost and complexity in the management of the operation, which can be overcome by substituting this document. In other means of transportation, the seller's company is provided, at the moment of delivery of the goods to the carrier, with the corresponding copy of the sender or consignor, which is the documentation that should be required in the documentary credit and that can be used, although it is not usual, with this means of payment, as stated in the UCP 600 rules.

2.4 Conclusions

The great versatility of the FCA rule makes it suitable for a wide variety of traffic and modes of transportation, making it advisable to apply it to:

- Full truckloads by road (national or international) door-to-door instead of EXW, since with FCA the seller loads the goods.

- LCL consolidated less-than-container-loads (LCL) through a freight forwarder or on an international carrier's truck, to whose facilities the seller must deliver the goods.
- Multimodal transportation in full container with sea (as a substitute for FOB) or rail phase, with loading at the seller's or forwarder's facilities near the corresponding terminal in the exporting country.
- Multimodal transportation by road and air, in which the goods are transported by road to the terminal docks or loading center at the airport of the selling company's country.

From a non-transportation point of view, this Incoterms rule is also suitable for transactions where:

- The buyer can obtain better transportation terms and costs, as well as control the entire logistics chain and ensure deliveries from its suppliers' facilities.
- Export clearance is required, and the selling company manages, pays for and controls this procedure for greater tax security in terms of VAT exemption.
- The seller has little experience in international sales and wants to limit their risks.

3 CPT (carriage paid to)

3.1 Overview and delivery

The CPT rule, like the CIP rule, provides for the delivery of the goods at the place of origin, with the peculiarity that the selling company, despite having contracted and paid for the transportation to the agreed place of destination, delivers the goods and transfers the risks to the purchasing company at the place of origin by placing the goods at the disposal of the carrier it has contracted.[5] This dichotomy is related to the widespread use of the Bill of Lading (BL) as a title document, which is why the CPT is particularly useful in multimodal transportation in containers with a maritime phase, although it can also be applied to other modes of transportation.

For all these reasons, both the place of delivery and the place of destination must be clearly defined in the contract of sale, since, in the absence of a specific place of delivery, it is understood that, in cases where several carriers are involved, the place of delivery and the transfer of risk occur when the seller delivers the goods to the first of them (similar to a delivery under FCA conditions at the seller's premises).

Consequently, any loss or damage in transit is the responsibility of the buyer, who, unless otherwise agreed in the contract of sale, must pay the seller and, if necessary, claim from the carrier or from any insurance that may have been taken out. If delivery is not to be determined this way, the contract of sale must clearly state the agreed place of delivery, which may be the terminal of the port of shipment or even the port of destination.

Moreover, in the preamble to CFR and CIF, the Incoterms discourage the use of these terms for containers and their replacement by CPT and CIP, which make the time of delivery coincide with the time when the seller makes the goods available to the carrier (whereas in CFR and CIF delivery does not take place until the container is loaded on board the vessel at the port of shipment). Although the costs are similar in both cases (e.g. between CPT and CFR), the difference in delivery and transfer of risk must be considered, since in CPT and

---

[5] This method of determining the place of delivery complies with the provisions of Article 31 of the United Nations Convention on Contracts for the International Sale of Goods or the Vienna Convention of 1980.

CIP it is fully clarified which party bears them in their entirety (the buyer), whereas in CFR and CIF delivery occurs when the goods are loaded on board, which may lead to a commercial dispute in the event of an unlocated incident (the condition of the goods is not checked when the container is loaded on board).[6]

As for customs clearance (if required) the general rule applies: the selling company clears for export and the purchasing company clears for import.

General formulation

CPT (designated place of destination). Incoterms 2020.

Writing examples

- CPT Pasir Panjang terminal, port of Shanghai, Shanghai. China. Incoterms 2020.
- CPT Tecon terminal, port of Santos, São Paulo. Brazil. Incoterms 2020
- CPT SPRBUN terminal, port of Buenaventura, Buenaventura, Colombia. Colombia. Incoterms 2020.

3.2   Main obligations and costs

- **Obligations of the selling company**
    1. To deliver the goods agreed upon in the purchase contract (after checking and verifying their quality) within the agreed term, to pack them properly for transportation and to mark the packaging properly (it is very convenient that these two aspects are specified in the purchase contract).
    2. Provide the commercial invoice and all other documents agreed in the purchase contract (as a proof of conformity).
    3. Notify the buyer that the delivery has been made and of any other requirement that allows the buyer to proceed with the reception of the goods.

---

[6] The reasons why CPT and CIP are preferable to CFR and CIF for containerized transport operations are the same reasons why FCA is preferable to FOB for the same type of operations. For further details, please refer to the FCA Incoterms analysis in the previous section.

CPT (carriage paid to) / CIP (carriage and insurance paid to)

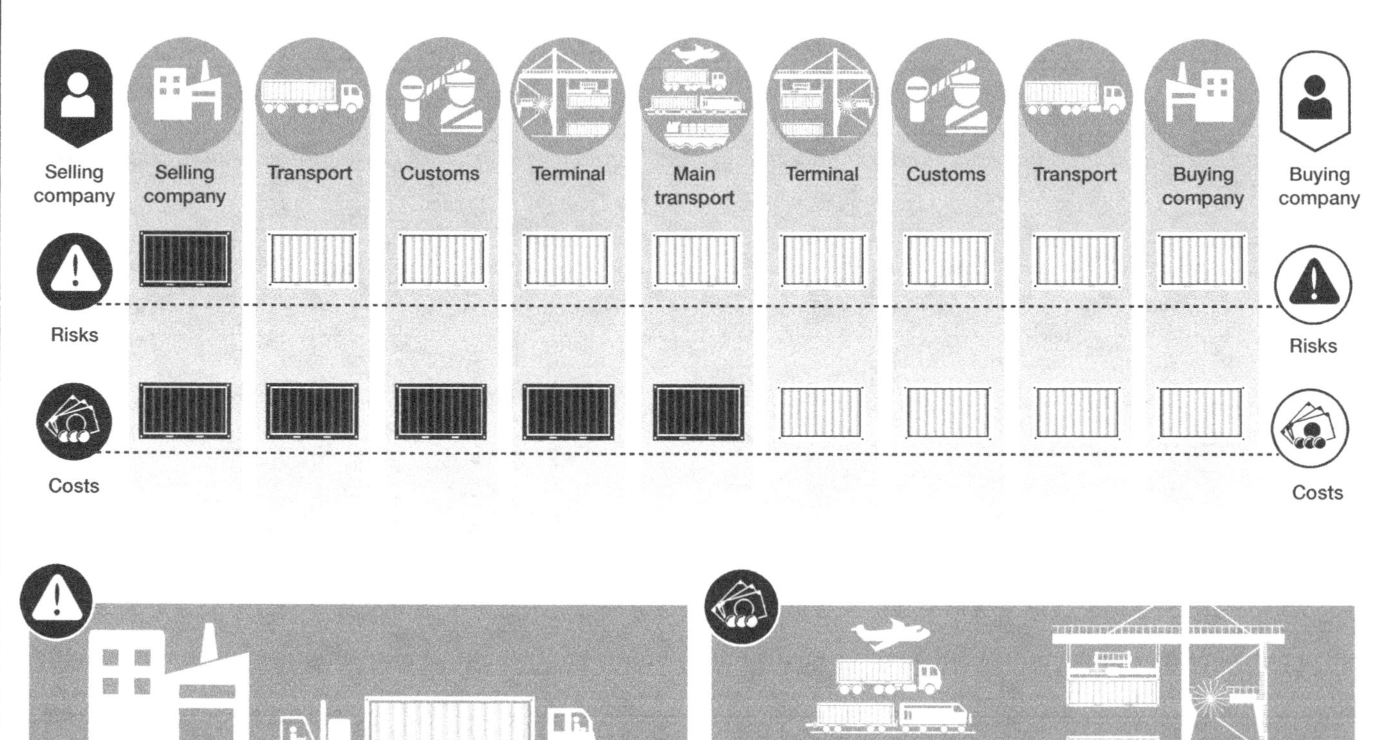

The selling company bears the transport costs to the designated place of destination (port or railway terminal, logistics center, etc.) although the delivery and transmission of risks to the buyer take place when the goods are made available to the first carrier at its facilities or another agreed place.

At the end of the maritime transport, the costs of unloading in the port of destination fall on the buying company unless the seller's contract of carriage includes them.

4. To arrange and pay for the transport to the named place of destination and to comply with any safety requirements related to such transport, e.g. verified gross weight (VGM) of the container, etc.
5. Export customs clearance (if required by the operation) and related formalities and costs: licenses, security clearance and inspections (red channel after the customs declaration has been filed, specific inspections based on the goods, such as phytosanitary, sanitary, pharmacological, safety, etc.). Also, assist the buyer in obtaining information and documents (at the buyer's expense) that may be required to manage the import clearance (and, where applicable, in transit countries), such as licenses, certifications or inspections.
6. If the seller bears the cost of unloading at the agreed place of destination, they cannot claim them from the buyer (this is the case in container shipping where the contracted freight includes the unloading of the container at the destination terminal).

- **Obligations of the purchasing company**
  1. Pay the price of the goods as agreed in the contract of sale (it should be noted that the means of payment is not regulated by the Incoterms).
  2. Proceed with the reception of the goods, i.e. receive them from the carrier designated by the seller at the place of destination specified in the Incoterms.
  3. Organize, manage and pay for the rest of the operations in the logistics chain after delivery of the goods: costs at the terminal or at the designated place of destination (including unloading of the vehicle, truck, ship, etc., if not included in the contract of carriage), import clearance in the country of destination (and, if applicable, in transit countries), final transport and unloading.

3.3 Considerations for effective use of the rule

3.3.1 Difference between place of delivery and payment of transport, and combination with Sea BL

The Group C rules present a dichotomy between the place to which the selling company must assume the transportation and the time of delivery (at origin).

This dichotomy is based on the appropriate and widespread use, in connection with maritime transport operations, of the BL as a contract of carriage.

This document, in addition to the functions of any bill of lading (receipt of the goods by the carrier and proof of the existence of the contract and its conditions), performs the function of a document of title, which implies the possibility of transferring the ownership of the goods to its legitimate holder by delivery of the document (if applicable, it may include an endorsement). In addition, the shipping company at the destination can only deliver the container to the person who presents an original BL and is its legitimate holder.

The BL may be issued in different ways depending on how the box relating to the consignee is filled in:

- *Nominative BL.* The consignee field contains the data of the purchasing company, the only one who can claim the delivery of the container to the shipping company or the freight forwarder at the destination by presenting one of the originals.
- *BL to the bearer.* The holder of an original can request delivery of the goods from the carrier at the destination (not used because of the risks and uncertainties associated with its use).
- *BL to order.* This is a BL with the words "to the order of" or equivalent in the consignee box. This last option is the one that allows the transfer of possession of the goods through the correct endorsement of the BL under the conditions of the bill of exchange and check law, a widespread practice, combined or not with means of payment such as documentary credit, which implies that the goods are sold at origin with transportation paid to destination and that the original consignee can endorse it to another, the last endorsee being the one who becomes the legitimate holder who can claim the goods at destination.

The original or originals of the Bills of Lading are sent by the selling company – who acts in the transport contract as the shipper (to whom the carrier delivers the complete set of BLs at origin) – to the buyer in coordination with the form of payment by documentary credit, direct shipment, freight forwarder, or pouch on the ship.

In any case, the delivery of the B/L at origin by the seller to the buyer (who, as the rightful owner, has access to the goods at destination) constitutes, in practice, the delivery and transfer of possession of the goods. It is logical, therefore, that it is the latter who assumes the risks of origin, since, upon receipt of the BL, it becomes at that moment the possessor ("virtual owner") of the goods. Finally, there is another type of bill of lading that does not combine the function of a document of title; it is the so-called "sea waybill". This document constitutes a contract of carriage with a mandate to the shipping company to deliver directly to the recipient company after identification at the destination, without the need to present the original bill of lading. In fact, sometimes only a copy is issued to the selling company as a receipt, while the rest of the documentation is replaced by electronic messages (express release or telex release) between the forwarding agents and the shipping company at origin and destination. The bill of lading is usually used in fiduciary operations and in short shipments that require administrative flexibility in order to avoid extraordinary costs at the port of destination due to a delay in the presentation of the bill of lading.

3.3.2   *Use with means of transport other than sea transport and bills of lading without title of value*

The Incoterms do not limit the use of CPT to containerized maritime transport but allow it to be applied to any mode or combination of modes of transport. Thus, transportation under CPT conditions is possible with these modes, even if the document in which the contract of carriage is formalized does not perform the function of a document of title. However, this combination must be made after first assessing some relevant aspects.

- **In road transportation**
  Road transport is the mode of transport in which there is the most negotiation of the contracting conditions between the shipper (in CPT terms, the selling company) and the carrier. In sea, air and rail transport, the shipper usually adheres to the general contract conditions issued by the carrier or an association of carriers, so that in practice a contract of adhesion is accepted.[7]

---

[7] A contract in which one of the parties can only accept or reject the covenant or agreement, without having the capacity to discuss or negotiate its content.

This significant negotiation possibility is due to market circumstances, where the shipping company is usually at least similar in size to the carrier, allowing negotiation of the contract terms without impositions. In any case, it is common for the shipper to impose them through a transportation provider selection process (tender) or via a load board on the internet. Additionally, the bill of lading is formalized at the time of loading the goods onto the vehicle in different formats and procedures (carbonless forms, printing from a management program, etc.). In this case, the shipper (the seller) and the carrier can agree on some key aspects in the transport contract that could negatively affect the buyer in case of a claim against the carrier, given that the delivery and transfer of risks occur at the origin when the truck is loaded. Some of these aspects may be:

- *Competent jurisdiction.* The rules applicable to the contract allow the shipper and the carrier to agree on the jurisdiction of certain courts or, alternatively, transport arbitration boards or similar bodies to resolve claims arising under the contract.
- *Other aspects that may affect the purchasing company:* convenience of agreeing on a declaration of value, insurance, etc.

Let us consider the case of a Spanish purchasing company in a contract of sale with its German supplier, concluded under the conditions of CPT Madrid and managed by road transport. The German seller, in compliance with its obligations under this rule, contracts with a Russian company, and the CMR consignment note contains a clause of submission to the Moscow courts. During transportation, the goods are lost, but the carrier does not respond to the claim of the buyer (as the party bearing the risk), and the buyer is obliged, in accordance with the terms of the transportation contract, to file a claim in the Moscow courts (this method of resolution was probably not known to the buyer, but it is the applicable one).

- **In other modes of transportation**
  In the rail and air modes, transport contracts are predefined, i.e. regulated by the corresponding regulations and formalized in waybills issued by the carrier itself (airline or IATA freight forwarder, rail operator, etc.). Consequently, there is not much room for negotiation (in any case, with regard to the price depending on the volume of contracting).

3.3.3 Coordination of the unloading at destination with transport contract

Under CPT conditions, unloading at the agreed place of destination is a cost to be borne by the buyer, unless it is included in the contract of carriage as a cost of the seller (in which case the seller cannot claim it from the buyer). This is usually the case in multimodal container transport with a maritime phase, as shipping companies usually work on liner terms, i.e. the freight includes loading and unloading of the container by container cranes at the ports of departure and destination. In air transport, the procedure is usually similar, as the freight includes the loading and unloading of the goods. For other modes, different situations may arise:

- In road transportation for full truck door-to-door, the CPT rule is followed, since the purchasing company usually performs the unloading.
- Rail transport offers a wide range of possibilities. For example, in container transport, the tariff offered by the rail operator usually specifies the conditions under which the container is picked up at each station. Thus, formulas include:

  - *Delivery on wagon:* the transport cost does not include unloading at the destination.
  - *Delivery on ground:* the transport cost includes unloading of the container from the container wagon to the terminal.
  - *Delivery on road truck:* the transport cost includes unloading at the terminal and loading onto a truck for further transportation or delivery at destination.

3.3.4 Other considerations for the use of CPT

- **Control of the logistics chain by the selling company**
  This company controls the transport and logistics chain to the destination, so it can select the most appropriate carrier in terms of quality of service and cost. As its volume of contracting increases, the seller can also benefit from better commercial terms.

This rule is very suitable for the seller when it is agreed that the seller's responsibilities (obligations and costs) end at the border (terminal) of the buyer's country.

This is particularly advisable in all those cases where the country of destination or the operation presents certain risks and difficulties: first operations with a customer or in a market (country), uncertain customs procedures, poor transport infrastructure, social or political risks, etc. In all these cases, through the CPT rule, the seller limits its obligations up to the arrival terminal in the country of destination and from there, the buyer can likely manage the specific characteristics of their market under better conditions. Consequently, the overall management of the operation is optimized.

- **Costs for the buyer at destination**
The CPT port-of-import rule can result in high costs for the purchasing company in the case of groupage containerized maritime transport (LCL) at the port of destination to access the goods. This is because freight forwarders and shipping lines exercise their right of retention under the terms of the CPT to refuse to release the container until all outstanding claims against it for port charges, etc. have been paid in full. In many cases, these costs are very onerous in relation to the stage or stages of the logistics chain that they represent. These situations are due to the abusive nature of certain non-standardized fees, concepts and cost components applied by some forwarders and operators as a condition of access to goods.

The best way to avoid these problems is to ask for an absolutely detailed quotation (indicating not only the amounts associated with certain components, but also the amount of all those that may exist, for example the cost of a possible scanner revision, etc.) before concluding the transaction, to prevent later application of abusive rates.

Purchasing companies can choose to apply the FCA (or FOB) rule at the port of export in order to know for sure the costs to be borne before contracting the transport from origin to their facilities, which can significantly reduce costs.

Another possibility is for each party to request fully itemized door-to-door quotations and exchange this information in order to select the best service at the lowest cost. The agreed Incoterms rule should then be determined, and the costs borne by each party should be communicated to the carrier. In any case, the forwarder will renegotiate the price to their convenience (collection management and deferment of payment, risk of non-payment, confidence in collection at destination, customs representation expenses, etc.), but the selling and purchasing companies will have largely avoided excessive increases in the amounts of some items because the party who must assume them has no choice (as is usually the case with the buyer in CPT port of destination conditions or CFR port of destination in cases of groupage, LCL).

- **The vendor provides a high level of service.**
  By placing the goods in the buyer's country, the seller greatly facilitates the management of the final phase of the international logistics chain.

- **Transport insurance**
  According to the Incoterms Group C rules, delivery takes place at the place of origin, meaning that, unless otherwise agreed, the buyer assumes the transportation risk from the time the seller makes the goods available to the first carrier at the seller's premises (when loaded on the first vehicle, similar to FCA).

  It is up to the buyer to assess the advisability of taking out insurance to cover these risks. In this case, the selling company is obliged to provide (at the buyer's request, risk and expense) the information necessary for the buyer to take out the insurance: number of packages, packaging, modes of transport and carriers to destination, route, vehicle data, etc. The buyer is not obliged to take out the insurance.

  As an alternative to the buyer taking out insurance, the same place CIP rule may be agreed, whereby the seller must take out insurance to cover the buyer's risks.

- **Documentation and proof of delivery**
  If agreed or customary, the seller must prove delivery by providing the buyer with the transport document or documents relating to the contract, dated within the agreed loading or shipment period and identifying the goods.

  The document must enable the buyer to claim the goods from the carrier. If such a document is negotiable (in the case of BL issued to order), the complete set of originals must be presented. In addition, the seller must notify the buyer that he has delivered the goods by making them available to the contracted carrier. This regulation of the delivery document differs across the modes of transport:

— *Contracting of container shipping with BL.* The selling company must provide the buyer (if applicable, through bank intervention in a documentary credit) with a complete set of correctly issued originals (nominative, to order, etc.) to enable the buyer to claim delivery of the container at the destination. The instructions for the BL also apply to the FIATA negotiable bill of lading for multimodal transportation (FBL).
— *Contracting a mode of transportation other than by sea with BL.* The bills of lading issued do not serve as document of title, so they cannot be endorsed, i.e. they are not negotiable documents. The carrier usually delivers a first copy (the one that serves as a receipt and proof of contract) to the seller, and two other copies are usually presented to the consignee for signature, one of which remains in the carrier's possession as proof of delivery at destination.

- **Transport documentation and documentary means of payment**
Two situations can be distinguished: transportation in containers with a maritime phase and transportation by other modes. In the first case, under CPT conditions, the selling company delivers at origin but must arrange transportation to the port of destination, so the documentation must prove the fulfillment of both obligations. In this way, this rule is adapted to the usual practice of documentary credits, which, according to the rules of UCP 600, require the complete set of originals of the contract of carriage. Usually, a BL issued under certain conditions is required, including specific provisions: date of shipment (not exceeding the maximum date of the credit), indication of prepaid freight, issued by a certain carrier, ports of origin and destination, description of goods and agreed Incoterms rule. Sometimes the BL is required to show the invoice number or the documentary credit number or other specific data of the transaction.

The formal conditions to be met by the BL must be agreed in the terms of the documentary credit and must balance two aspects: on the one hand, the purchasing company must be sure that with the presentation of this documentation it will be able to access the purchased goods (complete set of nominative originals or to order, conveniently endorsed, often at the importer's bank); and, on the other hand, the selling company must be able to obtain it, otherwise it will not be able to present it to the bank for collection. As the seller arranges maritime transport, they must inform the carrier of the formal requirements to be met by the BL according to the credit requirements.

By combining the two obligations (delivery at origin and contracting and paying for transportation to the port of destination), the process of obtaining the documentation is delayed with respect to the time of delivery (from the seller's facilities to loading on the ship). This is because the selling company must comply with the second obligation of the CPT rule, which is to contract and pay for the transportation and to allow the buyer access to the goods at the destination.

However, as previously mentioned, the letter of credit should ideally require the documents proving the fulfilment of the selling company's obligations, so that the right to payment is established upon presentation. It would be perfectly valid (and certainly more in line with the correspondence between the delivery and the document required in the credit) to require a multimodal BL (from the warehouse of origin to the port of destination) issued before the goods are shipped, when the carrier takes over the goods at the seller's warehouse.

3.4 Conclusions

CPT is a widely used rule (though less so than CFR), which, according to the recommendations of the Incoterms, should be used even more frequently in container transportation as a substitute for CFR. In fact, the fundamental difference between the two is that under CPT conditions, the selling company performs the delivery and the transfer of risk at its premises, whereas the CFR rule stipulates that this takes place when the container is loaded on board the container ship at the port of shipment.

The CPT rule is therefore very suitable for multimodal ocean container shipments, both full container load (FCL) and less-than-container load (LCL), where a Bill of Lading (BL) is used to transfer possession of the goods or manage the payment of the transaction through documentary payment (documentary credit, documentary remittance, or similar). This rule can also be used for the other modes of transportation (e.g. door-to-door LTL). However, in these cases, the bill of lading does not play the role of a document of title, and the purchasing company is obliged to bear the risks of transportation without having participated in its contracting, which means that any claims the buyer may need to make could be influenced by the terms of that arrangement.

Thus, with the exception of multimodal container transport operations with a maritime phase, it seems more logical to align the point to which the seller and the buyer arrange and assume transport with the point of delivery, as provided for in both the FCA and the DAP, DPU and DDP. Another alternative is to agree on the CIP rule, similar to the CPT in delivery and risk transfer, but CIP includes insurance that the seller must arrange to cover the transportation risks borne by the buyer.

4   CIP (carriage and insurance paid to)

4.1   Overview and delivery

The CIP rule differs only from CPT in that the selling company is obliged to take out insurance to cover the risks of the goods in transport that the buyer will bear from the time of delivery. Therefore, the analysis conducted for CPT is applicable to this rule, so its description will focus on this particularity.

The CIP/CIF value corresponds to the customs value calculation base (the taxable amount for applying the percentage or ad valorem tariff), which is more widely used internationally (following the proposal of the World Customs Organization).[8]

General formulation

CIP (designated place of destination). Incoterms 2020.

Writing examples

- CIP Pasir Panjang terminal, Shanghai Port, Shanghai. China. Incoterms 2020.
- CIP Tecon terminal, port of Santos, São Paulo. Brasil. Incoterms 2020.
- CIP SPRBUN terminal, puerto de Buenaventura. Colombia. Incoterms 2020.

4.2   Main obligations and costs

- **Obligations of the selling company**
  1. To deliver the goods agreed upon in the purchase contract (after checking and verifying their quality) within the agreed term, to pack them properly for transportation and to mark the packaging appropriately (it is highly desirable that these two aspects are specified in the purchase contract).

---

[8] Even so, there are countries such as the United States or Australia that use the FOB basis to determine the customs value and apply tariffs in ad valorem format.

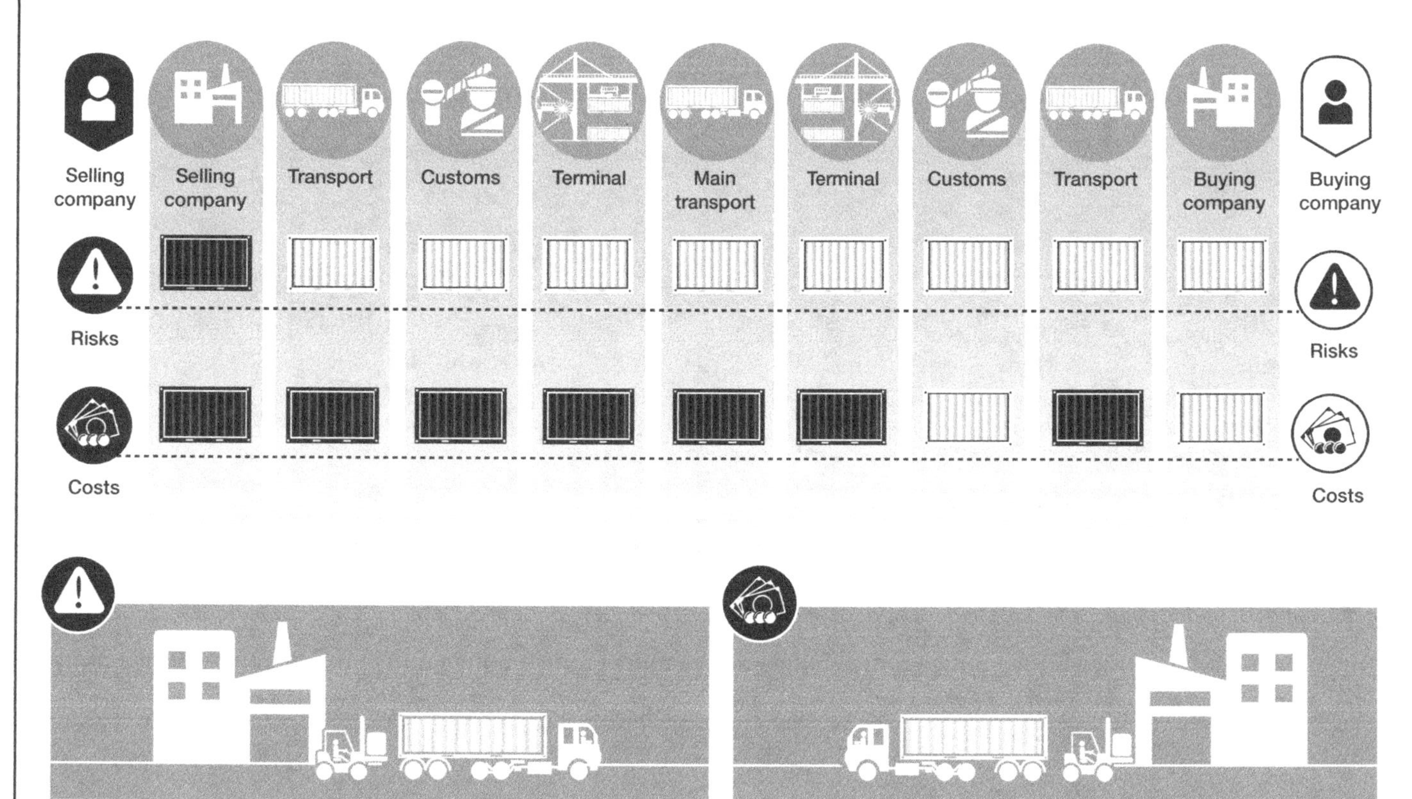

The selling company bears the costs of road transport to the designated place (usually the buying company's premises) although the delivery and transmission of risks to the buyer take place when loading the goods on the carrier's vehicle at its premises or another agreed place.

At the end of the road transport, the costs of unloading in destination fall on the buying company unless the seller's contract of carriage includes them.

2. Provide the commercial invoice and other documents agreed in the contract of sale (as a proof of conformity).

3. Notify the buyer that the delivery has been made and of any other requirements that allows the buyer to proceed with the acceptance of the goods.

4. Arrange and pay for transportation to the named destination and comply with any safety requirements associated with such transportation (e.g., Verified Gross Weight of Container or VGW).

5. Export customs clearance (if required by the operation) and related formalities and costs: licenses, security clearance and inspections (red channel after the customs declaration has been filed, specific inspections based on the goods, such as phytosanitary, sanitary, pharmacological, safety, etc.). The seller must also provide the Buyer with the necessary assistance to obtain the information and documents (at the Buyer's expense) that may be required to manage the import clearance (and, where applicable, in transit countries), such as licenses, certifications or inspections.

6. If the seller bears the cost of unloading at the agreed place of destination, they cannot claim them from the buyer (this is the case in container shipping where the contract of carriage includes the unloading of the container at the destination terminal).

7. To hire and pay, under the conditions established by the Incoterms rule, an insurance that covers the risks of the goods with regard to the transport that are borne by the Buyer from the moment of delivery at the place of origin (thus, the buyer assumes the role of policyholder in this contract, since it is the party that concludes and pays for the insurance contract). This is the new obligation of the seller under CIP that did not exist in CPT and will be discussed in detail below.

- **Obligations of the purchasing company**
  1. Pay the price of the goods as agreed in the contract of sale (it should be noted that the means of payment is not regulated by the Incoterms).
  2. Accept the goods, i.e. receive them from the carrier designated by the seller at the place of destination specified in the Incoterms.
  3. Organize, manage and pay for the rest of the operations in the logistics chain after delivery of the goods: at the terminal or at the designated place of destination (including unloading of the arriving vehicle, be it

truck, ship or any other), import clearance in the country of destination (and, if applicable, in transit countries), final transport and unloading.

4.3 Considerations for effective use of the rule

The selling company must take out an insurance policy to cover the risks of the goods during transportation, which must meet the following conditions:

- **Minimum coverage**
  It must comply with A-Mode of the ICC (Institute Cargo Clauses) clauses of the Institute of Insurers of London or other similar clauses. This is one of the novelties of the Incoterms 2020 rules, since until the 2010 version, the mandatory coverage for CIP was Type C. The ICC clauses, which are the most widely accepted and implemented internationally, adopt three types (A, B and C) that cover the following risks:

  - **Type C**. The lowest coverage. It includes fire, explosion, grounding, stranding, running aground, sinking, shipwreck, collision or impact, unloading in port, refuge and capsizing, jettison, derailment and general average sacrifice.
  - **Type B.** An intermediate coverage. In addition to the risks indicated in Type C, it adds dragging by waves, ingress of sea water, loss of packages during loading or unloading, damage caused by lightning, earthquakes and volcanic eruptions.
  - **Type A.** It covers any risk of loss or damage, with the exception of certain risks expressly excluded, such as malice of the insured, normal loss of weight or volume, wear and tear, inadequate packing and packaging, inherent vice, delays, insolvencies, radioactivity, war, strikes, and unseaworthiness.

- **Additional coverage by agreement**
  Although A-Mode is the highest of the three types of coverage, it is common (and advisable) for companies to agree to increase it to include other risks, such as war and strikes, in addition to those specific to each type of goods and operation. In this case, the cost of the additional coverages, which entails a higher premium to be paid by the seller, is passed on to the buyer through a higher price.

- **Quality and service of the insurance company**

  In order to meet the requirements of the agreed Incoterms rule, it is advisable to take out insurance with a well-established and experienced company that specializes in transport insurance and has a presence in the countries of origin or destination. It should be noted that the rules governing the insurance contract are not standardized by an international convention, but differ from one country to another. In some countries, in order to make a claim, the insurance must be taken out with a local company (established in the country of the claimant).

  The contract with a specific insurance company may be agreed and specified in the contract of sale and reflected in the terms and conditions of the documentary credit, if this means of payment has been used (requiring a policy or certificate issued by the same). The insurance must allow both the purchasing company and other interested parties to claim directly from the insurance company. The other interested parties may be, for example, the seller up to the moment of delivery of the goods (the insurance policy may then be endorsed to the buyer, making him the insured from that moment) or a third company to which the goods have been sold by endorsement of the bill of lading and to which the insurance is also endorsed when the risk is transferred to it.

- **Insured value coverage**

  The insured value, defined as the maximum limit of indemnity to be paid by the insurance company in the event of loss, must cover at least 110% of the purchase price and be contracted in the same currency as the contract. This concept corresponds to the value of the interest to be insured (for example, that of the goods transported). Since the selling company must include the cost of the insurance in the price itself, it can be calculated with a simple mathematical operation:

$$\text{Insured value} = 1.1 \times [(1 + c) \times \text{CPT}].$$

  - CPT: value of the goods under CPT conditions.
  - c: decimal of the insurance premium coefficient applicable to the operation.

> **Example of insurance cost calculation**
>
> If the selling price of the goods under CPT conditions is 200,000 € and the insurance company has quoted the premium at 0.75% of the insured value, the insured value including the CPT value plus insurance and 110% as stipulated in the Incoterms rule (110% CIP) can be obtained as follows:
>
> $$VA = 1.1 \times [(1 + 0.0075) \times 200,000] = 221,650 \text{ €}.$$
>
> Thus, the amount of insured value 221,650 € includes the value of the goods, insurance and 110 % of the above accumulated amount, i.e. 110 % of the CIP value.

- **Transport stages covered by insurance**

  The insurance must cover the risks of the goods during transportation from the geographical point of delivery (in case of multimodal transportation with more than one carrier, from the moment when the seller makes the goods available to the first carrier, i.e. from the loading of the container at their facilities, similar to delivery under FCA conditions) to, at a minimum, the designated destination, i.e. the place to which the seller contracts and assumes responsibility for transportation (e.g. the port of destination).

  At the time of publication of this book (2024), the most common Incoterms in connection with container transport are FOB and CIF. The change from CIF to CIP is relatively simple (considering that the minimum coverage established in CIF must be increased in CIP) and better aligns the operation, as it synchronizes the delivery by the selling company with the time up to which it controls the goods.

  Under both regimes (CIP and CIF), the cover starts at the moment of delivery, but while under CIP conditions the insurance must cover the transport from the seller's premises, under CIF conditions it must do so from the moment the goods are loaded on board the vessel. Therefore, if opting to transition from CIF to CIP, the seller must adapt their coverage to include the stages of transport from the moment of delivery to the first carrier, as provided for in the second rule.

- **Proof of insurance contract and direct claim of the purchaser**

  The formalization of the insurance contract must be made in writing and is specified in the corresponding policy, which includes general and specific conditions. The former are common to all policies of the same branch or sector (transport, life, automobile, etc.) and include the aspects of the insurance relating to definitions, purpose and scope of the insurance, general coverages, etc. The general ICC coverage clauses are an example of this.

The policy is completed by the Particular Conditions, which identify the parties to the insurance contract (policyholder, insured and beneficiary) and the insured value, and the risk coverages of the General Conditions are expanded and specified according to the specific characteristics of the operation (for example, the transportation of frozen products must include coverage for the risk of breakage of the refrigeration equipment of the vehicle, truck or container in which the goods are to be transported).

In addition to the full policy, the insurance company is usually required to issue a certificate of insurance to prove its existence. This certificate must show the policy number and the coverage provided (coverage clauses, risks and insured value). It is essential for the purchasing company to be able to claim directly from the insurer. In this regard, it should be noted that the insurance policy may be nominee (in the name of the buyer), to order (from the seller who assigns it by endorsement or directly from the buyer) or to bearer (assigning the right to claim to the insurer upon delivery of the insurance certificate).

- **Proof of insurance documentation and documentary means of payment**
  In addition to the information regarding the CPT rule, under CIP conditions, the presentation of the insurance certificate proving its contracting under the agreed conditions is usually added to the documentary payment methods:

  - Part and value insured.
  - Coverage contracted.
  - Stages of transport covered.
  - Date of issue proving the validity of the insurance from the place of delivery, etc.

All of this must comply with the requirements of Article 28 of the UCP 600 on insurance documents and their coverages. These requirements stipulate, among other things, that such a document (policy or certificate, as

specified in the credit terms): must be issued and signed by an insurance company or its agents (the signature of an agent must indicate that it is on behalf of the insurer); if issued in several originals, all
must be presented; it must indicate the insured amount (110% of the CIP or CIF value) and be expressed in the same currency as the credit; its date of issue must not be later than the date of shipment, etc.

- **Information to the purchasing company for additional insurance**
  The seller shall, at the buyer's request and expense, provide the Buyer with all information necessary for the buyer to take out additional insurance to cover, for example, voyages beyond the agreed place of destination (such as from the port of destination) or to enable the buyer, in the event that the seller limits itself to taking out compulsory ICC Type A insurance, to take out insurance against additional risks (war, strike, etc.).

4.4   Conclusions

The CIP rule is suitable for all operations where the use of CPT is also possible or recommended. The goods are delivered with transport insurance, an aspect that must be evaluated by the buyer. The conclusion of insurance contracts is subject to several factors that can cause controversy in areas where security is expected, such as the vagueness of the coverage, uncertainty regarding the terms of the contract, national laws that may interfere with the process of claiming from the insurance company, the manner in which the indemnity is determined and its payment materialized, etc.

Therefore, in the event that there is not full confidence in the fulfillment of the insurance function, there is an option to apply the CPT rule and that the purchasing company is the one that subscribes a policy under the conditions it considers most convenient, so that it assumes the functions of policyholder, insured and beneficiary of such insurance.

5 DAP (delivered at place)

5.1 Overview and delivery

The DAP rule (together with the discontinued DAT) was one of the new features introduced in the 2010 version of the Incoterms to replace the discontinued DDU (delivery duty unpaid). Under these conditions, delivery and transfer of risk by the seller occurs when the goods are placed at the disposal of the buyer on the means of transport without unloading at the named place of destination, so that the seller assumes all costs and risks of transportation to that point.

It is therefore crucial to define the designated place very precisely, as only based on it can the scope of this Incoterms rule, which can offer great versatility, be determined. For example, in the case of a maritime container transport operation, in the case of a DAP port of destination, the seller pays for the transport and bears the costs until the container arrives at the port of destination (without even unloading from the vessel of arrival). For the same operation, if the customer's warehouse DAP is agreed, in addition to the risks and costs indicated above, the costs of passage through the port terminal (handling, fees, etc.) and those of transport to the destination warehouse would be added. Delivery is made there without unloading from the arriving vehicle.

In any case, DAP is most commonly used in operations where the designated place is located beyond the terminal of entry into the country of destination (more typical in combinations with CPT and CIP or their variants CFR and CIF) and is usually arranged with the buyer's warehouse at destination or elsewhere.

Therefore, this arrangement is usually agreed upon when the selling company assumes the costs, transportation and risks already in the buyer's country (in the case of an international transaction). This has important implications for tax and control purposes, especially if customs clearance is required. Since the selling company assumes the costs and risks of transportation to the place of destination, this point should be clearly specified, as it may correspond to the buyer's facilities, the warehouse of a logistics operator contracted by the buyer, the facilities of a client company of the buyer, etc. If the seller contracts for transportation or ancillary operations that exceed the agreed Incoterms rule (e.g. unloading of the goods at the place of destination), the seller cannot claim the additional costs from the buyer, so it is advisable for the buyer to draw up transportation contracts that accurately reflect its obligations.

Assuming that the designated place is an inland point in the buyer's country, the seller must bear the costs and risks of transportation to the country of destination, the stay and handling of the goods at the destination terminal (port, railway station or airport), and the subsequent costs, which usually consist of another stage of transportation (by road or in combination with other modes) to the named place of destination. The selling company assumes these risks:

- It is the party that must claim from the carrier (if applicable) in the event of loss or damage to the goods during transportation.
- It must consider, even if it is not obliged to do so, the advisability of taking out insurance to cover the risks of the goods during transportation.

As for customs clearance (if necessary), the general criterion is followed: the seller clears for export and the buyer clears for import. In this sense, the management of import clearance by the buyer under DAP conditions is essential for the seller's compliance with the Incoterms rule.

General formulation

DAP (designated place of destination). Incoterms 2020.

Writing examples

- DAP 140, Gloucester Road, Wanchai, Hong Kong. China. Incoterms 2020.
- DAP Rua Hungría, s/n, Andar, Jardim Europa, São Paulo. Brasil. Incoterms 2020.
- DAP nave A1, parque industrial del Cauca, Cali. Colombia. Incoterms 2020.

5.2 Main obligations and costs

- **Obligations of the selling company**
    1. Deliver the goods agreed upon in the purchase contract (after checking and verifying their quality) within the agreed term, to pack them adequately for transportation and to mark the packaging properly (it is highly desirable that these two aspects are specified in the purchase contract).
    2. Provide the commercial invoice and other documents agreed in the contract of sale (as a proof of conformity).

DAP (delivered at place)

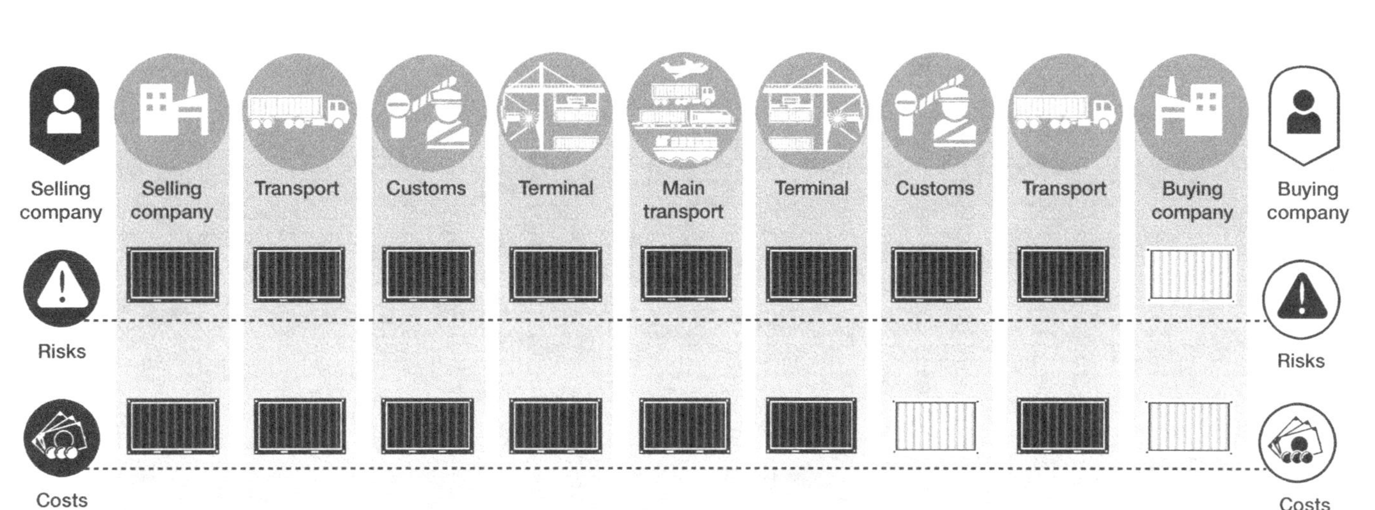

The selling company bears the costs and risks until the goods are delivered to the designated place of destination (terminal, logistics center, warehouse, etc.), without unloading them from the arrival vehicle. From that moment on, the costs and risks are borne by the buying company.

3. Notify the buyer that the goods can be received.
4. Arrange and pay for transportation (or arrange it with its own means) to the designated destination and comply with any safety requirements related to such transportation (e.g. verified gross weight of the container or VGM, etc.).
5. Carry out the export customs clearance (if required by the operation), assuming its formalities and associated costs: licenses, security clearance and inspections (red channel after the presentation of the customs declaration, specific inspections due to the goods, such as phytosanitary, sanitary, pharmacological, safety, etc.). They must also assist the buyer in obtaining the information and documents (at the buyer's expense) they may need to manage the import clearance (and, where applicable, in transit countries), such as licenses, certifications or inspections.
6. If the seller bears the cost of unloading at the agreed place of destination, they cannot claim these costs from the buyer.

- **Obligations of the purchasing company**
  1. Pay the price of the goods as agreed in the contract of sale (it should be noted that the means of payment is not regulated by the Incoterms).
  2. Take delivery of the goods, i.e. receive them from the carrier designated by the seller (it may be the seller's own means) at the place of destination specified in the Incoterms.
  3. Carry out the import customs clearance (formalities and taxes) and provide any information or documents requested by the Seller to carry out the export customs clearance (and, if applicable, in transit countries).
  4. Unload the goods from the arrival vehicle at the place of destination specified in the Incoterms.

5.3   Considerations for effective use of the rule

5.3.1   Application to road transport without customs clearance

The DAP conditions are very suitable for door-to-door full truckload and groupage shipments (e.g., palletized goods), since the selling company performs the loading at origin with their means and the buyer unloads the goods at destination with their means, which aligns with the express or default provisions of the rules governing these contracts at the national and international levels.

In areas where customs clearance is not required, the application of the DAP rule coincides with the carriage paid formula, by which the seller contracts and assumes the transportation and its risks up to the destination. In this way, they can negotiate the terms of the transport contract, such as jurisdiction (competent courts or arbitral tribunals, declaration of value, etc.), in order to adapt the contract to the needs of the operation and thus obtain legal certainty in the event of a claim against the transport operator.

5.3.2   Application to international operations and multimodal transports

The application of DAP in these circumstances presents some disadvantages for the selling company:

- **Purchasing company's dependence on import clearance**
  In operations with customs clearance, in order for the seller to manage and fulfill their obligations in the country of destination (transportation to the destination), they must manage the import clearance upon entering the customs territory of that country, because if a problem arises here, the goods may be held up at the customs office of the destination terminal (port, airport, etc.), thus generating costs.

  Among the most typical costs that can be applied in these cases for containerized transport operations are demurrage and detention charges. The demurrage is the surcharge applied to the shipper that signs the transportation contract when the time offered by the port terminal (in this case, import) by default (for example, seven days) is exceeded, while detention charges is the surcharge applied when the time offered by the shipping company to dispose of the container is exceeded. Once the offered time is exceeded, demurrage and detention charges are incurred and charged to the shipper (in this case, the seller) in accordance with the contract of carriage. Ocean quotations should (and usually do) include information on the time allowed and how the surcharges will be applied, e.g. seven free days at the terminal and beyond that, 20 €/$ per day of occupancy per 20-foot container.

In addition to these additional costs, the risk is also increased, as any delay or prolonged stay of the container at the terminal can obviously have a negative impact on the condition of the goods.

Therefore, these costs have two different implications:

a) Based on the contracts of carriage, these costs should certainly be borne (initially) by the selling company, even if their origin is the fault of the buyer. It would be necessary to analyze the terms of the transportation contract to determine its exact scope (details in the maritime quotation).

b) Taking into account the Incoterms rule, DAP indicates that the costs (see B9, e) and risks (see B3, a) for this circumstance are borne by the buyer.

In practice, this means that the extraordinary costs are paid first by the seller, who can then pass them on to the buyer (which may not be easy).

On the other hand, some importers take advantage of these circumstances to force a price reduction that exporters end up accepting as a "negotiated" lesser loss.

- **Assumption of additional costs at destination**
  In multimodal transport operations (usually containerized) under DAP conditions, it is common for the destination to be different from the terminal (port, railway station or airport) through which the goods enter the importing country, so that the exporting company has to contract and assume some services at the destination, subject to taxes that are difficult to deduct and to unknown regulations. For all these reasons, the management of these services is more complex for the seller than for the buyer, who is in a better position to manage them due to its geographical location and greater knowledge of procedures in their own country. Hence, these operations require a thorough assessment of both the destination market and the service and experience that freight forwarders can offer.

- **Uncertainty in operations carried out at destination**
  This arrangement should only be agreed if the selling company is sure that the logistical means and services at the destination (infrastructure, roads,

vehicles, etc.) are capable of guaranteeing the success of the operations for which they are responsible, which should be carried out with relative ease and without assuming any particular risks.

5.3.3   Other considerations for the use of DAP

- **Control and contracting of the logistics chain by the selling company**
  By controlling and assuming the transportation and logistics chain to the final destination, the seller is able to select the appropriate carriers and negotiate their contracts in a way that favors its legal position in case of a claim for an incident during transportation. These contracts also give the seller access to favorable rates and conditions that improve the competitiveness of its offers or allow it to benefit from higher commercial margins.

- **The selling company offers an optimal level of service.**
  The selling company delivers to the buyer's designated place in the buyer's market, so the buyer only has to arrange the import clearance and unload the goods.

- **Transport insurance**
  The selling company assumes the risks until the goods are positioned on the vehicle, at the agreed place of destination, ready for unloading. Consequently, they should consider the convenience of taking out insurance to cover the risks borne up to that point.

- **Documentation and proof of delivery**
  With regard to delivery documents, the seller must provide the buyer with the document that allows the buyer to receive the goods at the agreed place of destination. With respect to the seller's proof of delivery, in road transportation it is common for the seller, who hires the carrier, to require, as a condition of payment for the service, a copy of the consignment note signed by the consignee as proof of delivery. On the other hand, in the case of multimodal transportation, since the delivery at destination is made by subcontracted carriers in the importing country, it is more difficult to obtain this document (although it would also be a copy of the consignment note with signature as proof of delivery of the goods).

- **Transport documentation and documentary means of payment**
  The combination of Group D Incoterms rules with documentary credits creates some uncertainties that need to be studied. Sometimes they lead to situations where payment is made before delivery (risk for the buyer) or very late in relation to delivery (risk for the seller), especially in the case of multimodal operations involving containerized transport. Depending on the documents required by the means of payment, two situations can be distinguished:

  - *The means of payment requires a document of delivery at destination* (which would be logical, since the goods are delivered at that point). In order to coordinate the seller's obligation to deliver and the seller's right to collect, the seller must wait to obtain a document proving delivery at destination (copy of the bill of lading with the consignee's signature, certificate from the shipping company of delivery to the buyer at the port or terminal of destination, etc.).

    However, the seller may have difficulties in obtaining this document, which is required by the documentary means of payment in order to proceed with the collection.

    These difficulties will significantly delay the execution of the transaction, in relation to the time at which the seller has made the goods available to the carrier he has engaged for delivery at the terminal or place of destination.

    In this case, the seller also has little ability to act, since the goods have already been delivered to the buyer in the country of destination. If the seller includes a reservation in the consignment note, which serves as a receipt for the goods (note on the absence of or damage to the goods), it invalidates the documentary credit, which would a priori prevent the collection of the export by the seller (at least it would generate a discrepancy, which will involve costs and a delay in the operation).

    Another consequence is that the terms of the documentary credit must be properly specified. By default, the UCP 600 stipulates a maximum period of 21 days from the date of shipment for the selling company to present the documents to its bank, and the estimated delivery times on certain sea routes far exceed this period. This situation implies that the documentary means of payment, one of the main objectives of which is to make the commercial transaction conditional on the fulfillment of obligations that must be reflected in the agreed documentation, is somewhat undermined.

- *The means of payment requires a document of delivery at origin.* In this case, it usually requires a document proving that the goods have been placed at the disposal of the carrier at origin for transportation to the destination (e.g., a consigned BL or an appropriate copy of the international or air waybill).

  However, this documentation does not prove delivery at destination, which is the obligation that gives the seller the right to payment. Consequently, in this situation, the right to payment is advanced relative to the fulfillment of the obligations agreed in the contract of sale and stipulated by the agreed Incoterms rule.

  Thus, if the goods are not delivered at the place of destination, the seller will have been paid upon presentation of such documents to the intermediary bank, while the buyer, since the delivery has not taken place, should not have paid, as a result of which it can claim the amount wrongly charged.

  On the other hand, these circumstances may encourage certain fraudulent practices on the part of the seller, who may, for example, instruct the carrier contracted by them to deliver the goods to another company and thus charge for them twice; or, if they have taken out transport insurance, they may try to fraudulently obtain the indemnity corresponding to a claim, after having received payment for the sale by presenting the bank with the documents of delivery of the goods to the carrier at the place of origin.

5.4   Conclusions

The application of the DAP terms is appropriate in national or international road transport operations in full truck or groupage and carriage paid regime that do not require customs clearance, in whose destination market the seller company does not encounter difficulties in fulfilling its delivery obligations at the agreed place and where it can be sure that the buyer will effectively manage the import clearance. The use of this Incoterms rule is also appropriate in combination with any multimodal transport (containerized or not) in those cases where the seller can easily manage all the operations up to the delivery at the customer's warehouse.

Conversely, DAP should be avoided in destinations with complex customs and logistical procedures, where there is no experience or no guarantee that the seller can deliver to the designated place (customers or countries with which the commercial relationship is initiated, countries that do not offer legal security or with poor transport infrastructures, etc.).

Finally, as with DPU and DDP, this is not a rule that is adequately adapted to the requirements of documentary means of payment, since although the seller makes the goods available to the carrier at the point of origin, delivery takes place at the destination, a situation that causes inconveniences depending on the documentation required by the documentary credit.

6   DPU (delivered at place unloaded)

6.1   Overview and delivery

It is the only new Incoterms rule included in the 2020 version and is introduced as a reformulation (almost a name change) of DAT, which appeared in the 2010 version. This reformulation has basically consisted in giving it greater versatility by changing its name from Terminal (although the 2010 version stated that it should be understood as a broad term covering not only terminals at the border, but could also be an inland point) to Place, which also places it as a rule subsequent to DAP, given that with DPU the seller assumes an additional cost and risk consisting of unloading the goods at the designated place of destination.

In all other respects, DPU is the same as DAP, so we will only comment on this difference (as we did in the transition from CPT to CIP, where the difference was the seller's taking out of insurance). With DPU, the seller delivers when the goods are placed at the buyer's disposal, unloaded from the arriving means of transport at the place of destination. Up to this point, the costs are borne by the seller. Therefore, the seller bears all costs and risks of transportation until the goods are unloaded from the means of transport at the place of destination (at which point the risk passes to the buyer, usually at the buyer's warehouse).

It is also possible that the selling company manages the transportation to the destination with its own means (own fleet of trucks) and unloads the goods there.

In operations with customs clearance, the use of DPU presents the same potential problems (costs and risks) discussed in DAP.

In the case of DPU, the buyer manages the import clearance, but if it does not do it properly, it generates additional costs (delays, occupations, etc.), which can be charged to the seller (according to the terms of its transportation contract), although the Incoterms rule indicates that the costs and risks of non-compliance with the buyer's import clearance obligation are ultimately borne by the buyer.

Please see the comments on this subject in the DAP rule, as they also apply here. Unlike DAP, DPU requires the seller to deliver the goods unloaded at the place of destination, which has some implications that may have to do with the means of transportation used for final delivery.

> *General formulation*
>
> DPU (designated place of destination). Incoterms 2020.
>
> ---
>
> *Writing examples*
>
> - DPU 140, Gloucester Road, Wanchai, Hong Kong. China. Incoterms 2020.
> - DPU Rua Hungría, s/n, Andar, Jardim Europa, São Paulo. Brasil. Incoterms 2020.
> - DPU nave A1, parque industrial del Cauca, Cali. Colombia. Incoterms 2020.

6.2 Main obligations and costs

- **Obligations of the selling company**
  1. Deliver the goods agreed upon in the purchase contract (after checking and verifying their quality) within the agreed term, to pack them appropriately for transportation and to mark the packaging properly (it is highly advisable to specify these two aspects in the purchase contract).
  2. Present the commercial invoice and other documents stipulated in the contract of sale (as a proof of conformity).
  3. Notify the buyer that the goods are ready for receipt.
  4. Arrange and pay for the transportation (or manage it with its own means) to the designated place of destination, including unloading there, and comply with any related safety requirements (e.g. verified gross weight of the container or VGM, etc.).
  5. Customs clearance includes costs and licenses, security clearance (e.g. Verified Gross Weight of Container or VGW, Verified Gross Mass, etc.) and inspections, such as red channel after customs declaration and specific phytosanitary, sanitary, pharmacological, safety, etc. inspections.
  6. Unloading of the goods at the designated place of destination.

- **Obligations of the purchasing company**
  1. Pay the price of the goods as agreed in the contract of sale (it should be noted that the means of payment is not specified in the Incoterms).
  2. Take over the unloaded goods, i.e. receive them from the carrier appointed by the seller (this may be done by the seller's own means) at the place of destination specified in the Incoterms.

DPU (delivered at place unloaded)

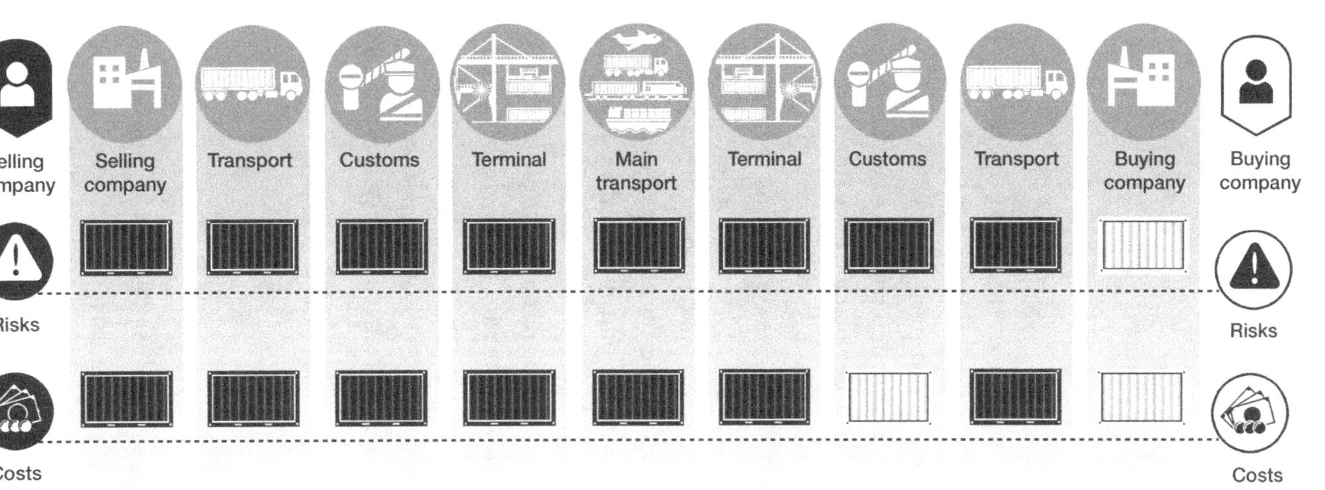

The selling company bears the costs and risks until the goods are delivered to the designated place of destination (port or airport terminal, logistics center, etc.), unloaded from the arrival vehicle. From that moment on, the costs and risks are borne by the buying company.

The selling company bears the costs and risks until the goods are delivered to the designated place of destination (warehouse, logistics center, etc.), unloaded from the arrival vehicle. From that moment on, the costs and risks are borne by the buying company.

3. Import clearance (formalities and taxes), as well as providing any information or documents requested by the Seller in order to carry out the export customs clearance (and, if applicable, in transit countries).

6.3   Considerations for effective use

6.3.1   Application to road transport of full truckloads (full truck)

The use of this rule is discouraged with road transport operations in full load, as it would require the driver to unload the goods at destination. This case raises the same controversy that occurs when comparing EXW with FCA, as it seems more logical to use the latter rule, since it determines that the personnel of the origin company (seller's warehouse or other place) is the one that carries out the loading operations for different reasons (safety, resources, etc.).

In the same way, the use of DPU in these operations would imply that the unloading would be done by the carrier hired by the seller, whereas it is advisable (due to security restrictions, etc.) for the destination warehouse personnel to perform the unloading. In addition, the regulations governing the contract of carriage state that both loading and unloading should be carried out by the sender and the consignee, unless expressly agreed otherwise.

This assignment changes in the case of parcels, where the rule usually indicates that these operations are carried out by the carrier. Therefore, as with EXW, DPU is advised only in road parcel transport operations (where the carrier unloads according to its contract). On the other hand, in road transport with full loads (full truckloads, pallets, etc.) it is likely more advisable to use DAP.

6.3.2   Application to the road transportation of parcels

DPU is a rule that is very compatible with road transport operations when sold on a "carriage paid" basis and when the carrier is responsible for unloading at the destination, i.e. in parcel operations or any other operations where the regulations governing the contract of carriage assign the responsibility for such unloading to the carrier (this assignment may depend on the regulations in force in each country).

6.3.3 Application to full container load transport (FCL)

The use of DPU in this type of operation has the following interpretations depending on the agreed port of destination:

a) If a DPU port of destination is agreed, the selling party pays for the transportation and bears the costs until the container arrives at the port of destination and is unloaded from the arriving vessel. This situation is in line with the usual formula for contracting liner services (liner conditions), which implies that the loading of the container at origin and its unloading by container cranes at destination are included in the freight (transport costs paid by the seller).

b) If the seller's warehouse DPU is agreed, unloading at destination would be done by the carrier, which does not seem logical since it is customary (or required by regulations) that the buyer's personnel unload the goods.

6.3.4 Application to the transport of goods in groupage containers (LCL)

DPU would be a perfect fit for this operation as the deconsolidating company (usually the forwarder) would unload the goods from the container in order to ship them from its facilities to the various final destinations.

6.3.5 Application in combination with other means of transport

For other modes, such as air or rail, the seller also bears costs and risks up to the agreed place (unloaded at the place of arrival, which would be an airport or rail terminal, or an inland point). In these cases, the versatility of the place further emphasizes that the designated place and the possible combinations of multimodal transportation will ultimately determine the costs and risks borne by the seller, since it could be agreed, for example, to a rail terminal PDU at an inland point downstream from the seaport of arrival in the country of destination.

6.3.6   Other considerations for DPU use

- **Purchasing company's dependence on import clearance**
  All of the above for DAP can be applied here, provided that the designated place of delivery is beyond the border or point of entry into the importing country where customs clearance takes place. This risk is reduced, but not eliminated, if the place of destination is the same as the place of customs clearance.

- **Assumption of additional costs at destination**
  In DPU transactions, the seller assumes an additional cost and risk compared to DAP, which consists of unloading the goods. In addition, as with DAP, the seller must contract and assume services at destination that are subject to taxes that are difficult to deduct, as well as unknown regulations, which adds an additional layer of complexity that may be relevant in countries with poor infrastructure, "unsafe" customs, and so on.

- **Insecurity in the operations carried out at destination**
  This arrangement, like DAP and DDP, should only be agreed if the selling company is sure that the logistics means and services at the destination will not hinder the development of the operation.

- **Control and contracting of the logistics chain by the selling company**
  As with DAP and DDP, this involves control of the logistics chain, with the advantages that this brings.

- **The vendor offers an optimal level of service.**
  The seller takes care of the delivery to the buyer's market, at the place specified by the buyer, and the unloading of the arriving vehicle, so that the buyer only has to take care of the import clearance. It is therefore advisable to consider taking out insurance to cover the risks up to that point, including unloading.

- **Transport insurance**
  The selling company bears the risk until the goods are delivered unloaded at the place of destination. It is therefore advisable to consider taking out insurance to cover the risks up to that point, including unloading.

- **Documentation and proof of delivery**
  See all provisions of the DAP rule.

- **Transport documentation and documentary means of payment**
  See DAP rule for further details.

6.4 Conclusions

Under the DPU rule, the seller contracts and pays for carriage to the agreed destination, including unloading, and the risk passes to the buyer when the goods are unloaded. Its combination with road should be limited to parcel shipments where the carrier provides unloading.

It is a very viable option for less-than-container-load shipments where the agreed place of destination is the warehouse of the deconsolidating company. It should not be used in countries with unsafe infrastructure for delivery at destination or with difficulties in import clearance to be performed by the buyer. In general, it should be used in known markets with sufficient and satisfactory experience. It is not appropriate to combine it with documentary credits, and if it is done, it should be done with caution.

7   DDP (delivered duty paid)

7.1   Overview and delivery

The DDP regime differs from the DAP only in that the selling company must handle and bear the import clearance and the resulting taxes. The analysis of DAP therefore applies to this arrangement and the description focuses on this feature. DDP imposes the maximum obligations on the seller, in contrast to EXW, where the seller bears the minimum obligations, although it includes one obligation less than DPU, namely unloading.

Under DDP, the seller delivers when the goods, cleared for import, are placed at the disposal of the buyer on the means of transport, without unloading, at the named place of destination. The seller bears all costs and risks of transportation until the goods are placed on the means of transportation at that place and upon arrival (at which time the risks are transferred). Therefore, the buyer only has to unload the goods from the arriving vehicle.

General formulation

DDP (designated place of destination). Incoterms 2020.

Writing examples

– DDP 140, Gloucester Road, Wanchai, Hong Kong. China. Incoterms 2020.
– DDP Rua Hungría, s/n, Andar, Jardim Europa, São Paulo. Brasil. Incoterms 2020.
– DDP nave A1, parque industrial del Cauca, Cali. Colombia. Incoterms 2020.

7.2   Main obligations and costs

- **Obligations of the selling company**
  1. Deliver the goods agreed upon in the contract of sale (after checking and verifying their quality) within the agreed term, to pack them adequately for transportation and to mark the packaging properly (it is very convenient that these two aspects are specified in the contract of sale).
  2. Provide the commercial invoice and any other documents agreed in the contract of sale (as a proof of conformity).

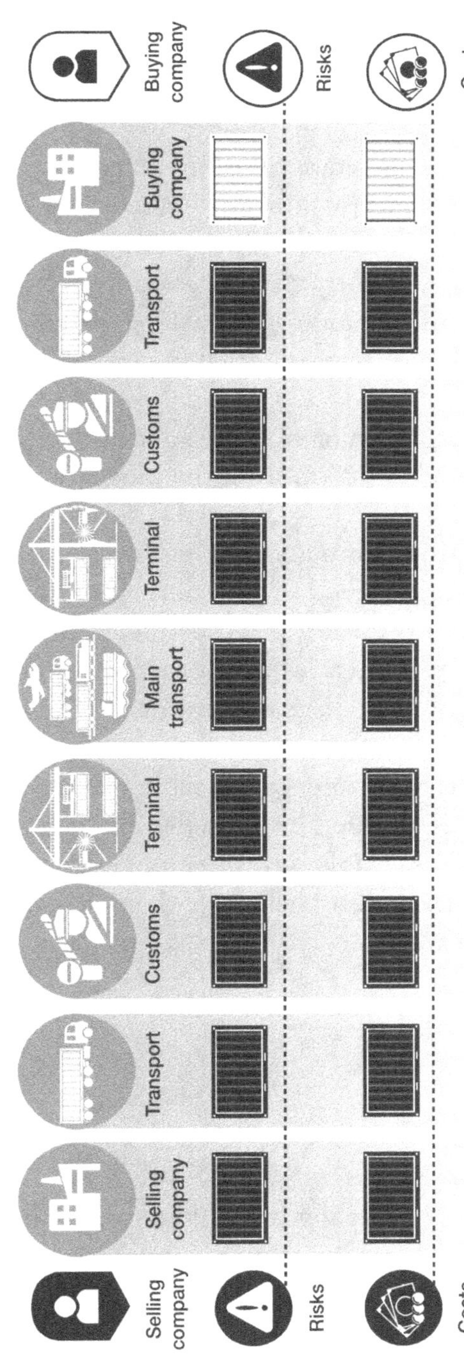

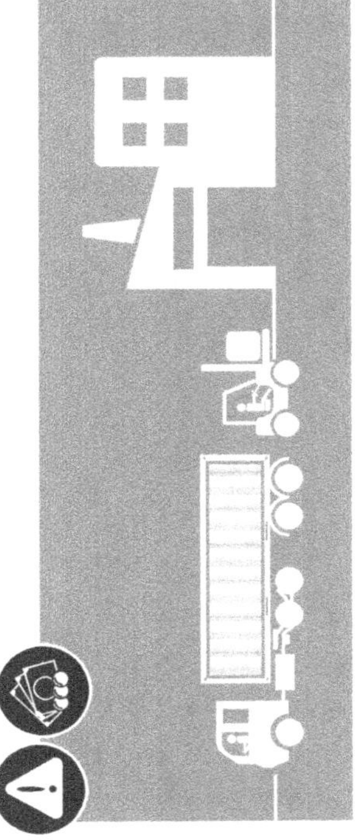

The selling company bears the costs and risks until the goods are delivered, import customs cleared, at the designated place of destination (the buying company warehouse or other), without unloading them from the arrival vehicle. From that moment on, the costs and risks are borne by the buying company.

3. Notify the buyer that he can receive the goods.
4. Contract and pay for the transportation (or arrange it with your own means) to the designated place of destination and comply with any related safety requirements (e.g. verified gross weight of the container or VGM, etc.).
5. Manage customs clearance (if required by the operation) for export, import and, if applicable, transit countries. Therefore, it must assume the formalities and costs associated with any customs clearance that may be applicable: licenses, security clearance and inspections (red circle after presentation of the customs declaration, specific inspections based on the goods, such as phytosanitary, sanitary, pharmacological, safety, etc.).
6. If the seller bears the costs of unloading the goods at the agreed place of destination, he cannot claim them from the buyer.

- **Obligations of the purchasing company**
  1. Pay the price of the goods as agreed in the contract of sale (remember that the means of payment is not regulated by the Incoterms rule).
  2. Accept the goods, i.e. receive them from the carrier designated by the seller (this may be done by the seller's own means) at the place of destination specified in the Incoterms.
  3. Assist the Seller (upon request and at the seller's expense) with any information or documents required by the seller for customs clearance in export, import and, if applicable, transit countries.
  4. Unload the goods from the arrival vehicle at the place of destination specified in the Incoterms.

7.3 Considerations for effective use of the rule

7.3.1 DDP and import clearance

Under DDP conditions, the selling company is required to handle the import customs clearance, which includes both the management and documentation of the import and the payment of the corresponding taxes.

There are usually two types of import taxes: the customs duty and the internal consumption tax (VAT or similar). Although there are several types of duties, the most common is the ad valorem duty, which is a percentage of the customs value. At the international level and according to the guidelines of the World Trade Organization, the latter is equivalent to the CIP or CIF value.[9] Thus, the regulatory framework for customs value usually starts from the invoice price and applies the necessary adjustments to determine that value.

For example, an FOB invoice will add transportation and insurance costs, and an FCA terminal invoice will add costs up to shipment, transportation and insurance.

The customs value is then adjusted by applying the customs duty, which depends on the goods and the country of origin (information usually recorded on a certificate of origin or invoice declaration).

Finally, VAT (or equivalent tax) is applied to the result of the customs value plus the duty, which usually adds up to significant amounts (although these are recovered through the VAT settlement systems established in each country).

There are other types of tariffs, such as specific tariffs (quantity per unit: ton, cubic meter, etc.), mixed tariffs (*ad valorem* plus specific), or compound tariffs (where there are maximum and minimum limits between different tariffs). In addition, certain products (alcohol, tobacco, hydrocarbons, etc.) may be subject to special taxes based on the nature of the goods (excise duties, etc.). Trade protection measures such as anti-dumping or anti-subsidy (countervailing) duties may also be applied.

Import duties and taxes are borne by the selling company. This can be detrimental to both the selling company and the buyer, resulting in limited use of the DDP rule.

Among other disadvantages, the following stand out:

- The regulations governing import clearance may impose requirements on the selling company that it is not in a position to meet (tax domicile in the country of destination, obtaining an import license that can only be requested by the buyer, etc.), thus making the use of this scheme unfeasible.
- Import taxes (usually customs duty and VAT) are charged by the seller on the invoice, but the buyer is in a better position to manage them and deduct some of them later. Customs duty is usually a non-recoverable cost, but VAT is usually neutral for "domestic" companies through the compen-

---

[9] General Agreement on Tariffs and Trade 1994 (WTO Agreement on Customs Valuation).

sation mechanism that is revealed in the periodic settlements (basically, the input VAT "charged" is subtracted from the output VAT "invoiced"). However, to the extent that the selling company cannot apply this compensation mechanism, but must carry out the import clearance, it will have to consider the VAT as a cost and include it in the price presented to the buyer, who, in case of managing the import clearance, could include it in this compensation mechanism (hence, in this case, both companies lose "competitiveness" in favor of the tax authority, represented by the customs on its collecting side).

- The import customs regulations are better known by the purchasing company, who is in a better position to comply with them. Therefore, in general, to the extent that the destination market presents greater commercial uncertainty, a lower degree of economic openness or less adaptation to the rules of international trade, it is preferable to avoid the use of DDP.

7.3.2   DDP variants

In the introductory note to this provision in the 2010 version (it does not appear in the 2020 version), it was stated that the VAT and taxes payable on importation must be borne by the selling enterprise, unless otherwise agreed in the contract of sale. This note reflects the practice of using variants such as DDP VAT unpaid or DDP VAT excluded, which delegate the payment of the internal consumption tax to the buyer, since the seller cannot recover it, as mentioned above, and the tax regulations usually designate the importing party as the taxpayer.

7.3.3   Other considerations for the use of DDP

- **Control and contracting of the logistics chain by the selling company**
  By controlling and assuming the transport and logistics chain to the final destination, the selling company is able to select suitable transport operators and negotiate their contracts in a way that is favorable to its legal position (especially in road transport) in case they need to claim for an incident during transport. These contracts also allows them to access favorable rates and conditions that improve the competitiveness of their

offers or provide them the opportunity to benefit from higher commercial margins.

7.4 Conclusions

The application of DDP terms is appropriate for transactions where the selling company, thanks to its experience and knowledge of the destination market, is able to offer a complete service through forwarding agencies able to guarantee the correct handling of import clearance, as well as for parcel and direct shipments of consumer goods where it is required to provide a complete service up to delivery (especially in transactions derived from electronic commerce).

However, as in the case of DAP and DPU, this rule is not sufficiently adapted to the requirements of documentary means of payment, since, although the selling company makes the goods available to the carrier at origin, delivery takes place at destination, a situation that generates losses depending on the documents required by the documentary credit.

The terms and conditions of the DDP are not compatible with national transactions or transactions within the same economic and fiscal zone, as it contravenes VAT rules, which require taxation at destination by the buyer. In practice, even if agreed upon, companies must apply the tax laws that are mandatory for them.

Chapter 5
How to use Incoterms 2020 rules for maritime transport

....

1 Introduction and applicability of Incoterms rules for maritime transport

The International Chamber of Commerce (ICC) classifies the Incoterms 2020 rules into two groups: rules for any mode or modes of transportation other than port-to-port (see Chapter 4) and rules for sea and inland waterways (hereafter referred to as maritime Incoterms). There are four rules in this second group:

- FAS (free alongside ship).
- FOB (free on board).
- CFR (cost and freight).
- CIF (cost, insurance and freight).

These latter rules are suitable for transactions where both the place of delivery of the goods and the place to which the goods are transported are ports.

Under the FOB, CFR and CIF rules, delivery- the transfer of risk from the seller to the buyer- occurs when the goods are loaded on board the vessel at the port of shipment, whereas under the FAS rule, delivery occurs when the goods are placed alongside the vessel at the port of shipment. As far as customs clearance is concerned, the four rules stipulate that export clearance is the responsibility of the selling company and import clearance is the responsibility of the purchasing company.

All kinds of goods are transported by sea, ranging from bulk cargo to ready-to-sell IT products. Broadly speaking, such goods can be divided into two groups:

- **Unitized goods**
  This group uses an intermodal transport unit (ITU), mainly the container and the semi-trailer, whose interior is typically loaded before its arrival at the port of shipment (in the warehouse of the selling company, in the facilities of the forwarding agency, etc.).

  Unitized cargo is handled and transferred between various modes of transportation in combination with sea transportation. This is the case for container traffic, which is handled in specialized terminals and loaded on board the ship by means of container cranes.

  It also includes roll-on/roll-off transport, in which the goods are wheeled onto the ship, mainly in road-ship combination transport, where either the whole truck or the semi-trailer is used as the UTI. The multimodal Incoterms rules are suitable for the transport of this group of goods (see chapter 4).

- **Non-unitized goods**
  This group includes trade not included in the first group, where it is appropriate to apply the Incoterms rules for sea and inland waterways: FAS, FOB, CFR and CIF. The group can be segmented into:

  - ***Bulks.*** They can be solids (cement, coal, wheat, etc.) or liquids (liquefied gas, hydrocarbons, etc.). They are handled at bulk terminals adapted to each type of goods by means of grab cranes, pipelines, etc.
  - ***General, conventional or fractional cargo*** (excluding containers). This traffic has declined as the use of containers has become more widespread. It includes shipments of non-unitized goods that are not included in bulk cargo, such as sacks, boxes, bales, drums, bundles, barrels, industrial parts, machinery, indivisible items of large volume or weight, etc. These goods are handled with specific means in general cargo, break bulk or multipurpose terminals, where mainly grab cranes operate, which adapt to the loading requirements of each cargo by placing slings, hooks, nets, etc. at their ends.

Unitized goods	Non-unitized goods	
	Bulks	**General cargo**
– Container – Semi-trailer	– 35,000 t of grain – 50,000 t of oil – 15,000 t of soybean oil	– 2,500 pallets[1] of citrus fruits to be transported by refrigerated vessel – 180 metal coils – 600 beams for construction – 4,500 cotton bales – 450 iron plates – 10 excavators

Table 5.1. Examples of unitized and non-unitized goods.

On the other hand, the contract for the transportation of non-unitized goods usually occupies the entire cargo capacity of a vessel, so that although there is a residual traffic of general cargo transported on a liner basis, such transportation is usually contracted under a chartering regime. In this case, the chartering company, which contracts the transport (the buyer, under FAS and FOB rules, or the seller under CFR and CIF rules), acts specifically according to the needs of the shipment. In the case of chartering, the supply of transportation consists of tramp vessels providing specific services according to demand, so that no liner service is offered and there are no fixed routes, fixed conditions or pre-established prices.[2]

The vessels that carry out these operations are adapted to them and tend to be tankers (for liquid and gaseous bulk cargoes), bulk carriers (specialized in the transport of solid bulk cargoes and usually equipped with their own loading and unloading equipment, such as grab cranes), other general or break-bulk cargo vessels (beams, coils, etc.) and some very specialized vessels, such as vehicle carriers or those for the transport of particularly heavy cargoes.

The maritime transport contract under a chartering regime, in which chartering agencies or brokers (chartering broker or ship broker) advise the chartering companies and shipping companies and draft the contracts, is documented

---

[1] Although the pallet can also be considered an ILU, when the shipment consists of a large number of such units, it can be treated as general non-containerized cargo, which is loaded on board the vessel by means of devices attached to grab cranes or by forklifts.

[2] Vessel dedicated to the transport of goods from the delivery points of the goods, without regularly covering a fixed route.

in a charter party. The charter can be agreed upon for a certain period of time, when the shipping company contracts for the use of the vessel for a certain period of time, or for a certain voyage, in which case it is related to purchase and sale transactions and the Incoterms are applied.

In the case of voyage chartering, the most commonly used model policy is the Baltic and International Maritime Council's (BIMCO)[3] GENCON.[4] With this document, a Bill of Lading (BL) is also issued, subject to the Charter Party BL, as proof of receipt of the goods by the carrier or shipping company, which is used to deliver the goods to the buyer at the destination, as it constitutes a document of title.

In this charter party, as a proof of the transportation contract, the contracting company (charterer) and the shipping company agree on all aspects negotiated in the maritime transportation:

- The loading and unloading ports.
- The date on which the vessel must report for loading at the port of departure.
- The vessel and cargo capacity.
- The cargo, laytime and demurrage.
- The freight (transport price), the expected loading and unloading time, etc.

The fact that the time and costs of loading and unloading are negotiated in the contract of carriage is connected with the conditions of transportation, which is a clear manifestation that the Incoterms rules for maritime transportation were designed to be applied to this type of operations. Nevertheless, one of these rules may be agreed for the sale and purchase of the described goods by any mode or modes of transport, but not vice versa, i.e. it is not convenient to agree on an Incoterms rule for sea and inland waterways in the case of, for example, multimodal container transportation (although it is very common).

---

[3] BIMCO is the largest private association of shipping companies, shipping agencies, and other types of agencies.

[4] A sample of such a charter party and an explanation of the contents of its boxes and clauses can be downloaded from the BIMCO website: www.bimco.org. There are other models of voyage charter policies, such as the Tanker Voyage Charter Party, or even specialized ones for certain types of goods, such as the 1999 Sugar Charter Party.

Thus, in the charter party, it must be agreed which party will bear the costs of loading operations in the port of shipment (loading and stowage of non-unitized goods), aspects which are not agreed in containerized transportation, because in these operations loading and unloading are included in the freight (under liner conditions), and the actual delivery of the goods by the selling company usually takes place at a point before the port (usually in its own warehouse). Charter parties also agree on the expected time for loading and unloading at the ports (laytime), which can result in demurrage or bonuses if not met.

The main shipping terms are as follows:[5]

- LIFO *(liner in free out)*. Freight[6] includes loading at the port of shipment, but not unloading at the port of destination.
- FILO *(free in liner out)*. Freight includes unloading at the port of destination, but not loading at the port of origin.
- FISLO *(free in and stowed / liner out)*. Freight does not include loading and stowing at the port of shipment but does include unloading at the port of destination.
- Liner terms. Freight includes loading and unloading from alongside the ship.
- FIO *(free in and out)*. Freight does not include loading and unloading.
- FIOS *(free in and out stowed)*. Freight does not include loading and unloading or stowage and unstowage.
- FIOST *(free in and out stowed and trimmed)*. Freight does not include loading, unloading, stowing, unstowing or trimming.[7]

Depending on the agreed Incoterms rule, the seller and the buyer must coordinate their obligations and the place of delivery with the terms of shipment

----

[5] The application of these shipping terms may vary from one port to another and is subject to the practices and customs of different geographical areas and countries. To familiarize yourself with their acronyms, you can follow these indications: the i (in) refers to loading at the port of origin, while the o (out) refers to unloading at the port of destination; the s refers to stowage, and the t to trimming; finally, the f (free) before an operation indicates that the freight does not include it, while in terms preceded by an l (liner) the operation is included in the freight contracted with the shipping line.

[6] Freight is the cost of transportation (sea or otherwise); in the case of chartering, freight is usually expressed by weight (e.g., per ton), volume, length, etc.

[7] Trimming, which complements the stowage of some solid bulk cargoes, consists mainly of smoothing and compacting the bulk to prevent cargo shifting during sea transport.

in order to adapt the freight to them. In this way, the following possibilities can be described, subject to change depending on the type of goods and the contracting party at the port of destination, which may be the shipping line or an external operator:

- If the FAS rule is agreed, the purchasing company (as charterer) must contract the transportation under LIFO or liner conditions, where the freight includes loading. Therefore, it is the shipping company's responsibility to carry out these operations, which connect with the seller's obligations to deliver the goods alongside the ship.
- If the FOB rule is agreed, the buyer must contract the transport under FIO, FIOS, FIOST, FILO or FISLO conditions, i.e. the freight does not include loading at the port of origin, since this management and its costs belong to the selling company, which delivers the goods once they have been loaded on the vessel. There is also the option for the seller to assume the loading on board of the shipping company contracted by the buyer under LIFO conditions, in which case it is advisable for the seller to know in advance the cost of loading they will have to assume to offer a price to the buyer.
- Under CFR and CIF conditions, the selling company, which in these cases contracts the transportation and acts as charterer, delivers the goods on board and pays the cost of transportation to the port of destination. Therefore, the transportation must be contracted on LIFO terms, which do not include unloading at destination, as this is already managed and paid for by the buyer.

If the shipping term does not include an operation that is included as an obligation of the seller or buyer under the Incoterms rule, this operation must be contracted externally to the shipping company, always coordinated (in terms of date and conditions) with the contract of carriage through a specialized operator (shipping agency, stevedoring company, etc.).

2   Assessment of the use of maritime Incoterms rules in containerized transport

Once the characteristics of the goods and the operations to which the maritime Incoterms rules apply have been outlined, it is worth explaining why these rules should not be used in container transport operations, despite the fact that in practice many of them are agreed under FOB and CIF conditions and, to a lesser extent, CFR.

2.1 Reasons why maritime Incoterms rules should not be used in containerized transport

- **Division of risks at the container transportation stage**

  Multimodal container transportation is most useful when it is treated as a single unit, i.e. as a single transportation phase. In these operations, the risks arising from the transportation —which can be carried out in different modes with their respective segments— should not be divided but assigned in their entirety (from loading and stowage of the goods in the container to their unloading at the place of destination) to one of the parties to the contract of sale, to the seller or to the buyer.

  Since this is a mode of transport characterized by the non-interruption of the loading unit from the loading and stowage of the goods at the origin (seller's or consolidator's warehouse) to the destination (deconsolidator's or buyer's warehouse), it seems appropriate that one of the parties should bear all the risks associated with this journey under the agreed Incoterms rule. This is because, in the event of a loss not occurring at destination, it may be difficult, if not impossible, to determine responsibility for the risks, depending on the time at which the incident occurred (before or after loading on board the vessel, the point of transfer in the FOB, CFR and CIF rules).[8]

However, the maritime Incoterms allocate the risks of container transport operations in accordance with the time of delivery. Under FOB, CFR and CIF terms, delivery occurs when the container is loaded on board the vessel at the port of shipment, whereas under FAS terms, delivery occurs when the container is placed alongside the vessel at the port of shipment. Thus, when applied to

----

[8] Non-localized loss is any incident involving loss or damage to the goods (wetting, damage due to crushing of the cargo or incorrect handling of the container, etc.) but where there is no clear evidence of the point where it originated (which would be the case in the event of a road accident or sinking of a ship).

container transport operations, the maritime rules divide the risk of the transport phase into pre-delivery and post-delivery (on-board loading).

This situation can lead to controversies as illustrated by the following example. Consider the case of a Spanish selling company that agrees with another Chilean company a container sale under FOB conditions in the port of Valencia. The goods are loaded and stowed in a container at the selling company's warehouse, located in an inland point in Spain, and then transported, for example, by road to Valencia. The container is handled and stored at that port, where it is loaded and stowed on board the ship, after which the seller transfers the risk to the buyer. Finally, it is transported by sea to the Chilean port, where it is unloaded, handled and stored until it is finally transported to the Chilean company's warehouse. When the Chilean company receives the goods, they open the container and check for any damage to the goods. In this situation, unless the damage is due to a localized loss (road accident, sinking of the ship, etc.), the controversy arises as to whether the damage occurred before delivery, when the container was loaded on board the ship in Valencia, or after delivery.

In these circumstances, the application of the multimodal Incoterms rules avoids disputes by assigning the entire transport risk to one of the parties, as in the following examples:

- **FCA full containerized vendor's facilities (FCL).** The seller loads and stows the goods in the container at its facilities, at which point it transfers the risks to the buyer company.
- **FCA facilities of the groupage transportation company (LCL).** The forwarding agency groups and loads the goods and consolidates the container at its facilities, at which time it transfers the risks to the purchasing company
- **CPT or CIP port or place of destination.** The seller contracts and pays for the transportation, but it is the purchasing company that assumes the risks from the moment the seller loads the container at its facilities or delivers the groupage to the carrier for consolidation.
- **DAP warehouse of the purchasing company.** The seller loads and stows the goods aboard the container at origin and bears the risk until the container is opened at the buyer's warehouse at destination.

Finally, it should be noted that some of these multimodal rules, although adapted to container transport, also share the risks. This is the case, for example, under DAP or DPU destination terminal conditions, where the goods are not unloaded from the container until they arrive at the buyer's warehouse. The transfer of risk should occur on arrival at the terminal (whether the goods are unloaded or not, depending on whether DAP or DPU is agreed) but there is still a journey to the final destination where the condition of the goods is checked.

- **Risk reasons for the selling company**
  Under FOB, CFR and CIF maritime rules, the seller does not transfer the risk to the buyer until the container is loaded on board the vessel at the port of departure; under FAS terms, which are rarely used in container transportation, delivery is made alongside the vessel. The container is a UTI by which the seller delivers the goods to the carrier well before loading on board the ship (at its own warehouses, in another place where the goods are consolidated and stowed, or upon arrival of the loaded container at the marine terminal), so that the application of the maritime Incoterms rules obliges the seller to bear the risks after the time of actual delivery over which it has control (usually that of loading the goods into the container).

  Thus, under FOB, CFR and CIF terms, the seller bears the risk until the container is loaded on board the vessel at the port of shipment. However, under FOB terms (as discussed in the analysis of the FCA rule as an alternative), this depends to a large extent on the shipping line contracted by the purchasing company (which, for economic reasons, may choose a shipping line with a lower frequency of port calls, e.g. fortnightly instead of weekly), the booking process of the transportation service, the freight forwarder who operates and coordinates the operation at the port of shipment, etc.

  These elements, which have a direct impact on the completion of the shipment on the scheduled date, are managed by the purchasing company and cannot be controlled by the selling company, which is, however, affected by them when it comes to fulfilling its obligation to deliver on board the vessel contracted by the buyer. Consequently, the alternative to the FOB rule is the use of FCA, which allows the selling company to control the delivery at its premises or elsewhere, so that it no longer depends on its loading on board the vessel but on the moment when the goods are delivered to the transport operator contracted by the buyer (usually a freight forwarder).

- **Cost reasons for the selling company**
  Comparing FOB terms with FCA, the use of FOB requires the seller to bear the costs until the container is loaded on board the vessel at the port of shipment. However, as mentioned above, these costs, which can be high (and increased by delays and other cost overruns due to poor transportation contracting by the buyer), are not controlled by the seller, who must still bear them in order to fulfill their obligation to deliver the container to the carrier contracted by the buyer.

  To avoid this problem, it is advisable that the price offered by the seller under FOB conditions be based on the transportation costs quoted by the freight forwarder or shipping company selected by the buyer to perform the transportation. These costs can vary significantly between different freight forwarders and shipping lines, so the seller may be able to offer a more competitive price by using its usual freight forwarder.

  The main difference between CFR terms and CPT terms lies in the cost of insurance (if any, as these terms do not require it) covering the first leg between the seller's premises and loading on board the vessel at the port of shipment. Under CPT terms with containers, delivery takes place at the time the goods are loaded into the container at the seller's premises, so the buyer can take out insurance from that point. On the other hand, under CFR conditions with container, the risks are divided: the seller assumes them until the container is loaded on board the vessel at the port of shipment, where they are transferred on to the buyer (in these circumstances, the insurance, if any, must be adapted to this point of delivery).

  Finally, considering the time of delivery, the compulsory insurance contracted by the selling company under CIF and CIP conditions covers a different route: in the former case, from its premises, and in the latter, from on board at the port of shipment. Under CIF conditions, the seller has the option of taking out insurance to cover his own risks from its premises to the place of delivery (once the container is loaded) or of taking out an endorsable insurance policy covering the entire voyage: until loading on board, the seller is the insured party, and once the container is loaded (when they receive the BL on board), they would endorse the policy to the buyer, positioning them as the insured party from that moment on.

2.2 Reasons why maritime Incoterms rules are used in containerized transport

- **Ease of allocating costs**

  The use of the Incoterms maritime rules facilitates the allocation of costs: under FAS and FOB conditions, the freight is borne by the buyer, while under CFR and CIF rules it is borne by the seller. However, it is important to note that the prior and subsequent costs incurred in the ports of shipment and destination (and in the segments before and after the maritime leg) correspond to the selling and purchasing companies, respectively, so that each bears the costs of its country or nearby area. This simplifies the work of the freight forwarder or shipping company, which has to invoice each party for the following reasons:

  - The costs are invoiced in their own currency and are are not affected by exchange rates between them.
  - Each party is familiar with the structure of the costs it must assume, as well as their corresponding denominations and definitions.
  - The volatility inherent in these transactions is borne by the company in the country where they are generated, which is more familiar with the circumstances that may arise from them (increase in port or transport costs due to changes in legislation or market evolution, etc.).
  - The use of certain multimodal Incoterms rules entails the sharing of upstream costs at the port of shipment between the selling and purchasing companies, which may raise problems of interpretation (e.g. under FCA conditions at the seller's premises, regarding which party should bear the cost of sealing the container, or the verified gross weight of the container, etc.).

  For example, the use of FCA Valencia port terminal, along with freight, for a shipment destined for Mexico may make it difficult to bill the costs incurred from the arrival of the container at that terminal by the freight forwarder to the Mexican purchasing company, for the following reasons:

- The appreciation of the Euro against the Mexican Peso may increase these costs relative to those paid in previous similar shipments.
- The buyer may be suspicious of the invoicing of certain cost components due to a lack of knowledge of their names and definitions in the country of origin.
- Costs may be increased at the port of origin and, in this case, rejected by the Mexican company.
- The sharing of certain cost elements may give rise to disputes as to the responsibility of one party or the other to bear them, as may occur, for example, with the expenses related to the fees for sealing containers, since this is done in the warehouse of the selling company.

- **Obtaining a shipped BL from the selling company**
  In FOB, CFR and CIF terms, the seller assumes the costs and risks until the container is loaded on the vessel (in CFR and CIF, the seller also assumes the transportation to the destination, but not its risks). This is evidenced by the issuance of a Bill of Lading (BL), which is usually required as a shipping document in documentary payments.

  Substitution of the FOB rule by FCA (e.g. with the seller's warehouse as the geographical point) is appropriate, but the required transport documentation must be changed if the means of payment is documentary. For example, it is appropriate to replace the shipped BL with a transport document that proves the delivery of the goods to the carrier at the seller's warehouse (inland bill of lading, forwarder's receipt certificate or FCR, etc.), or even with a multimodal BL (house pier) issued by the shipping company as responsible for the transport from the seller's warehouse, but without the "shipped" expression.

  This is in contrast to the usual practice of requesting the shipped BL, which is reinforced by the fact that the issuing bank of the letter of credit repeatedly requests a BL that largely guarantees collection by the importer, who must request it at the destination in order to request delivery of the goods, while the exporter must present it to the bank in order to collect the credit.

- **Force of habit**

  Many companies operate satisfactorily under FOB, CFR and CIF terms for their containerized shipments, so they do not need to change this dynamic. For these and other reasons, these rules will continue to apply to multimodal maritime container transportation.

  In these cases, the practical application of the Incoterms rules described in chapter 7 must be adapted to this type of transportation.

3　FAS (free alongside ship)

3.1　Overview and delivery

Under FAS terms, the seller must deliver the goods, cleared for export, alongside the vessel (on the quay under the loading crane) contracted by the buyer at the named port of shipment, usually in the country of export. This rule also allows for the possibility of "making available the goods so delivered", as is common in the case of chain sales of bulk goods during maritime transport.

Due to the high handling costs of these shipments of goods (bulk or breakbulk), it is essential to determine the exact loading point at the port of shipment from which the buyer company begins to bear the costs.

General formulation

FAS (puerto de embarque designado). Incoterms 2020.

Writing examples

– FAS south dock, Escombreras dock, port of Cartagena, Murcia. Spain. Incoterms 2020
– FAS bulk solids terminal, port of Valencia, Valencia. Spain. Incoterms 2020.

3.2　Main obligations and costs

- **Obligations of the selling company**
  1. Deliver the goods agreed upon in the purchase contract (after checking and verifying their quality) within the agreed term, to pack them adequately for transportation and to mark the packaging (except for bulk goods, which are the property of FAS) in an appropriate way (it is very convenient that these two aspects are specified in the purchase contract).
  2. Provide the commercial invoice and other documents stipulated in the purchase contract (as a proof of conformity).
  3. Place the goods (bearing the costs and risks until then) alongside the vessel designated by the buyer, in the port of shipment established (or procure the goods so delivered).

4. Notify the buyer that the goods have been delivered or that the vessel has not presented itself to receive the goods within the agreed time.
5. Clear customs for export (if required for the operation) and related formalities and costs: licenses, security clearance and inspections (red channel after presentation of the SAD, specific inspections due to the goods, such as phytosanitary, sanitary, pharmacological, etc.). It must also assist the buyer in obtaining (at the buyer's expense) the information and documents that the buyer may need to manage the import clearance (and, where applicable, in transit countries), such as licenses, certifications or inspections.

- **Obligations of the purchasing company**
  1. Pay the price of the goods as agreed in the contract of sale (it should be noted that the means of payment are not regulated by the Incoterms).
  2. Notify the seller of the name of the vessel, the place of loading (e.g. by specifying the terminal), if any, and the date of delivery within the term agreed in the contract of sale. If the buyer fails to do this, or if their carrier fails to receive the goods, the buyer shall bear all risks of loss or damage to the goods from the date or time agreed in the contract of sale for delivery, as well as any additional costs resulting from this situation (which may be additional costs of the seller until actual delivery can be made).
  3. Contract and bear the cost of loading operations at the port of shipment.
  4. Contract and pay for sea transportation as soon as the goods are alongside the ship at the port of shipment. The Incoterms provide the possibility for the seller to contract the transportation at the risk and expense of the buyer, if the buyer so requests or if it is customary practice. In any case, the seller may refuse to do so. In fact, this option is not recommended because it positions the seller as the shipper (charterer in the language of the charterparty) as opposed to the shipping line/carrier in the contract of carriage by sea.
  5. Organize, manage and pay for the rest of the operations in the logistics chain after delivery of the goods by the seller: loading on board the vessel at the port of shipment, sea transport between the ports of origin and destination, unloading at the port of destination, import clearance

FAS (free alongside ship)

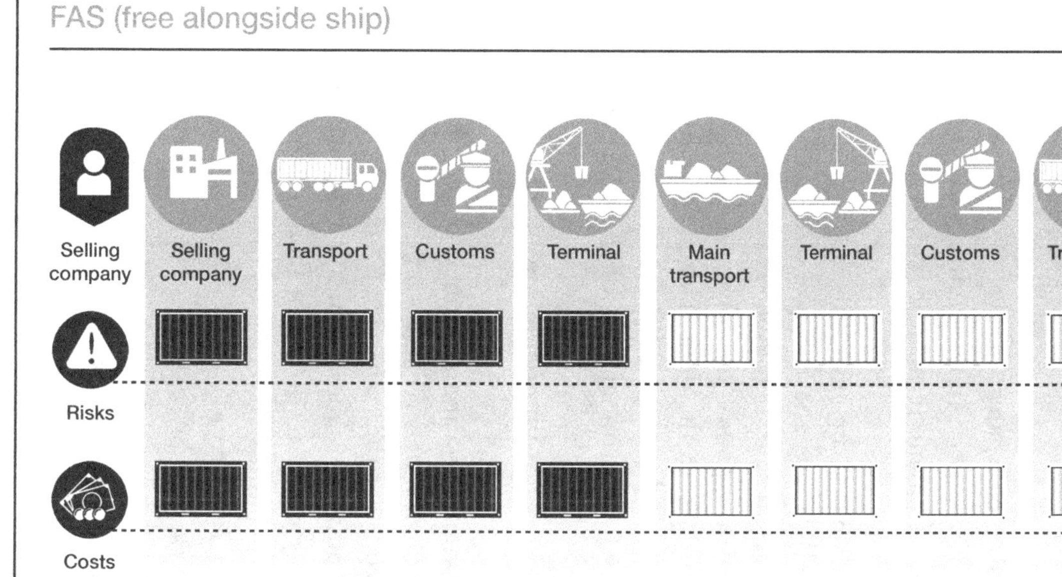

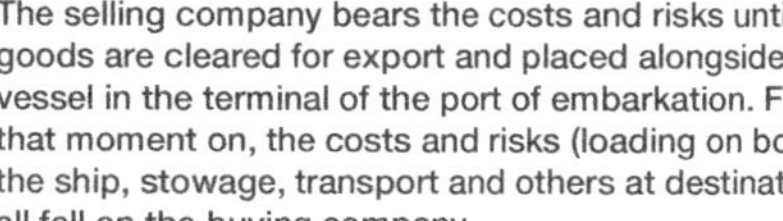

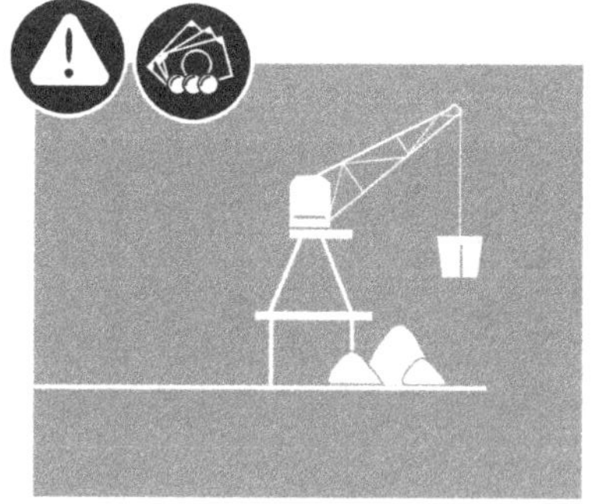

The selling company bears the costs and risks until the goods are cleared for export and placed alongside the vessel in the terminal of the port of embarkation. From that moment on, the costs and risks (loading on board the ship, stowage, transport and others at destination) all fall on the buying company.

FAS (free alongside ship): with container

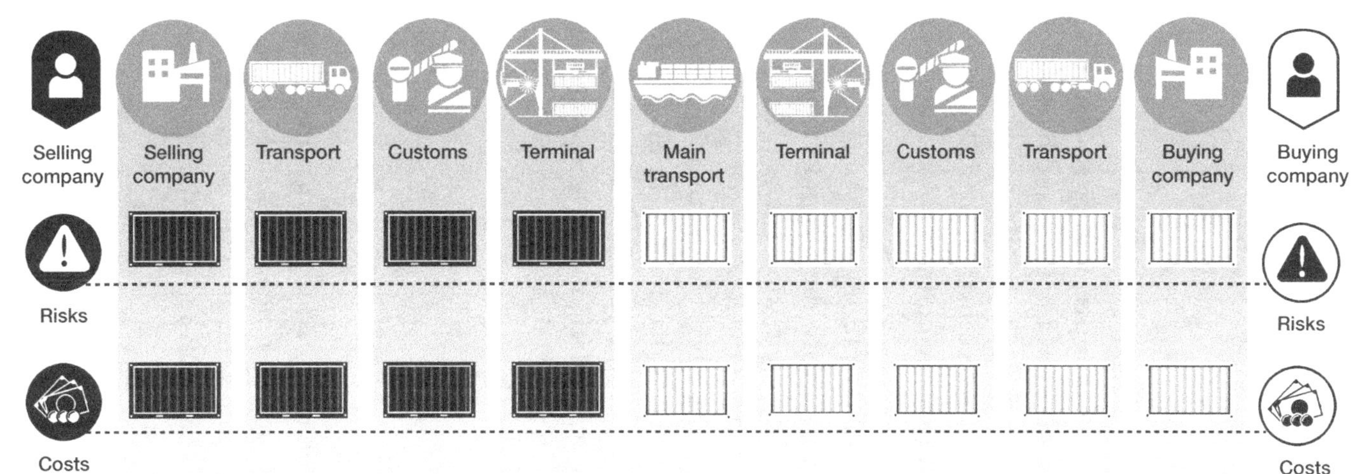

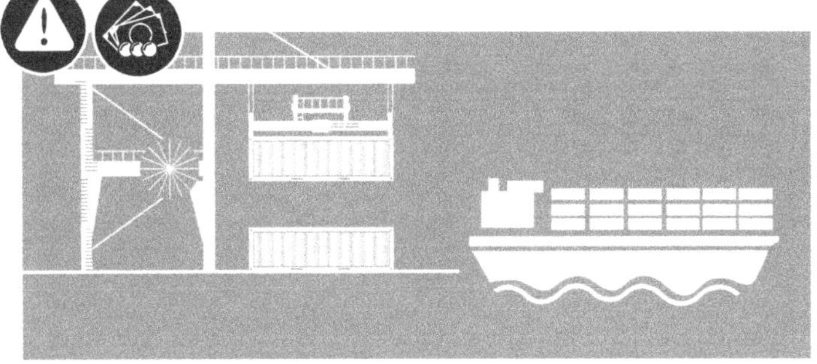

The selling company bears the costs and risks until the container are cleared for export and placed alongside the vessel in the terminal of the port of embarkation. From that moment on, the costs and risks (loading on board the ship, stowage, transport and others at destination) all fall on the buying company.

(and, if applicable, in transit countries) and subsequent costs up to the final destination.

3.3 Considerations for effective use of the rule

3.3.1 Use of FAS with non-unitized goods

- **Transportation contracts and other pre- and post- sea voyage costs**
  Selling and purchasing companies must manage and bear the costs in their respective countries. The exceptions are loading at the port of shipment and any ancillary operations required by the goods (stowage, trimming, etc.), which take place in the seller's country but are paid for by the buyer.

- **Contracting of maritime transportation**
  The buyer is obliged to negotiate with the shipping company or chartering agency the conditions of transportation (freight, dates, etc.) and the cargo (means of transportation, laytime, costs, delays, etc.).[9] In the case of chartered transportation, it is advisable for the buyer to contract the transportation with shipping terms that include in the freight the cost of loading and ancillary operations of the goods at the port of shipment, such as LIFO and liner. In this way, the freight paid to the shipping company already includes these operations, which are completed when the seller delivers the goods alongside the ship.

3.3.2 Use of FAS in containerized transport

FAS is one of the least used Incoterms. Its use in container transportation is not common, and the 2020 version recommends that it be replaced by FCA. However, if it is agreed, it implies the same obligations for the seller as under FOB conditions, although the risks are transferred to the buyer when the goods

---

[9] The period authorized for a vessel to load or unload at a port, which is stipulated in the charter party. Failure to comply results in demurrage payable by the charterer ("shipper" in a charterparty) to the shipping line (shipowner/operator).

are delivered alongside the ship and not after loading (as stipulated in the FOB rule).

As regards costs, it is common for shipping lines to operate under liner shipping conditions which include in the freight the cost of loading on board the vessel by container crane. These circumstances are therefore the same as those described under FAS terms. In any case, if the cost of loading is not included in the freight, it would have to be borne by the selling company.

3.3.3   Other considerations for the use of FAS

- **Transport insurance**
  The FAS rule does not oblige either party to take out insurance to cover possible risks to which the goods may be exposed during transportation. However, both parties, especially the buyer, must evaluate the advisability of taking out insurance to cover the risks assumed by each party (in the case of the seller, up to the point of placing the goods on the ship, where the risks are transferred to the buyer).

- **Documentation and proof of delivery**
  The seller's proof of delivery must be a document evidencing receipt of the goods at the port of shipment, such as a dock receipt issued by the relevant operator (shipping line, stevedore, freight forwarder or port authority). This Incoterms rule requires the seller to provide the usual proof of delivery. On the other hand, since the seller is not obliged to contract for carriage, he is not obliged to provide a contract of carriage (which is the case in CFR and CIF terms, where it is stipulated that the seller must provide the transport document).

  The seller is not obliged to produce a document proving delivery on board the vessel, a bill of lading constituting a contract of carriage, or a mate's receipt issued by the ship's first mate to prove loading of the goods on board the vessel.

- **Transport documentation and documentary means of payment**
  In case a documentary means of payment is agreed upon as a guarantee of collection of the transaction, the same transport document proving delivery under FAS conditions must be required. In the case of containerized

transport, it is common for the shipped BL to be delivered to the selling company, as it involves the same costs as under FOB conditions. However, it should be noted that it is the buyer who contracts the transport, so the seller must first ensure that it has access to the BL if it is required in the documentary credit (see the process in this regard under FOB terms).

- **Control of the logistic chain and service level of the selling company**
  The purchasing company controls most of the logistics chain and its costs. Especially when buying and selling bulk and non-unitized goods, it is important to keep in mind that ocean transportation accounts for a large portion of the total logistics costs. In return, the buyer has access to favorable prices and conditions when handling large volumes of shipments. The service level of the selling company is reduced, since this rule obliges the buyer to manage all operations once the seller places the goods alongside the ship at the port of shipment.

3.4   Conclusions

The FAS rule is rarely used. However, it is appropriate for non-unitized shipments such as:

- Bulk cargoes: animal feed, cereals, cement, coal, etc.
- Bulky and heavy material (indivisible parts, etc.).
- Machinery and capital goods.

Under these conditions, the selling company simply places the goods at the side of the ship, while the buyer contracts and assumes the loading on board, as well as the subsequent costs (transportation to the port of destination, costs at the port of destination, import clearance, etc.). It is also very convenient to contract the transport under the appropriate shipping conditions, so that the obligations and costs of both parties are coordinated.

4   FOB (free on board)

4.1   Overview and delivery

The FOB rule is one of the most commonly used rules for all types of shipments (bulk, containers, etc.). It means that the seller must deliver the goods, cleared for export, on board the vessel contracted by the buyer at the named port of shipment (usually in the seller's country).

Delivery also occurs when the seller "places the goods so delivered at the disposal of the buyer", as is the usual case in the chain sale of bulk goods by sea.

General formulation

FOB (designated port of embarkation). Incoterms 2020.

Writing examples

- FOB south terminal, Escombreras dock, port of Cartagena, Murcia. Spain. Incoterms 2020
- FOB solid bulk terminal, port of Valencia, Valencia. Spain. Incoterms 2020
- FOB container terminal, port of Barcelona, Barcelona. Spain. Incoterms 2020.

4.2   Main obligations and costs

- **Obligations of the selling company**
  1. Deliver the goods agreed upon in the purchase contract (after checking and verifying their quality) within the agreed term, to pack them adequately for transportation and to mark the packaging (except for bulk goods, goods suitable for FOB) in an appropriate manner (it is highly desirable that these two aspects are specified in the purchase contract).
  2. Present the commercial invoice and other documents agreed upon in the Contract of Sale (to prove that the goods conform to the Contract).
  3. Place the goods (at the buyer's expense and risk) on board the vessel designated by the buyer at the named port of shipment (or to procure the goods so delivered).
  4. Notify the buyer that the goods have been delivered or that the vessel has not taken over the goods within the agreed time.

FOB (free on board)

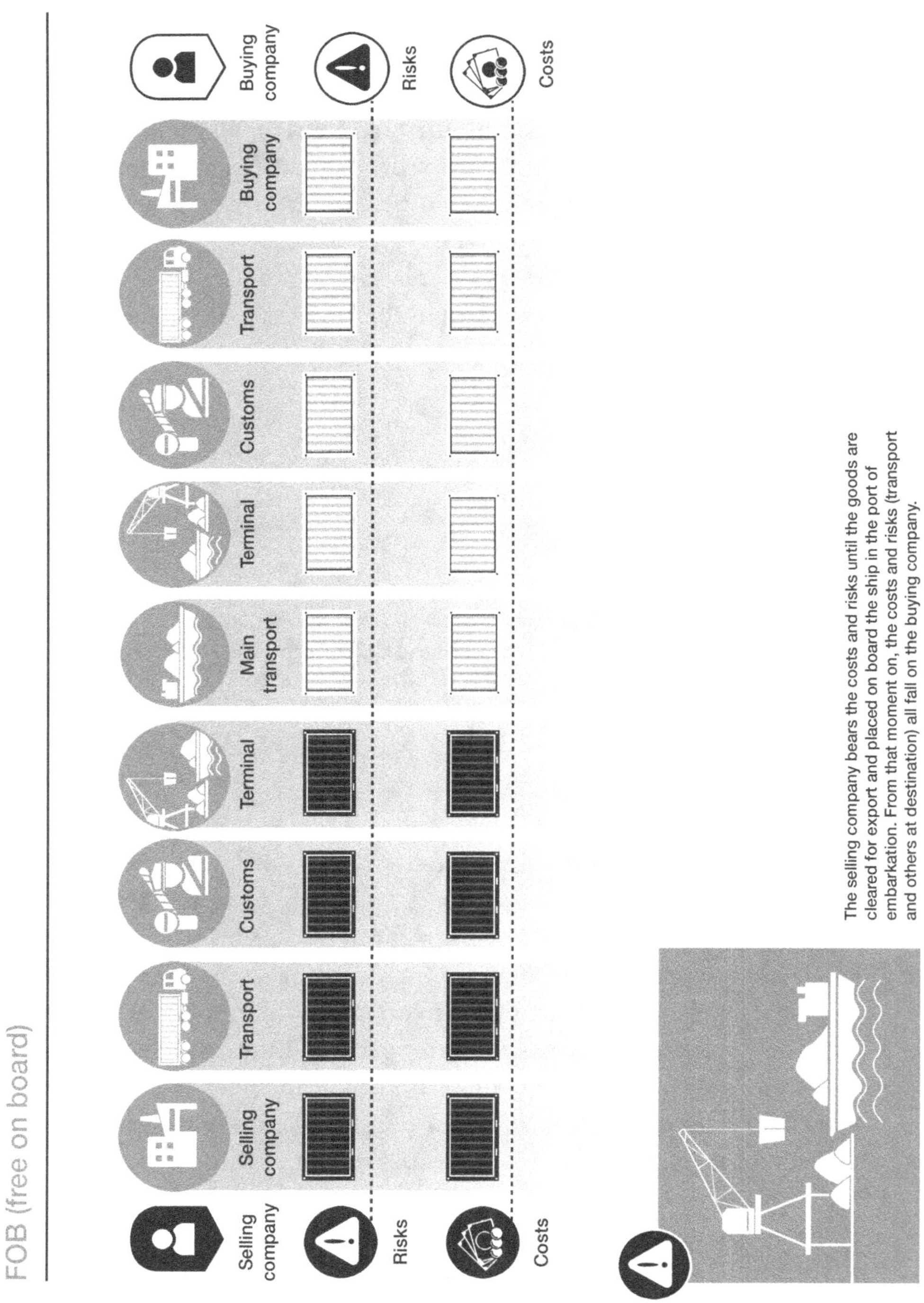

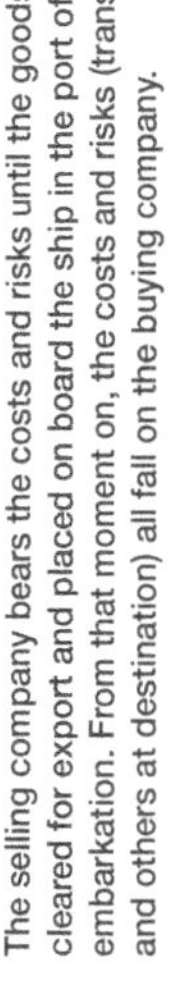

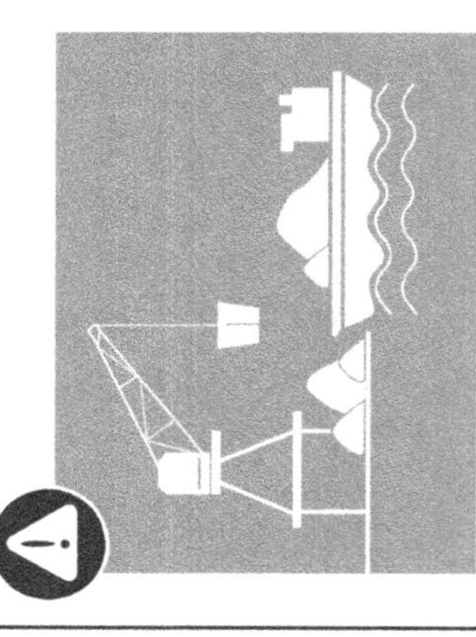

The selling company bears the costs and risks until the goods are cleared for export and placed on board the ship in the port of embarkation. From that moment on, the costs and risks (transport and others at destination) all fall on the buying company.

FOB (free on board): with container

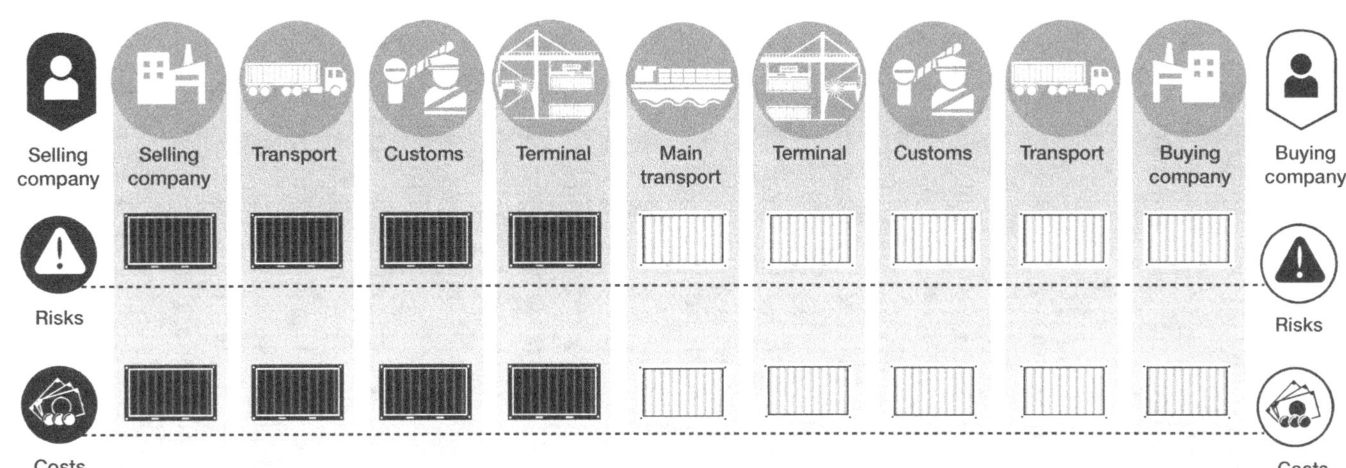

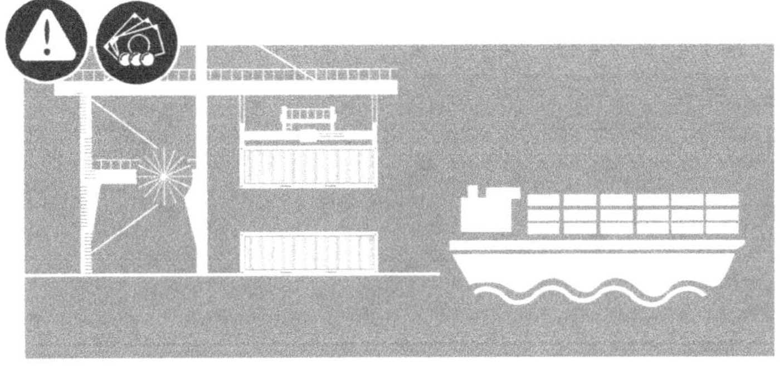

The selling company bears the costs and risks until the container is dispatched for export and placed on board the ship in the port of embarkation. From this point on, the costs and risks (transport and others at destination) all fall on the buying company.

5. Clear customs for export (if required for the transaction) and related formalities and costs: licenses, security clearance and inspections (red channel after presentation of the SAD, specific inspections due to the goods, such as phytosanitary, sanitary, pharmacological, safety, etc.). They must also assist the buyer in obtaining the information and documents (at his expense) that they may need to manage the import clearance (and, where applicable, in transit countries), such as licenses, certifications or inspections.

- **Obligations of the purchasing company**
  1. Pay the price of the goods as agreed in the contract of sale (it should be noted that the means of payment are not regulated by the Incoterms).
  2. Notify the seller of the name of the vessel, the place of loading (e.g. by specifying the terminal), if any, and the date of delivery within the term agreed in the contract of sale. If the buyer fails to do this, or if the carrier fails to receive the goods, the buyer shall bear all risks of loss or damage to the goods from the date or time agreed in the contract of sale for delivery, as well as any additional costs resulting from this situation (which may be additional costs of the seller until actual delivery can be made).
  3. Contract and pay for sea transport once the goods are on board the vessel in the port of shipment. The Incoterms rule provides for the possibility for the seller to contract the transportation at the risk and expense of the buyer, if so agreed in the contract of sale. In any case, the seller may refuse to do so (since it must be agreed). In fact, this option is not recommended because it positions the seller as the shipper (charterer, as opposed to the carrier) under the maritime contract of carriage.
  4. Organize, manage, and pay for post-delivery activities, including ocean freight between origin and destination ports, ocean freight unloaded at destination ports (and through countries, where applicable), and post-delivery expenses. The Incoterms provide for the possibility for the seller to arrange transportation at the buyer's risk and expense if this is the buyer's request or if it is customary practice. In any case, the seller may refuse to do so. In fact, this option is not advisable because it positions the seller as the shipper (charterer in the language of the charterparty, as opposed to the shipping line/carrier) in the contract of carriage by sea.

4.3 Considerations for effective use

4.3.1 Use of FOB with non-unitized merchandise

- **Transportation contracts and other pre- and post- sea voyage costs**
  Selling and purchasing companies must manage and bear the costs of transportation to and from the port in their respective countries or nearby geographical areas.

- **Contracting of maritime transportation**
  The purchasing company is obliged to negotiate with the shipping company or chartering agency the terms of transportation (freight, dates, etc.) and the cargo (means of transportation, laytime, costs, delays, etc.). However, it is possible for the selling company, in agreement with the buyer or at the buyer's request, to contract for the transport, which the buyer assumes (freight collect). Although this is not advisable because it positions the seller as the shipper in the contract of carriage, it is true that in this way, since the seller controls the operations of the freight forwarder and the shipping company, the risks of excessive costs arising from delivery to the carrier chosen by the buyer are reduced (see the heading "Cost reasons for the selling company" in section 2.1 of this chapter). If this alternative is chosen, it is usual for the operator to request the buyer's agreement in advance on the freight to be paid at destination, the cost of which, together with the costs after arrival at the port, should be carefully examined by the buyer.

  With regard to chartering, it is advisable for the purchasing company to contract terms that do not include loading at the port of shipment (an operation carried out and assumed by the seller), such as FIO, FIOS, FIOST, FISLO or FILO. The choice of shipping term depends on the type of goods and the requirements for their proper transportation (stowage, trimming, etc.), as well as the inclusion of unloading at destination in the freight contracted by the buyer with the shipping line (FISLO and FILO terms) or the exclusion of such unloading, in which case it must be contracted with an external operator, such as a shipping agency (FIO, FIOS and FIOST terms).

4.3.2   Use of FOB in containerized transport

The 2020 version of the Incoterms (as well as the previous versions) discourages container shipments on FOB terms and instead recommends the use of the FCA rule for the reasons given in section 2 of this chapter. Nevertheless, these operations are often carried out on FOB terms.

The use of FOB in containerized transportation requires the selling company to assume the costs and risks until the container is loaded on board the vessel at the port of shipment. From the buyer's point of view, the FOB rule avoids having to bear such costs and risks prior to the start of the maritime transport (delays and costs at the port due to bad sea conditions, costs of special administrative and operational costs at the port of shipment, etc.).

On the other hand, it gives them full control over the logistics chain (choice of shipping company or freight forwarder) and is a very common practice, for example, with Asian suppliers who have already standardized it.

4.3.3   Other considerations for the use of FOB

- **Transport insurance**
  The FOB rule does not oblige either party to take out insurance to cover the risks to which the goods may be exposed during transportation. However, both parties, in particular the buyer, must consider the advisability of taking out insurance to cover the risks assumed by each party (in the case of the selling company, until the goods are placed on board the vessel, at which time the risks are transferred to the buyer). The advisability of taking out insurance in this type of transaction is reinforced by the difficulty for the injured party (the party bearing the risk according to the Incoterms rule) to make a direct claim against the shipping company for damage occurring during transportation, due to the application of legal frameworks and the terms of the contract of carriage (imposed as a contract of adhesion), which are very favourable to the carrier.

- **Documentation and proof of delivery**
  The seller's proof of delivery must be a document showing that the goods were loaded on board at the port of origin, i.e., the usual proof that the goods have been delivered (as opposed to CFR and CIF terms, where the

seller must provide the bill of lading to satisfy the same obligation). Under FOB and FAS terms, the seller does not contract for transportation and is therefore only required to provide proof of delivery. However, in practice, and given that this party assumes the costs and risks until the goods are loaded on board, the usual proof of delivery document is the contract of carriage or the bill of lading (BL), a document that must be delivered to the seller as shipper of the goods at the port of export, in application of one of its main functions (receipt of the goods by the carrier).

However, under FOB conditions, it is the buyer who contracts the transportation and can therefore put pressure on the shipping company to deliver the BL, which can be detrimental to the seller if the document is required for collection, for example by documentary credit. In this case, the seller must first ensure that the document is delivered, either by making payment of the relevant costs conditional on the document being obtained, or by arranging for carriage at the buyer's expense.

The massive use of the FOB rule in many cases is a consequence of the fact that the BL is usually required to collect (in case of requesting it, for example, in a documentary credit) but, as we commented above when analyzing the FCA, there are many operations where, for various reasons (trust between the parties, operations between companies of the same group, payment in advance, etc.), in order to speed up the operation, it would be convenient to eliminate the issuance of a loaded BL with its function as a negotiable instrument and replace it (in the case of agreeing on FOB) with a BL without that function, the electronically issued bill of lading, which saves the costs of issuing and managing the BL and speeds up delivery at the destination since the buyer can claim it simply by identifying themselves.

If, after analyzing the circumstances of the transaction, it is decided to use FCA instead of FOB, a previous document such as example 1 of the Bill of Lading can be presented as proof of delivery. FOB delivery may also be evidenced by a bill of lading issued by the ship's first officer.

- **Transport documentation and documentary means of payment**
  In the case of agreeing on a documentary means of payment, it is common to require the document proving delivery of the goods (BL shipped or shipping receipt).

- **Control of the logistic chain and service level of the selling company**
  In FOB terms, the buyer controls most of the logistics chain and its costs, since ocean transportation costs, especially for bulk and non-unitized goods, represent a large portion of the total logistics costs. This allows the buyer to choose the transport operator (shipping line and freight forwarder), negotiate freight under better conditions (transit times, etc.) and access advantageous rates and conditions. On the other hand, compared to FOB, CFR limits the control of the buyer, who may find it difficult to access the goods and may have to bear high costs at the port of destination (especially in the case of consolidated shipments). To avoid these problems, both companies should request quotations that are as detailed as possible (including amounts for each item) in order to control the costs that will be invoiced later.

  The selling company's level of service is limited, as the buyer controls the costs and assumes the risks from the time of shipment on board.

  In any case, the choice between FOB and CFR will also depend, as we will indicate when outlining the criteria for choosing the optimal rule, on whether one or the other party (seller or buyer) has access to more competitive freight rates and transportation conditions than the other (in which case, the rule that allows this advantage to be demonstrated should be chosen).

4.4   Conclusions

Along with CIF, FOB is one of the most widely used Incoterms. However, according to the recommendations (explanatory notes for users) of version 2020, its use should be limited to shipments of non-unitized goods such as:

- Bulk solids (cement, coal, etc.) or liquids (liquefied gases, etc.)
- General cargo transported in coils, bales, drums, etc.
- Other general cargo consisting of sheets, pallets, etc.
- Bulky and heavy material (indivisible parts, etc.)
- Machinery and capital goods.

The contract of transportation under these conditions must be made using the appropriate shipping term that allows coordination of the obligations and costs of both companies. Although, for practical reasons, the use of FOB is very common in container transport, its application to this type of operation can give rise to controversies arising from the risks and costs assumed by the selling company up to the delivery of the container, over which it has no control.

Finally, in FOB terms, the buyer manages most of the logistical chain by contracting the maritime transport, a fact that can lead to greater competitiveness by allowing them to access advantageous rates and conditions thanks to the large volumes contracted.

5   CFR (cost and freight)

5.1   Overview and delivery

The use of CFR is very common in various types of operations (bulk, container, etc.). Under CFR terms, the selling company delivers the goods, cleared for export, on board the vessel and contracts and assumes responsibility for their transportation to the named port of destination. In the case of chain sales of bulk goods or goods obtained during the voyage, the seller may "provide" the goods so delivered. As with Group C rules, the CFR presents a dichotomy between the point of delivery and passing of risk (in this case, when the goods are loaded on board the vessel at the port of shipment) and the point to which the seller must contract and assume carriage (the named port of destination).

Therefore, although the seller is the one who pays for the main (maritime) transportation, the buyer is the one who bears the risks. Consequently, it is essential that both the place of delivery and the place of destination are clearly specified in the contract of sale, bearing in mind that if the former is not specified, it will be assumed that delivery takes place when the goods are loaded on board the vessel at the port of shipment. Likewise, it is essential to specify any place of delivery located in a different place (port of destination, place prior to the port of shipment, etc.).

For example, in a shipment made in Spain under a purchase and sale agreed under the conditions "CFR Terminal 1, Port of Valparaiso, Valparaiso. Chile. Incoterms 2020", the seller will have to contract and bear all costs until the goods are placed at the port of destination. However, if the loss occurs after the loading of the vessel in the port of shipment, the buyer bears the risks, with the consequent implications regarding the payment of the purchase and sale and the claim against the carrier. On the other hand, if the loss occurs before the goods are loaded on board the vessel, the seller bears the risk.

This cost/risk dichotomy relates to the use of the Bill of Lading (BL). Since it constitutes a security (unless it is issued without this function, in which case, as mentioned above, it is called a bill of lading), the seller must provide the buyer with the originals of this document as proof of delivery of the goods, which will enable the buyer to claim the goods from the shipping company at the place of destination. In this way, the buyer takes possession of the goods at the point of origin, and it is appropriate for them to bear the risks during transportation.

In the introductory notes to the CFR, the Incoterms 2020 advise against its use in container transport and recommend its replacement by the CPT, which makes it possible to synchronize the time of delivery and transfer of risk with the time when the seller makes the goods available to the carrier (usually in his warehouse when the goods are loaded into the container). This substitution clarifies the allocation of risks as they are fully borne by the buyer.

General formulation

CFR (designated port of destination). Incoterms 2020.

Writing examples

- CFR terminal 1, port of Valparaiso, Valparaiso. Chile. Incoterms 2020
- CFR pier 12, port of Buenaventura, Buenaventura. Colombia. Incoterms 2020
- CFR bulk terminal, port of Santos, Santos. Brazil. Incoterms 2020
- CFR container terminal, port of Veracruz, Veracruz. Mexico. Incoterms 2020.

5.2 Main obligations and costs

- **Obligations of the selling company**
  1. Deliver the goods agreed upon in the purchase contract (after checking and verifying their quality) within the agreed term, to pack them adequately for transportation and to mark the packaging (except for bulk goods, goods suitable for CFR) in a proper way (it is highly desirable that these two aspects are specified in the purchase contract).
  2. Present the commercial invoice and any other documents stipulated in the sales contract (as a proof of conformity).
  3. Contract and pay for transportation until the goods are placed at the port of destination, loaded on board the ship of arrival.
  4. Notify the buyer that the goods have been delivered so that they can receive them at the port of destination.
  5. Clear customs for export (if required for the operation) and its related formalities and costs: licenses, security clearance and inspections (red channel after presentation of the SAD, specific inspections due to the goods, such as phytosanitary, sanitary, pharmacological, safety, etc.).

CFR (cost and freight) / CIF (cost, insurance and freight)

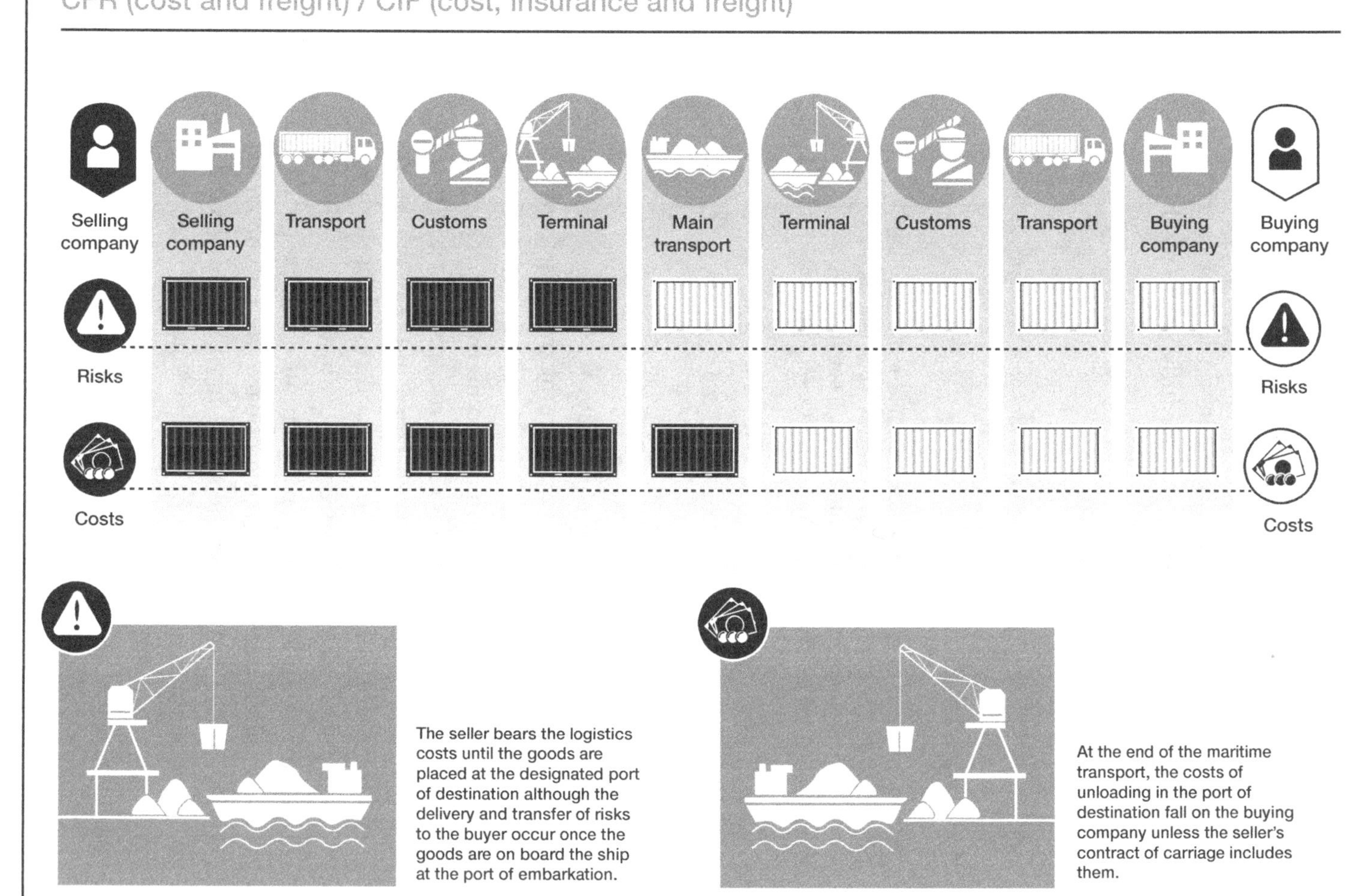

The seller bears the logistics costs until the goods are placed at the designated port of destination although the delivery and transfer of risks to the buyer occur once the goods are on board the ship at the port of embarkation.

At the end of the maritime transport, the costs of unloading in the port of destination fall on the buying company unless the seller's contract of carriage includes them.

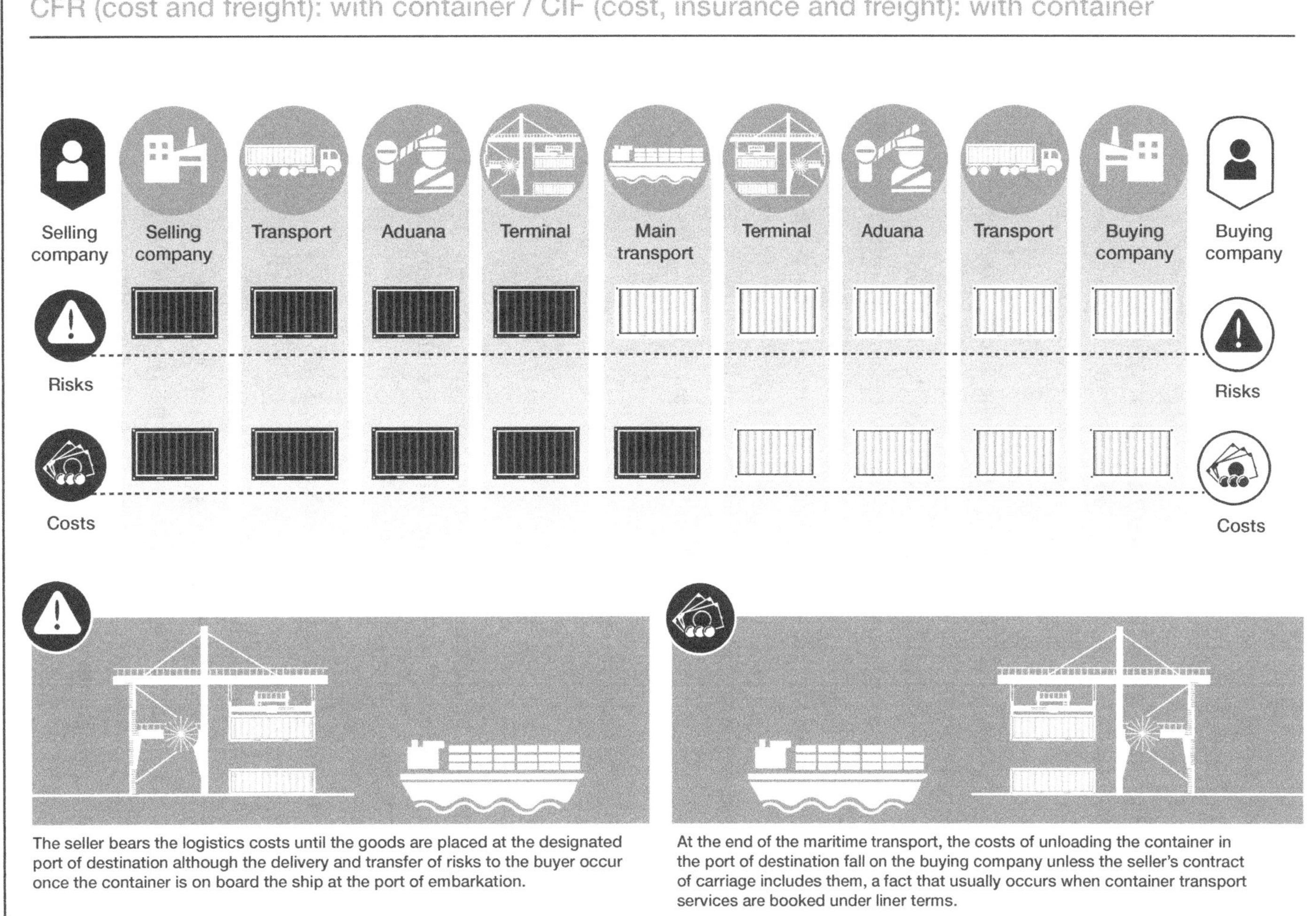

The seller bears the logistics costs until the goods are placed at the designated port of destination although the delivery and transfer of risks to the buyer occur once the container is on board the ship at the port of embarkation.

At the end of the maritime transport, the costs of unloading the container in the port of destination fall on the buying company unless the seller's contract of carriage includes them, a fact that usually occurs when container transport services are booked under liner terms.

It must also assist the buyer in obtaining (at the buyer's expense) the information and documents that may be necessary for the management of import procedures (and, where applicable, in transit countries), such as licenses, certifications or inspections.

- **Obligations of the purchasing company**
  1. Pay the price of the goods as agreed in the purchase contract (it should be noted that the means of payment is not regulated by the Incoterms rule).
  2. If agreed in the contract of sale, the buyer can determine the time of shipment or the place (specific terminal, etc.) where they will receive the goods at the designated port of destination.
  3. Organize, manage and pay for the rest of the operations in the logistic chain after the arrival of the goods at the designated port of destination: unloading at the port of destination and the rest of the costs at that port, import clearance (and, if applicable, in transit countries) and subsequent costs to the final destination.

5.3　Considerations for effective use

5.3.1　Use of CFR with non-unitized merchandise

- **Contracts of carriage and other pre- and post-shipment costs**
  Selling and purchasing companies must manage and bear the costs in their respective countries or nearby areas.

- **Contracting of maritime transportation**
  The selling company is obliged to negotiate with the shipping company or chartering agency the conditions of transport (freight, dates, etc.) and the cargo on board the vessel (means of transport, laytime, cost, delays, etc.). In the case of carriage under charterparty, it is appropriate for the seller, acting as charterer, to contract carriage on shipping terms that include loading at the port of origin, but not unloading at the port of destination (which is performed and assumed by the buyer), i.e. on LIFO or similar terms.

5.3.2 Use of CFR in containerized transport

Version 2020 of the Incoterms (and previous versions) discourages the use of CFR in container transport and recommends, as an alternative, the application of the CPT rule, according to which the transfer of risk occurs at a point up-stream of the port of shipment, i.e. at a place where the selling company can control the operation (e.g. when the goods are loaded into the container at the place of origin, usually at its warehouse). On the other hand, under CFR con-ditions, the transfer of risk occurs when the container is loaded on board the vessel at the port of shipment, which involves an element of risk for the selling company and, moreover, divides the containerized voyage into two risk legs to be borne by each company (see section 2. 1 of this chapter).

On the other hand, liner shipping is usually contracted on liner terms,10 so that the freight assumed by the selling company at the time of contracting the transportation includes the cost of unloading the container by container crane at the port of destination. From that point on, the cost is borne by the buyer. If the freight does not include unloading at destination, the cost is borne by the buyer.

5.3.3 Other considerations for the use of CFR

- **Delivery point in maritime transport with transshipment**
  As mentioned above, it is crucial that the parties clearly specify both the place of delivery and the place of destination, bearing in mind that if the former is not specified, it will be deemed to occur when the goods are loaded on board the vessel at the port of shipment (same as FOB). The parties may agree on another place of delivery, but they must specify it in the contract of sale (which is not common). This is especially important if, for example, there are two ocean legs in the international logistics chain of the transaction.

  Suppose a multimodal container transport in which a company from Murcia, Spain, agrees with a Mexican company "CFR port of Veracruz",

---

[10] This situation, although the most common, may vary depending on the customs and regulations of each port or geographical area.

Mexico. Incoterms 2020". Let us assume that the transport management contracted by the seller includes a road trip from Murcia to the port of Cartagena, a short sea trip from the port of Cartagena to the port of Algeciras (also in Spain), where a transshipment will take place in order to embark on a ship that will travel to the port of Veracruz (Mexico). The selling company pays the transportation costs to the port of Veracruz, but there is a reasonable doubt as to which port (after the goods are loaded on board the vessel) the risks are transferred from the seller to the buyer. The first option (recommended) is that the parties specify it in the contract of sale. The second option (if not agreed) is that the risks are transferred when the goods are loaded on board the vessel at the first port (in the port of Cartagena). This is an important aspect to be evaluated by the purchasing company, for example, when considering insurance.

- **Transport insurance**
  The CFR does not require either party to purchase insurance, although it is advisable that both parties consider the convenience of taking out insurance to cover their respective risks. In the case of the seller company, this would be until placing the goods on board the ship at the port of loading (or at the first port in the case of transshipment), at which point the risks are transferred to the buyer.

- **Documentation and proof of delivery**
  The seller must provide the buyer with a Bill of Lading (BL), a document that serves as proof of delivery and allows the buyer to claim the goods from the carrier at the port of destination.
  The BL must state "freight prepaid" or its equivalent to indicate that the freight has been paid by the seller. Unless otherwise agreed, the ocean bill of lading must be a negotiable document, i.e., one that allows the buyer to sell the goods by endorsement, and the seller must deliver the complete set of originals to the buyer.
  The shipping document must reflect the goods, be dated within the agreed shipping period, allow the buyer to reclaim the goods at destination and, unless otherwise agreed, authorize its resale by transfer of the document.
  This negotiable status (endorsable if issued to order) requires the seller to deliver the complete set of originals to the buyer. As mentioned above in FOB and FCA, in certain operations (between companies of the same

group with a high level of trust, when payment has been made in advance, etc.) it may be convenient to replace the prepaid BL with a sea waybill or a prepaid waybill, which makes the management of the operation easier and cheaper, since it allows delivery to the buyer at destination by mere identification.

- **Transport Documentation and Documentary Payment Method**
  If a documentary payment method is agreed upon, it is common to require a dispatched BL as proof of delivery, issued in accordance with the terms agreed in the letter of credit (nominative or to order, number of originals, carrier, etc.). It is customary for such a document to state that the seller is responsible for the cost of transportation by using the phrase "freight prepaid" or its equivalent.

- **Control of the logistic chain and service level of the selling company**
  Under CFR terms, the seller controls most of the logistics chain, which allows it to access advantageous rates and conditions when large volumes of transportation are contracted. This way, the seller can offer competitive service levels and delivery conditions by placing the shipment at the port of destination, from where the purchasing company can complete the operation without excessive complications. However, this company must consider and agree in advance the costs to be borne at the destination (see "Buyer's Costs at Destination" in Section 3.3 of Chapter 4) in order to avoid additional costs at the port of destination as a condition for access to the goods.

5.4 Conclusions

The CFR is widely used. According to the recommendations of the 2020 version of the Incoterms, its use should be limited to shipments of non-unitized goods (bulk, general cargo, machinery, heavy and bulky cargo, etc.). Therefore, its use in container transport operations is discouraged, where it is recommended to replace it with the CPT rule. The contract of carriage under these conditions should be concluded using the appropriate shipping conditions that allow for the coordination of the obligations and costs of both companies.

The application of the CFR in container transportation divides the risks of transportation into two phases corresponding to each party at the time of loading of the goods on board (a moment when the condition of the goods is not checked). In case of damage, this may lead to disputes if the exact location of the incident is unknown.

On the other hand, the use of CFR is appropriate in transactions where possession is transferred by virtue of the bill of lading's function as a document of title.

Finally, under CFR conditions, the selling company manages most of the logistics chain by contracting maritime transport, which can be a competitive factor by allowing it to access advantageous rates and transport conditions.

6   CIF (cost, insurance and freight)

6.1   Overview and delivery

The CIF rule differs from the CFR rule only in that it requires the seller to insure the goods against the risks of transport borne by the buyer. These risks correspond to the buyer from the time of delivery and transfer of risk, i.e. when the goods are loaded on board the vessel at the port (in the case of transshipment, at the first port). Transport risks prior to this point are borne by the selling company, which may cover them by insurance if it deems it appropriate. The CFR analysis is therefore applicable to this arrangement, so its description focuses on the difference described.

General formulation

CIF (designated port of destination). Incoterms 2020.

Writing examples

– CIF terminal 1, port of Valparaiso, Valparaiso. Chile. Incoterms 2020.
– CIF pier 12, port of Buenaventura, Buenaventura. Colombia. Incoterms 2020.
– CIF bulk terminal, port of Santos, Santos. Brazil. Incoterms 2020.
– CIF container terminal, port of Veracruz, Veracruz. Mexico. Incoterms 2020.

6.2   Main obligations and costs

- **Obligations of the selling company**
  1. Deliver the goods agreed upon in the purchase contract (inspected and checked for quality) within the agreed period, to pack them adequately for transportation and to mark the packaging (except for bulk goods, goods suitable for CIF) properly (it is highly desirable that these two aspects are specified in the purchase contract).
  2. Present the commercial invoice and other documents stipulated in the contract of sale (as a proof of conformity).
  3. Arrange and pay for the transportation of the goods to the named port of destination, loaded on board the arriving vessel.

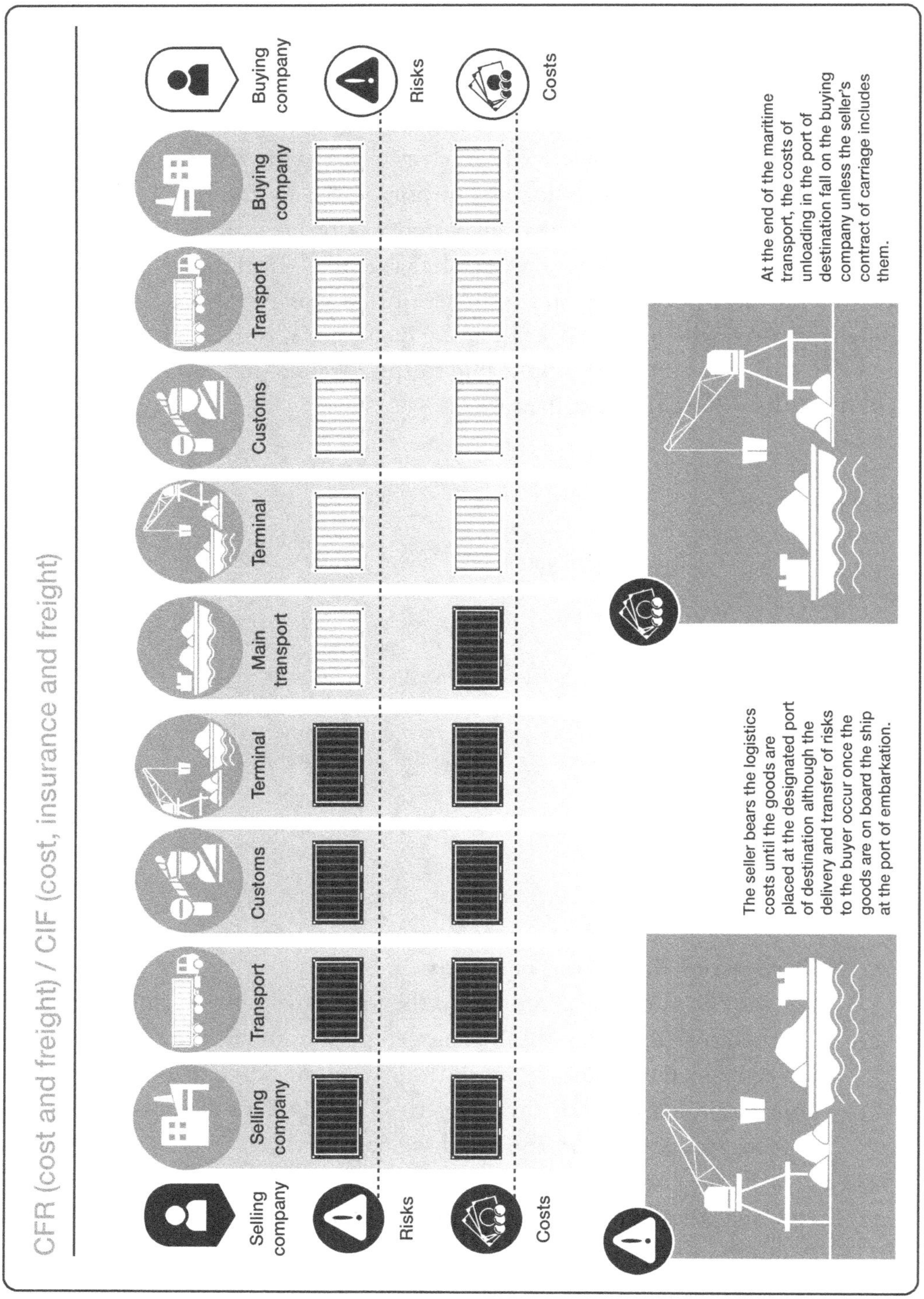
CFR (cost and freight) / CIF (cost, insurance and freight)
Selling company
Risks
Costs
Selling company
Transport
Customs
Terminal
Main transport
Terminal
Customs
Transport
Buying company
Buying company
Risks
Costs
The seller bears the logistics costs until the goods are placed at the designated port of destination although the delivery and transfer of risks to the buyer occur once the goods are on board the ship at the port of embarkation.
At the end of the maritime transport, the costs of unloading in the port of destination fall on the buying company unless the seller's contract of carriage includes them.

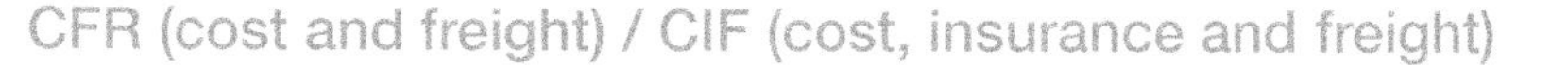

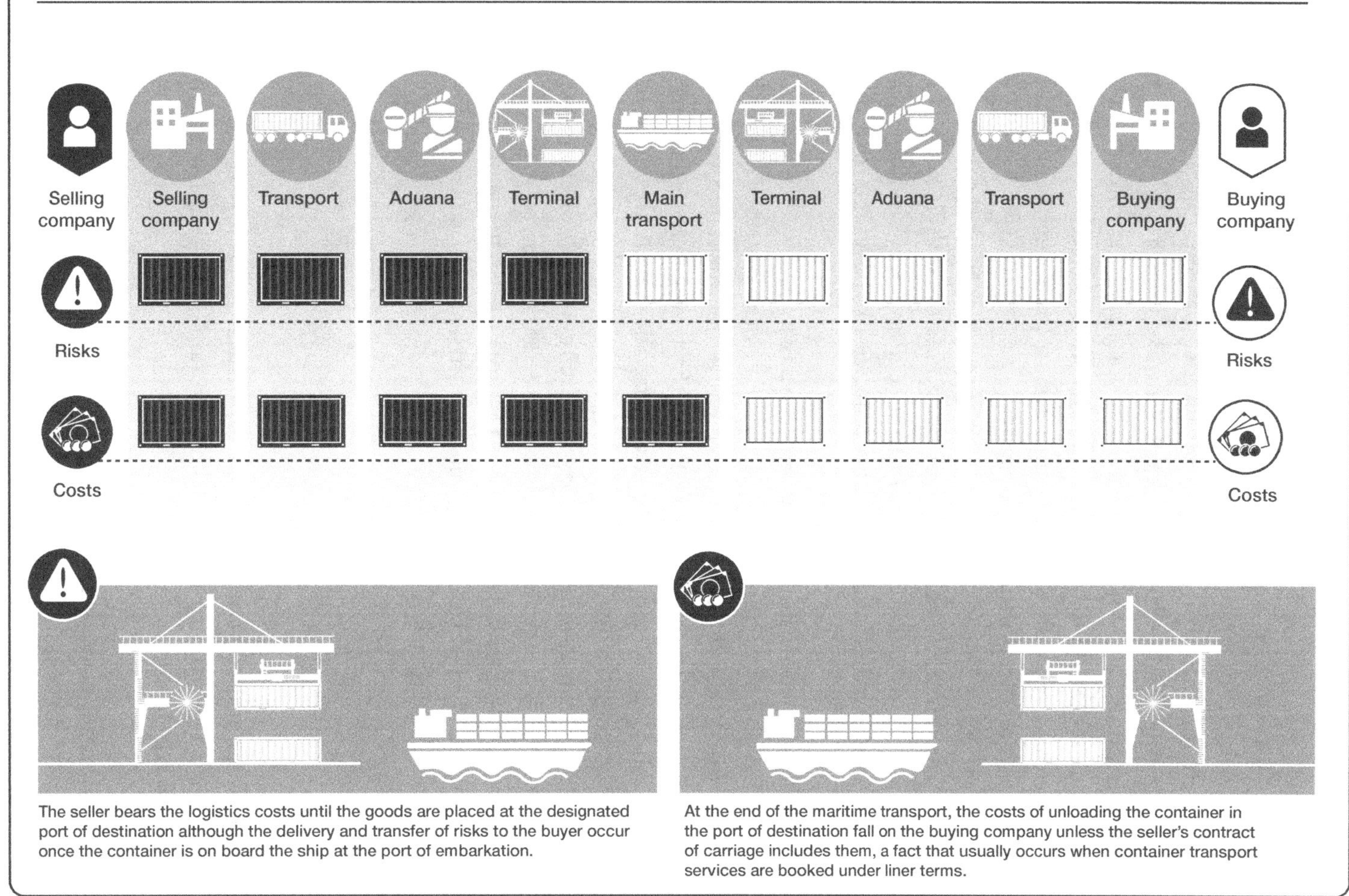

CFR (cost and freight): with container / CIF (cost, insurance and freight): with container
Selling company
Selling company
Transport
Aduana
Terminal
Main transport
Terminal
Aduana
Transport
Buying company
Buying company
Risks
Costs
Risks
Costs
The seller bears the logistics costs until the goods are placed at the designated port of destination although the delivery and transfer of risks to the buyer occur once the container is on board the ship at the port of embarkation.
At the end of the maritime transport, the costs of unloading the container in the port of destination fall on the buying company unless the seller's contract of carriage includes them, a fact that usually occurs when container transport services are booked under liner terms.

4. Notify the Buyer that the Goods have been delivered so that the Buyer can receive them at the port of destination.
5. Clear customs for export (if required for the operation) and the related formalities and costs: licenses, security clearance and inspections (red channel after presentation of the SAD, specific inspections due to the goods, such as phytosanitary, sanitary, pharmacological, safety, etc.). It should also assist the buyer in obtaining the information and documents (at the buyer's expense) that it may need to manage the import clearance (and, where appropriate, in transit countries), such as licenses, certifications or inspections.
6. Procure transportation insurance to cover the risks borne by the Buyer from the time of delivery of the goods until their arrival at the named port of destination. This insurance must meet certain requirements set forth in the Inco terms and conditions: coverage, insured value, etc.

- **Obligations of the purchasing company**
  1. Pay the price of the goods as agreed in the contract of sale (it should be noted that the means of payment is not regulated by the Incoterms).
  2. If agreed in the contract of sale, the buyer may determine the time of shipment or the place (e.g. the specific terminal) where it will receive the goods at the named port of destination.
  3. Organize, manage, and pay for the remaining operations in the logistics chain after the goods arrive at the specified port of destination: unloading and other costs at the port of destination, import clearance (and, if applicable, in transit countries), and subsequent costs to the final destination.

6.3 Considerations for effective use of the rule

The selling company must take out an insurance policy to cover the risks of the goods during transportation. The insurance policy must comply with the following conditions:

- **Minimum coverage**
  It must correspond to Type C of the Institute Cargo Clauses (ICC) of the Institute of London Underwriters or other similar clauses. The ICC claus-

es, which are the most widely accepted and implemented internationally, are divided into three types (A, B and C) covering the following risks:

- **Type C.** This is the lowest level of coverage. Includes fire, explosion, grounding, stranding, running aground, sinking, wreck, collision or struck by, unloading in port of refuge and capsizing, grounding, derailment and general average sacrifice.
- **Type B.** This is an intermediate coverage that adds to the risks of Mode C the following risks: dragging by waves, seawater intrusion, loss of packages during loading and unloading, damage caused by lightning, earthquakes and volcanic eruptions.
- **Type A.** Covers any risk of loss or damage, except for certain expressly excluded risks such as malice on the part of the insured, loss of normal weight or volume, wear and tear, improper packing and conditioning, inherent vice, delay, insolvency, radioactivity, war and strike, and unseaworthiness.

Given the limitations of Type C, which does not cover some of the most common risks to which goods are exposed in maritime transport (dragging by waves, seawater ingress, loss of packages during loading and unloading, etc.), it is usually agreed under CIF conditions to contract a higher level of cover.

- **Additional coverage by agreement**
  It is common for the parties to agree to take out insurance with a wider coverage, which in practice usually corresponds to Type A, including war and strike damage. In this case, the cost of the additional coverage is passed on to the purchasing company. This increase in insurance cover is particularly appropriate when CIF is used in multimodal container transport operations, since the goods transported in this way (in addition to being of higher value) are exposed to greater risks than those presented by bulk goods (for which the CIF rule is designed), such as theft, which is typical of container goods but not of bulk goods (a loss which is included in ICC "A" cover but not in "C").
  It should be noted that one of the new features of version 2020 is that the insurance coverage in CIP (a rule designed for multimodal transport) has been upgraded from ICC "C" to ICC "A". In most cases where CIP or

CIF rules were agreed prior to version 2020, coverage was already raised by mutual agreement and should now be done likewise.

- **Quality and service of the insurance company**

  In order to meet the requirements of the agreed Incoterms rule, it is advisable to contract the insurance with a well-established and experienced company, specialized in transport insurance and with a presence in the countries of origin or destination. The selection of the insurance company may be the subject of an agreement between the seller and the buyer.

  The insurance should allow both the buyer and other interested parties (e.g. the seller up to the moment of delivery of the goods, i.e. when the shipment takes place on board) to claim directly from the insurance company. The seller can then endorse the insurance policy to the buyer, configuring it as insured from that moment on. The seller can also claim from the insurer for a third company to which the goods have been sold through endorsement of the bill of lading, and the insurance has also been endorsed when the risk has been transferred.

  The interest of this point lies in the dichotomy between risk and cost that exists in CIF conditions, as well as in the fact that, by delivering (or endorsing) the bill of lading and the insurance policy to the purchasing company, the latter takes possession of the goods from the point of origin (after shipment), where it begins to bear the risks of transportation, and thus, from that moment on, it also appears as insured.

- **Insured value coverage**

  The insured value or sum insured is the maximum amount of compensation to be paid by the insurance company in the event of a claim. It must cover at least 110% of the purchase price and be in the same currency as the contract that establishes it.[11]

- **Transport stages covered by insurance**

  The insurance must cover the risks of the goods during their carriage from the geographical point of delivery, when the goods are loaded on board

---

[11] For the calculation of the insured value, see the section "Coverage of the insured value" in Chapter 4, Section 4.3.

the vessel at the port of shipment (in the case of several vessels per transshipment, when they are loaded on board the first vessel), to at least the designated port of delivery.

The application of this consideration to container transport is controversial because of the desirability of treating all stages of such transport as a unit in terms of risks and their corresponding allocation to one or the other party (see section 2 of this chapter). Thus, since the CIF rule requires the seller to take out insurance to cover the risks borne by the buyer from the time of delivery (the seller may optionally take out another policy to cover its own risks up to that point), in the event of a loss, disputes may arise as to the point in the logistics chain at which the loss occurred and, therefore, as to which party should bear the risk.

In contrast, in the transportation of non-unitized goods (bulk cargo, packages, etc.), the condition of the goods at the time of loading is usually certified and indicated in the BL by expressions such as "clean on board". Furthermore, it is common to require certificates of weight, quality and compliance with other parameters at the time of loading, which removes any doubt as to the loading of the goods on board, as well as their delivery and effective transfer of risk under proper conditions. These checks cannot be carried out in the case of container transport, where the container usually arrives at the port already loaded, closed and sealed.

- **Proof of insurance contract**
  The formalization of the insurance contract must be made in writing and is specified in the corresponding policy, which is made up of general and specific conditions. The former are common to all policies in the same branch or sector (transport, life, automobile, etc.) and include the aspects of the insurance relating to definitions, purpose and scope of the insurance, general coverages, etc. In the transportation sector, an example of this is the general ICC coverage clauses. The latter complete the policy by specifying the characteristics of the contract (parties, insured value, specific risks included, etc.).

  The insurance policy may be issued in the name of the buyer (nominative), to the order of the seller who assigns it by endorsement, or directly to the buyer it has been shipped and the risk transferred, or to the bearer (assigning the right to claim from the insurer upon delivery of the insurance certificate).

It is customary to request from the insurer a certificate confirming the existence of the insurance policy and its main aspects (coverage clauses, risks and insured value).

- **Proof of insurance documentation and documentary means of payment**
When using a letter of credit as a means of payment, it is necessary to specify in the letter of credit whether the full policy is required as evidence or whether a certificate of insurance is sufficient. In addition, the requirements of Article 28 of the UCP 600 (Documentary Credit Regulation) regarding the "Document of Insurance and Coverage" must be taken into account, which requires, among other things, that such a document (policy or certificate, as specified in the terms and conditions of the credit):

  - Must be issued and signed by an insurance company or its agents (the signature of an agent must indicate that it is for the account of the insurer).
  - If issued in several originals, all must be presented.
  - It must indicate the sum insured (110% of the CIF value).
  - It must be expressed in the same currency as the credit.
  - Its date of issue must not be later than the date of shipment, etc.

- **Information to the purchasing company for additional insurance**
The seller must provide the buyer, at the buyer's request and expense, with all the information necessary for the buyer to take out additional insurance, for example to cover subsequent voyages to the agreed port of destination, or to enable the buyer to take out a policy with greater coverage.

  However, because of the convenience of taking out insurance and the fact that it may be difficult to adapt it to the risks and requirements of the operation, the seller, using CFR as an alternative to CIF, can provide the buyer with all the information necessary to take out insurance to cover the risks to be borne. In this way, the purchasing company becomes the policyholder, insured and beneficiary of the insurance policy contracted, which undoubtedly facilitates the indemnification process in the event of a loss covered by such insurance.

6.4   Conclusions

Along with FOB, CIF is one of the most widely used Incoterms. Its application should be limited to shipments of non-unitized goods (bulk, general cargo, machinery, heavy and large-volume cargo, etc.), according to the recommendations of the 2020 version of these rules.

The CIF rule is widely used in shipments of industrial and other non-unitized goods of medium or high value, as well as in containerized shipments of consumer goods. Its widespread use in these operations is due to the fact that the insurance covering the risks during transportation allows for an indemnity element in case of loss.

The contract of transportation under these conditions must be made using the appropriate shipping terms that allow for the coordination of the obligations and costs of both companies.

The use of CIF in container transport divides the risks of transport into two phases corresponding to each party. This can lead to disputes in the event of damage if the exact location of the damage is unknown.

On the other hand, the use of CIF is appropriate in operations where the ownership of the goods is transferred, since the bill of lading acts as security.

CIF terms allow the seller to take control of most of the logistics chain, improving its competitiveness through access to better rates and terms.

Chapter 6

Criteria for choosing the optimal Incoterms rule and applying it to the sales contract

1 Determining factors in the choice of the optimal Incoterms rule

The choice of an Incoterms rule entails obligations, management, costs and risks for both the seller and the buyer. Therefore, the choice of the optimal rule must be the result of a process in which different options, criteria and factors, sometimes incompatible, must be properly evaluated. Each company must prioritize what it considers necessary in the negotiation that regulates the sale and purchase. The following are the most relevant factors in choosing the optimal Incoterms rule.

1.1 Matching the Incoterms rule to the mode of transport and its operation

Incoterms are divided into multimodal and maritime rules. The latter (FAS, FOB, CFR and CIF) should be applied only to operations where the goods are loaded over the side of the ship (bulk, break bulk, etc.). Under these rules (except under FAS conditions), the seller must deliver the goods on board the vessel designated by the buyer at the port of shipment. The use of maritime rules is not appropriate for other operations (including container transport) that are to be carried out under multimodal transport conditions (EXW, FCA, CPT, CIP, DAP, DPU and DDP). In view of the widespread use of the FOB and CIF rules in container transport, it is therefore necessary to consider the advantages in terms of costs and risks, especially for the selling company, of replacing the FOB rule by the FCA rule (where the goods are delivered for risk transfer when it is made available to the carrier long before being loaded on board) and of replacing the CIF rule by the CIP rule (or its uninsured variants, CFR by CPT).

The application of maritime Incoterms is also inappropriate for other modes of transport (road, rail or air) because they are not adapted to the characteristics of their operation, since delivery does not take place in any case when the goods are placed alongside the vessel or loaded on board at the port of shipment. Another element that can optimize the choice is the use of Incoterms rules that synchronize the cost of transport and the assumption of risk. We therefore recommend combining the use of FCA and DAP with road transport. In both cases, the obligation to contract and pay the cost of transportation and to assume its risk is assigned to the buyer (in FCA) or to the seller (in DAP). Thus, if one of the parties has to claim damages from the carrier, it will do so with full knowledge of the conditions under which the transportation was contracted, since it is named as the shipper in the contract.

In other cases, such as CPT or CIP, the buyer bears the risk of a loss, but if they need to claim from the carrier, they will do so under the terms of the contract of carriage agreed with the seller, which the buyer was unaware of (such as arbitration or competent courts for the settlement of disputes, etc.). Finally, it is essential to agree on a set of Incoterms in accordance with the operations carried out by each company. In this respect, it should be noted that, in practice, many operations for which the EXW rule has been agreed are carried out under FCA conditions, since the selling company loads the goods onto the first vehicle. These inconsistencies can lead to avoidable costs and disputes by choosing the Incoterms rule that fits the operational specifics of each case.

1.2 Complexity and specific characteristics of the operation

Transport operations may have certain characteristics that increase their complexity, such as the following:

- Unforeseen problems arising from access to a new market, such as requirements for product marketing, insufficient infrastructure to meet the operation's transportation obligations, etc.

- Distrust in a new supplier or customer in terms of payment, customs, stability of the operation, etc.
- New aspects in the logistics chain due to a change of transportation mode, port, carrier, etc.
- Transportation of goods with specific risks, such as hazardous, controlled temperature, etc.
- The need to perform customs clearance, as opposed to the less complex operations performed in the same economic-fiscal region.
- Risks of a military, commercial, political, financial, administrative nature, etc..

These situations increase the uncertainty of the success of the operations, so companies try to minimize the potential risks that may arise from them. This explains the preference of the selling company to agree on short-range rules, such as FCA or FOB, while the buyer tends to propose broader conditions, such as CPT, CIF or other rules in the same group.

On the other hand, the use of Group D Incoterms should be limited to transactions in which the seller has maximum assurance about fulfilling their obligations at the destination, with no special risks arising from it. Therefore, it is not advisable to agree on these terms unless there is sufficient experience in the destination market and it does not present complexities and uncertainties resulting from the factors described above.

1.3 Control and identification of the risks in containerized transport

Containerized transportation offers its greatest advantages in door-to-door operations, where the goods, once loaded into the container at the warehouse of origin, are not handled until they reach their destination. However, in this type of operation, there is a risk of damage or loss at a point in the transport that is difficult to identify, not attributable to a localized incident.

Thus, choosing Incoterms rules that clearly assign the risks of containerized transport to the appropriate party facilitates the attribution of responsibilities in the event of a loss or damage that is not localized. In this regard, the rules EXW, FCA, CPT, CIP, DAP, DPU, or DDP are particularly suitable. In other transactions (e.g., FOB, CFR, and CIF), depending on the design of the logistics chain, delivery and transfer of risk may occur at an intermediate point in the containerized voyage, which can lead to disputes in determining liability for non-localized loss or damage.

1.4   Risk minimization

Risk minimization can be viewed from two perspectives. According to the first, if a company has to choose between two rules that are equivalent in terms of costs, it should try to agree on the terms that minimize its risks. For example, in the case of a choice between CIP and DAP, the selling company should opt for CIP because it transfers the risks of origin to the buyer. The buyer, on the other hand, should prefer to operate under DAP conditions, where they assume no risk until the goods are delivered at the designated destination.

The second approach is to minimize risk by taking out the proper insurance to cover the transportation risk (see section 2 of this chapter).

1.5   Means of payment

Although means of payment are excluded from the scope of Incoterms, this aspect is particularly relevant when documentary means of payment are agreed. The most common is the so-called "documentary credit" or "letter of credit". Under these conditions, the transport documents play a fundamental role, together with the other documents required by the agreement. As a general rule, these means of payment require the presentation of the documents obtained by the selling company at the time of delivery of the goods, so that, after proving the fulfillment of its delivery obligation, it is entitled to collect the sale by means of the documentary credit.

In view of the usual practice of requiring a transport document (e.g. a Bill of Lading or BL shipped) in these payment methods, it may be advisable to apply the maritime rules of Group C (CFR or CIF), which guarantee that the selling company obtains such a document. In any case, this document must meet the requirements of the credit.

Conversely, documentary means of payment are not suitable with the rules included in Group D, which do not often fit their operational needs.

In the analysis of each rule (see chapters 4 and 5), the documents required by the different means of payment are specified.

1.6 Customs clearance and international taxation

One of the general criteria of the Incoterms rules is to assign the export clearance to the seller (except for EXW terms) and the import clearance to the buyer (except for DDP terms). In this sense, it is best to avoid the use of EXW or DDP unless the respective companies are highly confident—through market knowledge, experience, and legal certainty—that they can meet the stipulated obligations.

Under EXW conditions, by not clearing for export, the seller may not have the document proving the export of the goods for tax purposes (SAD or similar document supporting VAT-exempt invoicing).

Similarly, under DDP conditions, the seller may not be able to comply with some of the requirements for import clearance. In addition, this company may not be able to deduct the taxes paid for this purpose (e.g., VAT), while the purchasing company could. As a result, the seller would have to include the VAT in the price, which would make both companies less competitive. This problem can also arise in other transportation conditions, such as DAP customer's warehouse, when the seller tries to recover the taxes paid in the destination country for import-related services, such as inland transportation.

Another interesting aspect to consider is the VAT exemption on intra-community shipments (sales to another EU member country). Under the current European VAT system, such sales are exempt if two conditions are met: first, the buyer is a VAT-taxable company (with an intra-Community operator number), and second, the goods are transported from the seller's country to the buyer's country. This transport is evidenced, for example, by a CMR bill of lading signed by the consignee (when the goods have been received), a document that the seller obtains when selling under CPT, CIP, DAP, DPU or DDP conditions, but not under EXW or FCA. Therefore, from this point of view, the selling company may prefer the first Incoterms rules.

1.7 Minimization of the overall cost of the logistics chain

Reducing these costs is one of the fundamental principles of logistics management, along with time and the need to be agile and flexible in responding to the market as key factors in the design of supply chains. To achieve this objective, it is necessary for the parties to request transport quotations in accordance with the conditions established by the various Incoterms rules, on the basis of which different prices can be offered, in order to choose the one that minimizes the total cost of the product's logistics chain. This is the only way to maximize the chances of competing in the target market and to carry out new operations in the future.

In general, the best prices can be obtained on the basis of two parameters: proximity and volume of contracts. On the one hand, each company is able to obtain better prices in those negotiations and operations (transport, customs clearance, etc.) that are carried out in its vicinity, due to its better knowledge of its own market, regulations and customs, its relations with suppliers of different services, etc. On the other hand, the volume of contracts is one of the main variables that allows both the selling and the purchasing company to have access to better transport conditions and rates.

Therefore, if one of the parties is able to access better transportation costs, it is advisable to agree on sales conditions in accordance with this situation.

1.8   Control of the logistics chain and level of service provided

Every organization should strive to control as many segments of the supply chain as possible, unless there are factors that increase its complexity (discussed in Section 1.2 of this chapter). The benefits of doing so (i.e., selling on Group C or higher terms and buying on Group E or F terms) include the following:

- *Optimal design of the supply chain.*
- *Greater control of the logistics flow, pickup and delivery times, and resolution of incidents during transportation.* For example, if the freight forwarder is contracted by the selling company, it is easier to reassign the shipment to another consignee if the buyer does not accept the goods at the import port or simply refuses to pay.
- *Greater control over compliance with customs and tax regulations,* since they are handled by the freight forwarder, whose services usually include those of a customs agent (customs broker).
- *Greater control over obtaining the documents required by the letter of credit.* Since the selling company contracts and manages the transportation to the destination, it is foreseeable that it will have no problems in accessing the documents that are usually required, such as the bill of lading.

- *Greater control over taking out the appropriate transport insurance to cover its own risks (as a seller under Group D conditions) or those of the purchasing company.* Under CIP or CIF conditions, it can be the only means of collection in the event that the company can only pay for the purchase and sale if the insurance compensates it by means of the corresponding indemnity. The competitive advantage of this choice can be illustrated by the following example. Suppose we sell on FOB terms with documentary credit. The purchasing company, due to a complex economic situation, decides to reduce costs and not to take out insurance to cover its risks from the time of shipment on board. Once on board, we present to the bank the documents required by the credit but discrepancies arise, causing us to lose the payment guarantee from the issuing bank. During the voyage, the ship sinks and the goods are lost, and the buyer, who has not taken out insurance, will find it difficult to obtain compensation for this (note that it is very difficult to obtain compensation from the shipping company and, if this happens, it is very likely that it will not cover the real value of the goods), which, combined with their poor economic situation, may prevent him them from paying the seller (even if the latter has delivered). However, if sold on CIF terms, the seller would have provided insurance to cover the economic loss of the goods and would allow payment to the buyer and thus collection from them. Similarly, agreeing to a Group F rule allows the buyer to choose the most appropriate insurance to cover its risks up to destination.

- *Choosing transporters located in the same country as the seller or the buyer who hires them.* This factor favors the development of logistics services provided by national companies, which strengthens them, brings foreign currency into the country of origin of the shipment through the export of services, and makes an important contribution to their international presence. In the medium and long term, this strategy of cooperation between exporting companies and transporters in the same geographical and economic area allows for more efficient proximity logistics services, facilitating the expansion of production companies in international markets.

- *Adapting packaging to the means of transport.* By managing the logistics chain (or most of it), you can determine and use the optimal packaging for the chain.

- *Obtaining more competitive transportation quotes and services, and transportation costs that are less subject to operational incidents.* For example, under CIP or CIF conditions, the selling company knows in advance the exact cost to the destination, whereas when selling under FOB conditions, unforeseen costs may arise due to operational incidents (delay in loading on board, etc.), which it will have to bear and which it has not included in the price offered to the purchasing company.

All of these aspects provide greater control and security to operations, and at the same time represent an important competitive advantage that allows the company to adapt to the needs of its customers, who in many cases choose to work with suppliers capable of delivering products to their respective markets.

Thus, these factors are fundamental to a company's internationalization strategy, given their close relationship with optimizing and increasing the level of customer service. From the point of view of importing companies, they make it possible to purchase from suppliers with little or no capacity to manage the necessary steps in the logistics chain.

1.9   Company size and international experience

A large organization has sufficient resources to carry out the steps involved in controlling the supply chain, as explained in section 1.8. Therefore, as a selling company, it can choose to apply Group C or even D rules, or propose purchases under Group E or F conditions, since it has access to very competitive transport offers and the necessary management capacity to operate efficiently.

SMEs, on the other hand, are less likely to be able to cope with the consequences of a contract which gives them control over a large part of the logistics chain, especially if they lack experience in export trade.

Consequently, if they are a selling company, they should opt for short-distance transportation terms such as EXW, FCA or FOB. In the latter case, it is particularly important for SMEs to have easy access to information and training resources, which can be provided both by public administrations and by associations of transport operators.

1.10   Increased bargaining power or legal enforcement

Regardless of whether each party in an international sale evaluates the criteria presented and offers or requests prices under certain conditions based on different parameters (experience, situation, size, etc.), it is common for the agreed Incoterms rule to be the one proposed by the company, seller or buyer, with greater negotiating power.

We have mentioned that Incoterms rules cannot contravene laws, so their interaction must be considered when choosing them; for example, if the seller is not able to handle import customs clearance in the country of destination, the DDPs may be difficult or impossible to implement.

Another striking example is the case of Algeria, which has decreed that sales to this country must be made on an FOB or less (EXW and FCA) basis, in order to exert greater control over the operations and to force the contracting of Algerian transport, which will obviously be reflected in a greater inflow of foreign currency into its balance of payments (the ultimate objective of such a measure).

Consequently, one could ask whether there is an ideal or best Incoterms rule for all cases. The answer is that there is not, but rather that the choice is the result of an assessment of the characteristics of the transaction and the criteria used (company profile, mode of transport, origin and destination, customs requirements and the influence of international taxation, means of payment, etc.). In fact, a company should not apply the same rule to all its operations, but rather adapt it to the factors and criteria involved in each of them. Similarly, even if it is more convenient for the selling company to operate under short-term conditions (EXW, FCA or FOB) in order to minimize its obligations and risks, it should not fail to consider the possibility of being more competitive and offering its products with greater added value on the international market.

For this reason, it is usually advisable for the selling company to operate under Group C conditions (CFR, CIF, CPT and CIP) and for the purchasing company to agree on Group F conditions (FCA supplier's warehouse or FOB port of export). This will save costs by obtaining better transport prices (thanks to the increase in the volume of contracts) and by controlling the logistics chain, thus eliminating the risk of non-compliance with delivery deadlines (since it prevents the supplier company from inadequately managing the transport contract when the goods are received in the country of origin), as well as gaining access to the advantages and avoiding the disadvantages described in section 1.8 above. All this can give the company access to more favorable transportation offers and allow it to work with carriers that offer better services in terms of reliability, location, complementary services, etc. These factors allow the company to operate in international markets with greater guarantees of success. Finally, there must be effective coordination between the commercial and logistics departments in determining the optimal Incoterms rule. In many cases, the commercial department, in its logical eagerness to close contracts, may agree on inappropriate rules that later pose enormous challenges and complexities for the logistics department. Therefore, contracts must be evaluated by both parts of the organization before they are signed.

2 Criteria for the application of Incoterms rules to the sales contract

Here is some guidance on how to apply this rule to various aspects of your purchase agreement.

- **Correctly drafting the Incoterms rule**
  When drafting the rules, the three initials identifying each of them in English must be used, followed by the specific place to which they refer (port, terminal or warehouse). Note that although a new version does not repeal the previous ones, it is advisable to refer to the most recent version, as shown in the drafting examples.

  The place referred to in the Incoterms rule must be specified as precisely as possible, since it determines (almost always) two key aspects of the agreed terms: the place of delivery and transfer of risk, and the place where the selling company ceases to bear the costs of the logistics chain.

  If you do not want to draft an excessively long description of this place, a more general (and shorter) description can be made in the Incoterms rule, but the long description must be written in the sales contract. (For example, if "Cundinamarca" is indicated, it is agreed that the geographical point that specifies the rule is "Calle 2#18-93, Vía Mosquera, Parque Industrial San Jorge, Bodega 57, Mosquera, Cundinamarca. Colombia". If this is not the case, the wording should be as accurate as possible.

  Based on these recommendations, here are some examples of proper wording:

  - FCA APM Terminals Callao, Peru. Incoterms 2020.
  - FOB south pier, Escombreras dock, port of Cartagena, Murcia. Spain. Incoterms 2020.
  - CIF terminal 1, port of Valparaiso, Valparaiso. Chile. Incoterms 2020.

- **Do not use variants of Incoterms rules**
  Since these are non-standardized terms of sale, the variations of the Incoterms rules, in case of their use, require clarification and detailing of their scope and meaning in the sales contract. Thus, if conditions such as EXW loaded or DDP VAT unpaid, among others, are agreed, it is essential to clearly specify in the sales contract the implications of these variants with respect to the general rule from which they derive.

- **Indicate the agreed Incoterms rule on all sales documents**
  Regardless of the format and means of sending these documents (paper, electronic, etc.), it is highly advisable to indicate the agreed terms of sale in the various documents of sale and purchase: offer, purchase order or sales contract, invoice, list of contents, certificates, transport documents, customs documents, letters of credit, etc.

- **Informing the carrier of the agreed Incoterms rule and coordinating its obligations and costs with those of the transport company**
  The sales contract and the transportation contract are independent. However, they must be coordinated to achieve two basic objectives:

  - Adjust the obligations of the Incoterms rules to the transport contracts in the best possible way.
  - Prepare cost projections that will allow tenders or price comparisons to be made to ensure the profitability of the planned operations.

  It is therefore essential to inform the carrier of the agreed Incoterms rule and to request quotes that are as detailed and comprehensive as possible so that costs can be allocated between the parties according to the agreed terms and conditions and the total cost of the logistics chain can be optimized. This is particularly useful in certain scenarios, such as those described below:

  - **Under FOB terms,** the selling company must quote prices based on the costs it will incur up to the point of delivering the goods on board, which it can only do if it has obtained the calculation of these costs from the buyer's carrier (freight forwarder or shipping line), since it is the carrier to whom it must deliver the goods. If the selling company offers a very competitive price on the basis of a quotation from its carrier, it may later find that it has to bear higher costs than expected.

— **Under CIF conditions,** before confirming the transaction, the purchasing company must ask for quotations on the costs it will have to bear, so as to avoid unforeseen and disproportionate costs when the goods arrive at the port of destination (this is usually the case with consolidated shipments).

- **Specify the aspects that are not covered by the Incoterms rule and specify the rest as well as possible.**
It is particularly important to specify the following aspects, which are not regulated by the Incoterms:

— **The means of payment.** They can directly influence the choice of appropriate sales conditions.

— **The transfer of title and the law and jurisdiction applicable** to any disputes arising under the contract of sale. To the extent that the parties are free to agree, it is advisable to specify the applicable legal framework and the courts (or arbitration tribunal in the case of arbitration) to which they submit.

It is also highly advisable to specify in as much detail as possible other aspects governed by the agreed terms and conditions, such as:

— **Packaging and packing.** In general, the Incoterms require the seller to pack the goods in a manner suitable for transportation. It should be noted that the buyer may make specifications in this regard, and it is appropriate to specify the packaging considered suitable for the operation. This option becomes more relevant when the goods have specific characteristics such as hazardous (must comply with the relevant regulations), fragile, controlled temperature, etc.

— **Documentation and customs procedures.** The previous study, by both companies, of the export and import customs procedures that affect an operation is key to its development since lack of prior information often causes the paralysis of the logistic chain to stop at customs, resulting in high costs that usually lead to difficult-to-resolve disputes. For this reason, there is a need for cooperation and mutual exchange of information and assistance between the two parties.

- **Consider the time of delivery and transfer of risks and plan their insurance coverage under optimal conditions**

  Each Incoterms rule defines in detail the time of delivery and the transfer of risk, so that each party must be aware of the risks it assumes in the transportation of the goods. It is therefore advisable to consider taking out insurance to cover these risks and, in any case, to take out cover appropriate to the risk profile of the transaction, depending on the origin, destination, type of goods, mode of transport, etc.

  The only two rules that require insurance (CIP and CIF) establish a minimum coverage that may be insufficient (types A and C of the ICC clauses in the CIP and CIF rules, respectively), so it is advisable to study the advisability of extending the risks covered depending on the characteristics of the operation (for example, in CIP, extending to ICC "A" coverage the risks due to war and strike).

Chapter 7
Case studies

....

1 Pricing and risk allocation according to the Incoterms rule

Price is one of the most important tools in a company's commercial policy, and its calculation involves many factors (product positioning, corporate image, competitors' prices, commercial strategy in each market, etc.).

In any case, the price must be profitable, i.e. it must cover costs and generate profits. This chapter applies this criterion to the different Incoterms rules depending on the distribution of costs between the selling and purchasing companies, and proposes a series of guidelines for determining sales prices and comparing alternatives with regard to different purchase offers.

1.1 Determining selling prices according to the Incoterms rule

To determine the selling price that the selling company can offer, the starting point is the "cost price of the goods" known to the company. Then, if it is calculated on the basis of a percentage of the above amount, the "commercial margin" is added. This avoids applying this margin to ancillary costs (transport, customs, etc.) which are not part of the core business of the organization and which it is advisable to pass on to the same extent as they are borne by the selling company.

Then there are the "operational costs" (loading and unloading, transportation, customs clearance, documentation, insurance, etc.).

Table 7.1 shows a cost structure or scale for calculating the price according to the rule applicable to the operation. This is a general tool that must be adapted according to the characteristics of each operation, which determine variants of the calculation procedure described below.

Note that although the following structure reflects the use of all Incoterms rules, some of them are only applicable to certain types of operations.

1.2   Choosing the optimal purchasing alternative

In order to choose the optimal purchase alternative, it is necessary to compare the offers associated with different Incoterms rules presented by various suppliers. This procedure is also valid for choosing the best offer when comparing prices offered by the same supplier using different rules.

In all cases, it is advisable to adopt a single criterion on which to base the choice, which should consist of identifying the costs already included in each price (according to the Incoterms rule under which it is offered) and adding those that the purchasing company must assume according to that rule up to the same point in the logistics chain (e.g. its warehouse).

Table 7.2 makes it possible to compare the different prices offered and to determine the optimal purchase alternative, understood as the one that allows the purchasing company to receive the product at its facilities at the lowest total cost. In any case, the choice of the optimal Incoterms rule will result from the weighting between the best alternative according to this criterion and the application of other relevant criteria, such as risk minimization, the highest level of control of the logistics chain, the fastest delivery (shortest travel time or transit time), the global purchasing conditions with each supplier, etc.

1.3   Attribution of risk in the event of a loss during transport

When goods are lost or damaged during transport, it is essential to locate the incident in order to allocate the risks to the company concerned, depending on the point in the logistics chain where the transfer of risk has taken place, as stipulated by the agreed Incoterms rule.

Table for calculating sales prices according to the Incoterms Rule		
	Concept	**Remarks**
	Cost of goods manufactured price	This is the cost of manufacturing the merchandise or the cost price of a product ready for sale (in the case of distribution companies). To this price must be added, as appropriate, the following costs, as follows.
+	Container and packaging suitable for transport	
+	Specific export costs (certificate of origin, certificate of inspection, technical certificate, etc.)	
+	Other costs (credit insurance, exchange rate insurance, financial costs of deferment of payment, etc.)	
=	**Export manufacturing cost price**	
+	Commercial agency commission	This commission should not be made dependent on the Incoterms rule, for example, by paying it per unit sold or applying it (if calculated as a percentage of the price) to the manufacturing cost price for export. This discourages the commercial agency from agreeing to broad Incoterms rules to increase its commission.
=	**Base price for export**	Cost basis to which the markup is applicable (as a percentage of this basis or according to a given amount)
+	Commercial margin or profit expected to be obtained from the transaction	This margin can be calculated as a percentage of the manufacturing cost price for export or as an amount to be added to the manufacturing cost price for export.
=	**EXW facilities or premises of the selling company**	
+	Vehicle loading (truck, container, etc.)	This is normally an internal cost of the selling company and is therefore not reflected in the case studies.

Continued

Continued

	Concept	Remarks
+	Export clearance (if applicable)	
=	**FCA facilities or premises of the selling company**	
+	Inland transportation to the facilities of the transport operator contracted by the purchasing company.	
=	**FCA other location: carrier's warehouse**	
+	Inland transportation to the export terminal	Applicable in the event that FCA another location does not include transportation to the export terminal and this second transportation is required to that point.
=	**FCA other location: carrier's warehouse, port terminal, airport or railway station**	
+	Handling and expenses at the export terminal	In the case of a designated port terminal. These costs generally include: – Terminal handling charges (THC). In containerized transport, this concept includes the unloading of the arrival vehicle at the terminal, its transfer to the container yard and its handling at the terminal until it is loaded on board the container ship. – Port taxes or wharfage. – Security charges related to the application of the International Ship and Port Facility Security Code (ISPS). – Other terminal costs: storage, demurrage, weighing, etc.
=	**FAS port of shipment**	
+	Cargo on board the vessel	In containerized transport, this concept is included in the freight, while in bulk and general cargo transport it must be considered separately.

	Concept	Remarks
=	**FOB port of embarkation**	Although the Incoterms rules do not recommend its application to containerized transport, this rule is included here due to its widespread use in this type of transport.
+	Main transport	This amount corresponds to: - In maritime transport, with the cost of transport between ports (freight). In the specific case of containerized maritime transport, it is necessary to specify what freight includes with respect to loading and unloading (by container crane). In addition, it should be noted that the freight rate is increased by different surcharges: fuel surcharge (BAF), congestion surcharge (CS), currency adjustment (CAF), destination charge, canal crossing, piracy, high season, hazardousness (IMO), safety (ISPS surcharge), etc. - In road transport, with the cost of door-to-door transport and with the costs from the FCA warehouse of the selling company to the DAP warehouse of the customer company. - In air transportation, with the cost of transportation between the airports of origin and destination and their surcharges. - In rail transportation, with the cost of transportation between the origin and destination railway stations and its surcharges.
=	**CPT terminal/port of destination/ airport/railway station (= CFR port of import = DAP port of import)**	DAP parece diseñada para llegar hasta un punto interior más allá del puerto pero la P indica place y su polivalencia permite usarla en combinación con un puerto marítimo u otro tipo de terminal de llegada al país de destino
+	Premium for freight insurance	
=	**CIP terminal/port of destination/ airport/railway station (= CIF port of import)**	Although ICC does not recommend the use of CFR and CIF with containerized transport, their combination is very common, especially in the case of CIF.

Continued

Continued

Concept		Remarks
+	Unloading at the destination terminal	This cost must be added in DPU terminal arrival prices if it is not included by default in the contract of carriage. In such a case, the selling company cannot recover it from the buyer. In containerized maritime transport, the unloading of the container by container crane may (unless it is operated under liner conditions, which is the most common) not be included in the freight, but in the handling charges at destination, in which case it is borne by the selling company. Therefore, it is necessary that both companies request detailed quotations in order to clearly allocate the costs (the seller assumes the unloading and the buyer, the rest of the costs) and avoid duplicate payment of this or any other concept.
=	**DPU terminal/port of destination/ airport/railway station**	DPU appears to be designed to reach an inland point beyond the port but the P indicates place and its versatility allows it to be used in combination with a seaport or other type of arrival terminal in the destination country.
+	Terminal/port of destination/airport/ railway station costs (dockage, handling, fees, etc.)	
+	Inland transportation to the purchasing company's warehouse or other location (logistics platform, etc.)	
=	**DAP purchasing company's warehouse or other location (if applicable)**	
+	Unloading at destination	This unloading is usually carried out by the purchasing company's personnel and would involve an internal cost, so it will not be reflected in the case studies.
=	**DPU purchasing company's warehouse or other location (if applicable)**	

	Concept	Remarks
-	Unloading at destination	DDP does not include the download, so it must be subtracted.
+	Import clearance and payment of taxes (customs duties and other import taxes, such as VAT or equivalent, excise duties, etc.)	
=	**DDP Purchasing company's warehouse (or other location designated by the purchasing company)**	

Table 7.1. Cost structure for calculating sales prices according to the Incoterms rule.

Comparative table for the choice of the optimal purchase alternative				
Items already included or to be assumed by the acquiring company, in each case	Prices offered by supplier companies associated with different Incoterms rules (compare as many prices as necessary)			
	Price Incoterms rule 1	Price Incoterms rule 2	Price Incoterms rule 3	Price Incoterms rule 4
Cost 1	Already included/include (add)	Already included/include (add)	Already included/include (add)	Already included/include (add)
Cost 2	Already included/include (add)	Already included/include (add)	Already included/include (add))	Already included/include (add)
Cost 3	Already included/include (add)	Already included/include (add)	Already included/include (add)	Already included/include (add)
Cost 4	Already included/include (add)	Already included/include (add)	Already included/include (add)	Already included/include (add)
Overall cost per comparison	Overall cost 1	Overall cost 2	Overall cost 3	Overall cost 4

Table 7.2. The choice of the optimal purchasing alternative should be based on the comparison of offers associated with different Incoterms rules.

If the incident occurs after delivery of the goods, the risks are borne by the buyer, as these are transferred to it by the seller at the time of delivery. In this case, although it is not specified in the Incoterms, the buyer must pay for the purchase (although this may depend on the terms of the sale and transport contracts) and, if applicable, may claim against the carrier, provided that the latter is liable according to the agreed terms, the particularities of the incident and the applicable provisions of the transport contract.

On the other hand, if the incident occurs before delivery of the goods, the seller is considered to have failed to deliver and must therefore bear the risks and costs of the loss, which cannot be passed on to the buyer. In these circumstances, the buyer may have a claim against the carrier. Table 7.3 summarizes these two situations.

It should be noted that, despite the close relationship between the two contracts, the Incoterms rules govern the terms of the contract of sale, but not those of the contract of carriage, which is governed by the applicable legal framework and its own conditions. In any case, the party determined to have borne the risk and suffered the damage would be entitled to claim damages from the carrier, provided that its liability can be proven. This compensation is specified and limited in the rule applicable to each contract of carriage according to the mode of transport used.

The identification and allocation of risks by the agreed Incoterms rule is independent of whether they are covered by insurance and is the key to initiating the dispute resolution process.

In the event that the risks of transportation are covered by insurance of the seller, buyer or carrier companies, and that such insurance provides coverage for the damage that occurred, the way to resolve the property damage must be

Situation	Consequence
The claim occurs after delivery	The selling company has transferred the risks, so the purchasing company must pay for the sale and purchase.
The claim occurs before delivery	The selling company has not transferred the risks, so the purchasing company has no obligation to pay for the sale and purchase.

Table 7.3. The attribution of risk in the event of a loss depends on the point in the logistics chain where the loss occurred in relation to the delivery of the goods.

the subsequent claim to the insurance company to pay the compensation that corresponds to the company that assumed the risk at the time of the damage and has to face that loss.

2 Practical cases of price calculation and risk allocation

The following pages present four practical cases that illustrate the guidelines proposed in this chapter. They concern sales transactions carried out in different modes of transport. For ease of presentation, the wording of the Incoterms rules has been simplified and the prices have been expressed in values that can be assimilated, without exact translation, to the euro or the US dollar.

Each of the cases is divided into three phases:

1) Case presentation,
2) Price calculation or choice of the optimal purchase alternative, and
3) Determination of the party that must assume the risks for the various damages that may occur during transportation.

Transaction data

A company based in Requena, a city west of Valencia (Spain), needs to calculate the selling prices of a shipment of toys in response to a purchase request from a potential Mexican customer. The shipment is to be containerized and the final destination is Puebla, a city located 400 km west of the port of Veracruz, Mexico.

The container for the shipment measures 40 feet, and there are 26 boxes to be shipped in it, with the appropriate packaging and packing for the operation and its transportation. Each box has a unit weight of 250 kg and the shipment consists of a total of 600 toys.

The selling company estimates that it can apply a commercial margin of 8.5% to the manufacturing cost price for export, adding in each case, depending on the different Incoterms rules, the costs it must bear.

The purchasing company has requested prices under the following conditions:

- FCA Requena.
- FCA Terminal Marítima Valenciana.
- FOB port of Valencia.
- CPT port of Veracruz.
- CFR port of Veracruz.
- CIP port of Veracruz.
- CIF port of Veracruz.
- DAP Puebla.
- DDP Puebla.

After contacting several carriers and in accordance with the terms of the best offer (15-day transit time, direct service, and weekly frequency), the selling company obtained relevant data for calculating the selling prices, which are shown in Table 7.4.

Determining sales prices according to the Incoterms rule

By applying the cost structure, the following sales prices are obtained under the conditions required by the purchasing company.

Concept	Price (€/$)
Unit cost price per toy	15.60
Packaging suitable for export	150
Certificate of origin required for export	70
Transportation by container truck from Requena to the port of Valencia	229
Export clearance	40
Handling charges (THC) and demurrage at the Valencia terminal	175
Port taxes at the port of Valencia (T3 tariff)	70
Security surcharge at the port of Valencia (ISPS surcharge)	19
Formalization and shipment of bill of lading (BL)	100
Ocean freight from Valencia to Veracruz (including BAF and CAF)	1,840
Freight insurance premium to Veracruz (including BAF and CAF)	50
Transport insurance premium Handling charges (THC) and terminal stay in Veracruz	120
Security surcharge at the port of Veracruz (ISPS surcharge)	15
Port charges at the port of Veracruz	35
Overall import customs clearance costs (taxes included)	1,835
Transportation by container truck from Veracruz to Puebla	500

Table 7.4. Relevant data for the calculation of sales prices for a containerized export operation from Spain to Mexico.

- **FCA Requena**
  To determine the FCA price, start with the manufacturing cost price and add the costs listed in Table 7.5.

	Manufacturing cost price: 600 toys × 15.60	9,360
+	Packaging suitable for export	150
+	Certificate of origin required for export	70
=	Export manufacturing cost price	9,580
+	Commercial margin or profit expected to be obtained from the operation: 0.085 × 9,580	814
=	Base price for export	10,394
+	Export clearance	40
=	**FCA Requena**	**10,434**

Table 7.5. Calculation of the selling price under FCA Requena conditions.

- **FCA Terminal Marítima Valenciana**
  To calculate the price under terminal FCA conditions, transportation to that point must be added, as detailed in Table 7.6.

	FCA Requena	10,434
+	Transportation by container truck from Requena to Valencia port	229
=	FCA Valencia Maritime Terminal	10,663

Table 7.6. Calculation of the selling price under FCA Valencia Maritime Terminal conditions.

- **FOB port of Valencia**
  Under these conditions, the shipping line or freight forwarder usually collects the bill of lading and delivers it to the ocean carrier. If Group C rules are agreed, the selling company pays for and receives the bill of lading on a regular basis. However, it is very common to proceed in the same way under FOB conditions, even if the seller chooses to contract carriage

forward in accordance with the alternative proposed in the Incoterms. In any case, the selling company must ensure that the BL is obtained if it is an essential document for the collection of the sale. The costs are detailed in Table 7.7.

	FCA Valencia Maritime Terminal	10,663
+	Handling charges (THC) and terminal stay charges at Valencia terminal	175
+	Port taxes at the port of Valencia (T3 tariff)	70
+	Surcharge for security at the port of Valencia (ISPS surcharge)	19
+	Formalization and shipment of the BL	100
=	FOB port of Valencia	11,027

Table 7.7. Calculation of the selling price under FOB conditions at the port of Valencia.

- **CPT port of Veracruz**
  The change from group F to group C conditions obliges the selling company to contract and pay for the main transportation, as detailed in table 7.8.

	FOB port of Valencia	11,027
+	Ocean freight from Valencia to Veracruz (including BAF and CAF)	1,840
=	CPT port of Veracruz	12,867

Table 7.8. Calculation of sales price under CPT conditions at the port of Veracruz.

- **CFR port of Veracruz**
  Prices under CPT and CFR conditions are similar. The main difference lies in the time of delivery when combined with container transport: in CPT conditions, delivery takes place when the goods are placed at the disposal of the first transport company (in this case, in Requena), whereas in CFR conditions, delivery takes place when the goods are loaded on board the vessel (in the port of Valencia). This circumstance may result, under CFR conditions, in a difference in the cost of the optional insurance

contracted by the selling company to cover its risks until the container is loaded (cost difference not included in the present calculation shown in Table 7.9).

	CPT port of Veracruz	12,867
=	CFR port of Veracruz	12,867

Table 7.9. Calculation of sales price under CFR conditions at the port of Veracruz.

- **CIP port of Veracruz**
  With respect to the CPT rule, CIP obliges the selling company to contract and assume a transport insurance covering the buyer's risks under the stipulated conditions, as shown in table 7.10.

	CPT port of Veracruz	12,867
+	Transportation insurance premium	50
=	CIP port of Veracruz	12,917

Table 7.10. Calculation of sales price under CIP conditions at the port of Veracruz.

- **CIF port of Veracruz**
  Although in this case they have been considered similar, as can be seen in Table 7.11, the prices under CIP and CIF conditions may vary for the same reasons as those given for the calculation of the sales price under CFR conditions at the port of Veracruz. This is due to the fact that for CIF terms, the insurance must cover the risks from the moment of delivery on the vessel (at the first port of shipment, if there are several for transshipment), and for CIP terms, from Requena, which may increase the premium.

	CIP port of Veracruz	12,917
=	CIF port of Veracruz	12,917

Table 7.11. Calculation of sales price under CIF conditions at the port of Veracruz.

- **DAP Puebla**

  With respect to CIP and CIF rules, DAP Puebla obliges the seller to pay the costs at the port terminal of destination and transportation to the buyer's warehouse. In this case, we assume that the seller, in order to cover their risks, will choose the same insurance under CIP conditions to insure those of the buyer (otherwise these costs can be deducted), which may now include subsequent trips to the port of destination. The costs are shown in Table 7.12.

	CIP/CIF port of Veracruz	12,917
+	Handling charges (THC) and Veracruz terminal stay costs	120
+	Surcharge for security at the port of Veracruz (ISPS surcharge)	15
+	Port fees at the port of Veracruz	35
+	Container truck transportation from Veracruz to Puebla	500
=	DAP Puebla	13,587

Table 7.12. Calculation of sales price under Puebla WTP conditions.

- **DDP Puebla**

  The DDP rule requires the selling company to manage and bear the cost of import clearance, as shown in Table 7.13.

	DAP Puebla	13,587
+	Overall import customs clearance costs (including taxes)	1,835
=	DDP Puebla	15,422

Table 7.13. Calculation of sales price under Puebla PDO conditions.

Assigning risks in the event of a claim

The Incoterms rules determine which party bears the risk of loss or damage to the goods in the event of an incident during transportation at each of these five points in the logistics chain:

a) During the road transport between Requena and the terminal of the port of Valencia.
b) During the stay and handling of the container at the Valencia terminal.
c) During the sea transport between the ports.
d) During the stay and handling of the container at the terminal in Veracruz.
e) During the road transport between the port of Veracruz and the warehouse in Puebla.

Table 7.14 shows the allocation of risk in the event of a loss at each of the points described, depending on whether it is borne by the seller or the buyer. Note that if the loss occurs in situation b), under FOB terms, the seller does not deliver the goods until the container is loaded on board the vessel at the port of export, whereas under FCA terms at the Valencia terminal, delivery takes place when the truck arrives at the container terminal, without having to unload.

Under CPT conditions, in relation to situations a) and b), it should be noted that the Incoterms rule provides for delivery and transfer of risk when the goods are placed at the disposal of the first carrier in the case of multiple carriers, as occurs in multimodal container transportation.

Location of loss	Incoterms rules								
	FCA Requena	FCA Valencia	FOB Valencia	CPT Veracruz	CFR Veracruz	CIP Veracruz	CIF Veracruz	DAP Puebla	DDP Puebla
a)	○	●	●	○	●	○	●	●	●
b)	○	○	●	○	●	○	●	●	●
c)	○	○	○	○	○	○	○	●	●
d)	○	○	○	○	○	○	○	●	●
e)	○	○	○	○	○	○	○	●	●

● Selling company.
○ Purchasing company.

Table 7.14. Attribution of risks in the event of a loss at different points in the logistics chain.

Therefore, delivery occurs when the goods are placed at the disposal of the first carrier, the road carrier, in the warehouse of the selling company (in this case, in Requena). On the other hand, under CFR conditions, delivery does not take place until the container is loaded on board the ship at the port of export. The same difference can be seen when comparing the CIP and CIF alternatives.

Case 2
Choosing the optimal purchasing alternative: containerized imports from Chile to Spain

Transaction data

A food distribution company located in Manresa, a city northwest of Barcelona (Spain), has asked a company based in Santiago de Chile for a proposal to buy a shipment of canned meat with different prices associated with different Incoterms rules. The Spanish company has to analyze the prices offered by the supplier company and determine the optimal alternative for the agreement of the operation.

Using the criterion of optimizing the costs of the logistic chain, the sales conditions are chosen that allow the shipment of tinned meat to be received in the Spanish warehouse at the lowest cost. The shipment consists of 400 trays, each containing 10 cans of canned meat, ready to be marketed in the Spanish market. The entire shipment can be transported in a 40-foot container. Table 7.15 shows the prices offered by the Chilean supplier under different selling conditions.

In order to choose the optimal purchasing alternative, the Spanish company

FCA Santiago de Chile	43,890
FCA San Antonio port container terminal	44,215
FOB port of San Antonio	44,832
CIF port of Barcelona	47,638
DAP Manresa	48,117

Table 7.15. Prices offered in a containerized import operation from Chile to Spain.

Transportation of container from Santiago de Chile to the port of San Antonio	462
Handling charges (THC) and other costs (ISPS security surcharge) at San Antonio terminal	110
Export clearance	40
Ocean freight from San Antonio to Barcelona (including BAF, CAF, Panama Canal passage, security, etc.)	2,575
Formalization and shipment of bill of lading (BL)	100
Transport insurance	175
Handling charges (THC) at Barcelona port	200
Security surcharge at Barcelona port (ISPS surcharge)	20
Port charges at Barcelona (T3 tariff)	70
Import clearance management	95
Inland transport (carriage) by road from Barcelona to Manresa	299

Table 7.16. Relevant data for the transport quotation in a containerized import operation from Chile to Spain.

has requested transportation quotes from several freight forwarders. In the end, it decided to load the container at the port of San Antonio (near Santiago de Chile) and ship it to the port of Barcelona on a weekly direct service with a transit time of 42 days. Table 7.16 shows the relevant data for the transportation quote.

Choosing the optimal purchasing alternative

The following is a breakdown of the sourcing alternatives for comparison to determine the terms that will allow the purchasing company to receive the goods at its facilities at the lowest total cost.

Table 7.17 shows the prices offered by the supplier company and the cost to the importer in each case. It should be noted that customs clearance is not considered in the selection of the optimal purchase alternative, since under all sales conditions the seller company clears the export, and the buyer clears the import.

On the other hand, in order to know the total cost, the import clearance must be considered. Comparing the different alternatives offered by the selling company, it can be seen that the optimal terms of sale for the buyer correspond to the Incoterms FCA San Antonio terminal rule. This implies that this company will have to take into account, in addition to the price offered by the Chilean company, the costs not included in it, as shown in Table 7.17.

Comparative table for the choice of the optimal purchase					
Items already included or to be assumed by the acquiring company, in each case	FCA Santiago de Chile 43,890	FCA San Antonio terminal 44,215	FOB port of San Antonio 44,832	CIF port of Barcelona 47,638	DAP Manresa 48,117
Ground transportation from Santiago de Chile to San Antonio	462	Already included	Already included	Already included	Already included
Handling charges (THC) at San Antonio terminal	110	110	Already included	Already included	Already included
Sea freight	2,575	2,575	2,575	Already included	Already included
Formalization and shipment of BL	100	100	Already included	Already included	Already included
Transport insurance	175	175	175	Already included	Already included
Handling charges (THC) at the port of Barcelona	200	200	200	200	Already included
Security surcharge at the port of Barcelona	20	20	20	20	Already included
Port taxes in Barcelona (T3 tariff)	70	70	70	70	Already included
Inland road transport from Barcelona to Manresa	299	299	299	299	Already included
Overall cost compared	47,901	47,764	48,171	48,227	48,117

Table 7.17. Comparative table of overall purchase costs
for the choice of the optimal Incoterms rule.

Finally, if the overall comparison cost shown in the table (47,764) is added to the import clearance management (95) and the import taxes (assumed to be 1,230), the final cost that the purchasing company must assume to receive the goods in its facilities is 49,089.

Assigning risks in the event of a claim

Depending on the different conditions offered, it is then determined which party bears the risk of loss or damage to the goods in the event of an incident occurring during transport at each of these five points in the logistics chain:

a) In ground transport from Santiago de Chile to the port of San Antonio.
b) During handling and stay at the San Antonio port terminal.
c) During maritime transport between San Antonio and Barcelona.
d) During handling and stay at the Barcelona port terminal.
e) During overland transport from Barcelona to Manresa.

Table 7.18 shows the attribution of the risks in the event of a loss at each of the described points, according to whether they should be assumed by the selling or the purchasing company.

Location of loss	FCA Santiago de Chile	FCA San Antonio	FOB San Antonio	CIF Barcelona	DAP Manresa
a)	○	●	●	●	●
b)	○	○	●	●	●
c)	○	○	○	○	●
d)	○	○	○	○	●
e)	○	○	○	○	●

● Selling company.
○ Purchasing company.

Table 7.18. Attribution of risks in the event of a loss at different points in the logistics chain.

Transaction data

A flower exporting company located in Puerto Lumbreras (Murcia, southeastern Spain) has established commercial contact with a potential customer, an importing company located in Mosquera, near Bogota (Colombia).

Unit cost price per cutting	3.30
Packaging suitable for export	70
Certificates of origin and phytosanitary certificates required for export	50
Trade margin applicable to the manufacturing cost price for exports	35 %
Road transport from the export company's warehouse to the cargo terminal at Barcelona airport	100
Export clearance	40
Handling charges at Barcelona airport	28
Airport taxes at Barcelona airport	17
Air freight from Barcelona to Bogota	250
Fuel surcharge applicable to freight	304
Air transportation insurance premium	43
Handling charges at Bogota airport	24
Airport taxes at Bogota airport	15
Import clearance and taxes	620
Ground transportation (hauling) from Bogota to Mosquera	92

Table 7.19. Relevant data for the calculation of sales prices
for an export operation from Spain to Colom-bia.

The company needs to calculate the selling prices for the shipment of a consignment of cut flowers, consisting of 1,000 cuttings, to be transported from its facilities by road to Barcelona airport and from there by air to Bogota airport. The operation ends with a final road transport to Mosquera. Table 7.19 provides the relevant data for the calculation of selling prices.

Prices should be calculated using the following selling conditions:

- FCA Puerto Lumbreras warehouse.
- FCA cargo terminal at Barcelona airport.
- CPT cargo terminal at Bogota airport.
- CIP cargo terminal at Bogota airport.
- DAP Mosquera warehouse.
- DDP Mosquera warehouse.

Determining sales prices according to the Incoterms rule

By the application of the proposed cost structure, the following sales prices will be obtained under the required terms and conditions.

- **FCA Puerto Lumbreras warehouse**
  To determine the price under SCF conditions, start from the manufacturing cost price and add the costs detailed in Table 7.20.

	Manufacturing cost price: 1,000 cuttings × 3.30	3,300
+	Packaging suitable for export	70
+	Certificates of origin and phytosanitary certificates required for export.	50
=	Export manufacturing cost price	3,420
+	Commercial margin: 0.35 × 3,420	1,197
+	Export clearance	40
=	FCA Puerto Lumbreras warehouse	4,657

Table 7.20. Calculation of the selling price under FCA conditions in the Puerto Lumbreras warehouse.

- **FCA Barcelona airport cargo terminal**
To calculate the price under terminal FCA conditions, transportation to that point must be added, as can be seen in Table 7.21.

	FCA Puerto Lumbreras warehouse	4,657
+	Road transport from the export company's warehouse to the cargo terminal at Barcelona airport	100
=	FCA Barcelona airport cargo terminal	4,757

Table 7.21. Calculation of the selling price under FCA conditions at Barcelona airport cargo terminal.

- **CPT Bogota airport cargo terminal**
The change from FCA terminal to CPT conditions obliges the selling company to bear the costs at the terminal and the main transportation to the destination, as shown in Table 7.22.

	FCA cargo terminal at Barcelona airport	4,757
+	Handling charges at Barcelona airport	28
+	Airport taxes at Barcelona Airport (E2/GTC)	17
+	Air freight from Barcelona to Bogota	250
+	Fuel surcharge applicable to freight	304
=	CPT cargo terminal at Bogota airport	5,356

Table 7.22. Calculation of the selling price under CPT conditions at the Bogotá airport cargo terminal.

- **CIP Bogota airport cargo terminal**
In accordance with the CPT rule, the CIP requires the selling company to take out and maintain transport insurance covering the buyer's risks under the conditions set out in Table 7.23.

	CPT cargo terminal at Bogota airport	5,356
+	Air transportation insurance premium	43
=	CIP cargo terminal at Bogota airport	5,399

Table 7.23. Calculation of the selling price under CIP conditions
at the Bogotá airport cargo terminal.

- **DAP Mosquera warehouse**
  According to the CIP rule, the DAP obliges the selling company to bear the costs at the destination airport terminal and transportation to the buyer's warehouse, as shown in Table 7.24. In this case, we assume that the seller, in order to cover its risks, chooses the same insurance that it has taken out under CIP conditions to cover those of the buyer. Otherwise, these costs can be deducted.

	CIP cargo terminal at Bogota airport	5,399
+	Handling charges at Bogota airport	24
+	Airport taxes at Bogota airport	15
+	Ground transportation (hauling) from Bogota to Mosquera	92
=	DAP Mosquera warehouse	5,530

Table 7.24. Calculation of the selling price under WTP conditions in the Mosquera warehouse.

- **DDP Mosquera warehouse**
  The DDP rule requires the selling company to manage and bear the cost of import clearance, as shown in Table 7.25.

	DAP Mosquera warehouse	5,530
+	Import clearance and taxes	620
=	DDP Mosquera warehouse	6,150

Table 7.25. Calculation of sales price under DDP conditions Mosquera warehouse.

Assigning risks in the event of a claim

Below is a discussion of which party bears the risk of loss or damage to goods during transportation at each of the following five points in the logistics chain, depending on the terms offered:

a) During transportation between Puerto Lumbreras and the Barcelona airport terminal.
b) During the stay and handling of the shipment at the Barcelona airport terminal.
c) During air transportation.
d) During the stay and handling of the shipment at the Bogotá airport terminal.
e) During road transportation between Bogotá Airport and Mosquera.

Table 7.26 shows the allocation of risks in the event of a loss in each of the described points, depending on whether they are to be assumed by the selling or the purchasing company.

Location of loss	FCA Puerto Lumbreras	FCA Barcelona	CPT Bogotá	CIP Bogotá	DAP Mosquera	DDP Mosquera
a)	Purchasing	Selling	Purchasing	Purchasing	Selling	Selling
b)	Purchasing	Purchasing	Purchasing	Purchasing	Selling	Selling
c)	Purchasing	Purchasing	Purchasing	Purchasing	Selling	Selling
d)	Purchasing	Purchasing	Purchasing	Purchasing	Selling	Selling
e)	Purchasing	Purchasing	Purchasing	Purchasing	Selling	Selling

● Selling company.
○ Purchasing company.

Table 7.26. Attribution of risks in the event of a loss at different points in the logistics chain.

Transaction data

A Spanish company located in Seville is preparing to calculate the sales prices to be applied to a shipment of chrome-plated crystal chandeliers to a Moroccan company located in Rabat. The company operates in this market through a commercial agent. The importing company has requested prices under the following conditions:

- FCA warehouse of the selling company in Seville.
- CPT Rabat.
- CIP Rabat.
- DAP Rabat.
- DDP Rabat.

Unit cost price per lamp	675
Packaging suitable for export	289
Commercial agency commission applicable to the manufacturing cost price for export	2 %
Commercial margin or profit expected to be obtained from the transaction	3,100
Certificate of origin required for export	60
Export clearance	30
International road transport from Seville to Rabat	1,800
Premium for international road transportation insurance	73
Import clearance and taxes	934

Table 7.27. Relevant data for the calculation of sales prices
for an export operation from Spain to Moroc-co.

The order, consisting of 30 chrome-plated glass lamps, can be transported by road in a trailer as a full truckload.

Table 7.27 shows the data required to calculate selling prices.

Determining sales prices according to the Incoterms rule

By applying the cost structure, the following sales prices are obtained under the required conditions.

- **FCA seller's warehouse in Seville**
  To determine the price under FCA conditions, start with the manufacturing cost price and add the costs listed in Table 7.28.

	Manufacturing cost price:30 lamps × 675	20,250
+	Packaging suitable for export	289
+	Certificate of origin required for export	60
=	Export manufacturing cost price	20,599
+	Commercial agency commission: 0.02 × 20,599	412
=	Base price for export	21,011
+	Commercial margin or profit expected to be obtained from the transaction	3,100
+	Export clearance	30
=	FCA warehouse of the selling company in Seville	24,141

Table 7.28. Calculation of the selling price under FCA conditions
warehouse of the selling company in Seville.

- **CPT Rabat**
  The change from FCA warehouse to CPT destination conditions requires the selling company to bear the cost of the main transportation to the destination, as shown in Table 7.29.

	FCA warehouse of the selling company in Seville	24,141
+	International road transport from Seville to Rabat	1,800
=	CPT Rabat	25,941

Table 7.29. Calculation of the selling price under CPT Rabat conditions.

- **CIP Rabat**

  With respect to the CPT rule, the CIP requires the selling company to purchase and assume transportation insurance covering the buyer's risks under the conditions specified, as shown in Table 7.30.

	CPT Rabat	25,941
+	Premium for international road transportation insurance	73
=	CIP Rabat	26,014

Table 7.30. Calculation of sales price under CIP Rabat conditions.

- **DAP Rabat**

  The selling company may decide not to take out insurance, in which case the premium can be deducted from the CIP price. Assuming that under DAP conditions the selling company decides to take out the same insurance to cover its risks at the same cost as it previously took out under CIP conditions to cover the buyer's risks, the result is as shown in Table 7.31.

	CIP Rabat	26,014
=	DAP Rabat	26,014

Table 7.31. Calculation of sales price under DAP Rabat conditions.

- **DDP Rabat**

  The DDP rule requires the selling company to manage and bear the cost of import clearance, as shown in Table 7.32.

	DAP Rabat	26,014
+	Import clearance and taxes	934
=	DDP Rabat	26,948

Table 7.32. Calculation of the selling price under DDP Rabat conditions.

Assigning risks in the event of a claim

We will now determine which party bears the risk of loss or damage to the goods in the event of an accident during road transport from Seville to Rabat, depending on the different conditions offered. Table 7.33 shows the allocation of risks according to whether they are borne by the seller or the buyer.

Location of loss	FCA Sevilla	CPT Rabat	CIP Rabat	DAP Rabat	DDP Rabat
In road transport from Seville to Rabat	○	○	○	●	●

● Selling company.
○ Purchasing company.

Table 7.33. Attribution of risks in the event of a claim in road transport from Seville to Rabat.

Tests on knowledge and application of the Incoterms rules

On the following pages you will find four quizzes to test your knowledge of the correct and effective application of the Incoterms 2020 rules. At the end, you will find the solutions for self-assessment.

Choose the correct answer (or the incorrect answer, if given) from the options presented in each of the following questions.

1. International trade offers:

   a) Only great benefits without any risk.
   b) High risks with no benefits.
   c) Low benefits and high risks.
   d) Great benefits, but also risks that must be minimized.

2. International sales transactions involve greater risks and complexity than domestic transactions for the following reasons, among others (mark the incorrect one):

   a) Different regulations of the sales contract in each country.
   b) More complex and extensive transportation within the logistics chain.
   c) Procedures and documentation related to export and import customs clearance.
   d) Greater trust between the seller and the buyer regarding the fulfillment of each party's main obligations related to the sale and purchase: delivery of the agreed product and payment of the price.

3. The function of Incoterms is:

   a) To determine the means of payment to be used in international sales.
   b) By applying them to a sales contract, to automatically assign to the parties (seller and buyer) some of the main obligations related to the performance of such contract.

   c) By applying them to a sales contract, to automatically assign to the parties (seller and buyer) absolutely all the obligations related to the performance of such contract.

   d) To regulate the obligations of the seller and the buyer in the sales contract even beyond the provisions of the laws and regulations in force.

4. The obligations specified by the Incoterms are, inter alia, the following (mark the incorrect one)

   a) The term and means of collection/payment of the sale/purchase.

   b) The transportation contract (which party, seller and buyer, and to what extent).

   c) The delivery of the goods and the transfer of risk from the seller to the buyer with regard to damage to the goods caused during transportation.

   d) The party responsible for managing the export or import customs clearance (administration, documents to be presented, customs taxes, etc.).

5. Among the most important aspects of the contract of sale, which are not regulated by the Incoterms, we can mention the following (mark the incorrect one)

   a) The quality and technical characteristics of the goods to be purchased and sold.

   b) The term and means of collection/payment of the purchase and sale.

   c) The contract of transportation (which part each, seller and buyer, and to what extent).

   d) The law for the settlement of disputes, the competent jurisdiction and the transfer of ownership.

6. The publication of Incoterms 2020 sets out the obligations of the parties (seller and buyer) to the contract of sale in an outline format, in which the obligations are arranged in the order of the seller's obligations versus the buyer's obligations in relation to:

   a) Eight key aspects (obligations) of the sale and purchase agreement.

   b) Twelve key aspects (obligations) of the sale and purchase agreement.

   c) Ten key aspects (obligations) of the sale contract.

   d) Six key aspects (obligations) of the sale and purchase agreement.

7. In accordance with the relationship between the Incoterms rules and the conclusion and management of transportation of goods (indicate the incorrect one):

   a) The contract of transportation is independent from the contract of sale (although it is closely related to it), and therefore it is closely related to the Incoterms.
   b) They are not related, and the contract of carriage is outside the scope of Incoterms.
   c) The contract of carriage is subject to the terms and conditions agreed therein (between the shipper and the carrier) and to the relevant legal framework depending on the means of transport used.
   d) Incoterms have a decisive influence on the conclusion and performance of the contract of carriage.

8. The relationship between the contract of sale and the contract of carriage is very close and is evidenced in many aspects, such as (point out the incorrect one):

   a) The bill of lading indicates the conditions of transfer of ownership of the goods, which are also regulated by the Incoterms.
   b) The Incoterms themselves specify the obligations and costs of the seller and the buyer in relation to the carriage of the goods and the allocation of their risks in the event of loss.
   c) The Incoterms themselves refer to certain documents or contracts of carriage as proof of delivery and receipt of the goods.
   d) Waybills (formalization of the contract of carriage) usually reflect the Incoterms rule agreed in the transaction.

9. Regarding the relationship between the Incoterms agreed in the contract of sale and purchase and the contract of insurance of the goods during transportation, we can state the following (point out the incorrect one)

   a) Obligations A2/B2, A3/B3, A4/B4 and A5/B5 (delivery and receipt, transfer of risk, transportation and insurance) should be considered first.
   b) Insurance is compulsory for the seller only in the CIP and CIF rules (to cover the risks of the buyer and under certain conditions).

c) For Incoterms other than CIP or CIF, there is no obligation to take out insurance, which does not mean that it is not advisable to take out insurance, or at least to explore the possibility of doing so.

d) No Incoterms rule states anything about the obligations of the seller or the buyer in relation to taking out insurance for the carriage of the goods.

10. With regard to the conclusion of transport insurance, it is worth mentioning some aspects such as the following (mark the incorrect one):

a) It is common for carriers to offer shippers the possibility of taking out transportation insurance in their offers.

b) In no case do carriers offer shippers the possibility of taking out transportation insurance.

c) The insurance contract and the transport contract are independent of each other, so that a transport operator responsible for a damage, according to the terms of the contract and the applicable legal framework, cannot refuse to pay the corresponding compensation on the grounds that its insurance company refuses to pay it.

d) The insurance contract is a very complex formal contract, and it is therefore recommended that all aspects of the contract be examined in detail before signing it.

11. It is advisable to consider taking out transport insurance for various reasons, such as the following (mark the incorrect one)

a) The carrier responsible for the loss is unwilling (or unable) to pay compensation. In this case, the insurance would pay the compensation and claim it from the carrier.

b) The value of the goods exceeds the limit of the carrier's indemnity stipulated in the agreement or regulation governing the contract of carriage, and through the insurance we can agree that the sum insured covers the full value of the goods.

c) The value of the goods is always covered by the carrier's limit of indemnity stipulated in the agreement or regulation governing the contract of carriage.

d) The damage is due to a cause that exonerates the carrier from liability (e.g. force majeure such as floods, etc.), and if the insurance covers such a cause, we may be indemnified.

12. The relationship between the customs regulations and the Incoterms is specified in the following obligations regulated in the latter (mark the incorrect one):

    a) A7, Export/Import Clearance: the Seller's obligations with respect to these formalities (including, where applicable, the obligation to assist the Buyer and to provide any documents that may be required for customs clearance).
    b) A1/B1, general obligations: delivery of the goods for the seller and payment of the price for the buyer.
    c) B7, Export/Import Clearance: the buyer's obligations with respect to these formalities (including, where applicable, assisting the seller and providing any documents may be required for customs clearance).
    d) A9/B9, Cost Sharing: indicates who will bear the cost of customs clearance.

13. With regard to the parties obliged to perform customs clearance, the Incoterms rules indicate that:

    a) In all rules, the seller always clears the export shipment.
    b) In all rules, the buyer always clears the import shipment.
    c) Both export and import shipments are always handled and paid for by the exporting company.
    d) The seller clears for export (except in EXW) and the buyer clears for import (except in DDP).

14. Regarding the relationship between the Incoterms rules and the means of payment of the sale and purchase, we can indicate that (point out the incorrect one):

    a) Incoterms rules do not directly specify the means of payment/collection of the transaction.
    b) Although the rules do not indicate the means of payment/collection to be used in the sale/purchase, there is a very close relationship between them, especially in the case of the use of documentary means of payment.
    c) The Incoterms rule specifically states the means of payment/collection to be used in the sale/purchase transaction.

d) The relationship between the Incoterms rules and the documentary credit is based precisely on the fact that there should be correspondence and synchronization between the documents required by the documentary credit, the agreed Incoterms rule and the (documentary) performance of the seller's main obligation, i.e. the delivery of the goods sold.

15. Regarding the relationship between the Incoterms rules and the documentary credit, we can state that (point out the incorrect one):

a) The relationship is based on the fact that there should be correspondence and synchronization between the documents required in the documentary credit, the agreed Incoterms rule and the (documentary) performance of the seller's main obligation, i.e. the delivery of the goods sold.

b) When negotiating the terms and documents of the letter of credit to be presented by the exporting company, the document that the exporting company receives when it delivers the goods should be required, since at that moment it has fulfilled its main obligation under the sales contract and should therefore be entitled to collect the letter of credit by means of the said transport document.

c) There is no relationship whatsoever and the documents required in the letter of credit as proof of delivery of the goods are irrelevant with respect to the Incoterms rule agreed in the sale and purchase.

d) It is essential that the parties agree on the documentation to be presented in the letter of credit and its requirements. This documentation must be necessary for the importing company to have access to the goods and to clear them for import, and may be for various reasons: delivery, import clearance and trade security.

Choose the correct answer (or the incorrect answer, if specified) from the options presented in each of the following questions.

1. The multimodal Incoterms rules are:

   a) EXW, FCA, FOB, CIF, and DAP.
   b) EXW, FCA, CPT, CIP, DAP, DPU, and DDP.
   c) EXW, FCA, FAS, FOB, CPT, CFR, CIP, CIF, DAT, DAP, and DDP.
   d) FAS, FOB, CFR, and CIF.

2. In the seven multimodal Incoterms rules:

   a) Export and import clearance by the seller.
   b) Export and import clearance by the buyer.
   c) Export clearance by the buyer and import clearance by the seller.
   d) Export clearance by the seller and import clearance by the buyer, except for EXW (export clearance by the buyer) and DDP (import clearance by the seller).

3. The Incoterms rule EXW:

   a) The seller delivers the goods by placing them at the disposal of the buyer at the seller's premises or elsewhere, without loading them onto the means of transport contracted for and sent by the buyer or clearing them for export (if required).
   b) The seller shall deliver the goods cleared for export to the carrier (trucking company, freight forwarder, international logistics company, etc.) designated by the buyer, who shall collect the goods at the agreed place specified in the rule.

c) The seller arranges and pays for transportation to the buyer's warehouse.

d) The seller controls most of the logistics chain and provides the buyer with a high level of service in the delivery of the goods.

4. With Incoterms FCA rule:

a) The buyer clears the goods for export.

b) The seller delivers the goods cleared for export to the carrier designated by the buyer (trucking company, freight forwarder, international logistics operator, etc.), who will collect the goods at the place agreed and specified in the rule.

c) The seller pays for the main transport to the buyer's warehouse.

d) The Seller clears for import.

5. In the Incoterms FCA rule:

a) The seller never bears transportation costs, regardless of the geographical location, accompanying and specified by the Incoterms rule.

b) The buyer pays for export clearance if customs clearance is required in the country of origin.

c) The seller clears the import if customs clearance is required in the country of destination.

d) In case of FCA at the Seller's premises, the Seller shall not bear the transport costs and formalities, but in case of FCA at another place, the Seller shall bear the costs, formalities and risks of transporting the goods to that place.

6. In the FCA Incoterms rule:

a) Neither party is obliged to take out transport insurance, although, in any case, it would be in the buyer's interest to take out insurance to cover the risks from the place of delivery to the place of destination. In the case of FCA to another place, the seller also assumes the risk up to that place and may therefore choose to insure it.

b) The buyer is obliged to take out insurance to cover the risks of transport.

c) The seller is obliged to take out insurance to cover the risks of transport.

d) The seller has a high degree of control over the logistics chain up to the place of destination.

7. Regarding the Incoterms CPT rule:

   a) The seller must contract and pay for transportation to the place specified in the rule and deliver the goods for the purpose of passing the risk to the buyer when the goods arrive at that place.
   b) The seller must contract and pay for transportation to the place specified in the rule, but delivers, for the purpose of passing the risk to the buyer, when the goods are placed at the disposal of the carrier contracted by the seller. In the case of multimodal transportation involving more than one carrier, and unless the parties (seller and buyer) have agreed otherwise, delivery is made when the goods are placed at the disposal of the first carrier.
   c) The seller is obliged to take out transport insurance.
   d) The buyer is obliged to clear the goods for export if this is required in the country of export.

8. Regarding the Incoterms CPT rule:

   a) Neither party is obliged to take out transport insurance, although, in any case, it would be in the buyer's interest to take out insurance to cover the risks from the place of delivery (origin) to the place of destination and, if it considers it appropriate, also for subsequent transports.
   b) The buyer controls most of the logistics chain.
   c) The seller shall bear the costs of export and import customs clearance, if required by the transaction.
   d) The seller is obliged to take out insurance to cover the transport risks borne by the buyer.

9. Regarding the Incoterms CIP rule:

   a) Neither party is obliged to take out transport insurance, although, in any case, it would be in the buyer's interest to take out insurance to cover the risks from the place of delivery (origin) to the place of destination and, if deemed appropriate, also for subsequent transports.
   b) The buyer must contract and pay for the transportation from the place of origin to the place specified in the Incoterms.
   c) The buyer has a high control over the logistic chain.

d) The seller is obliged to contract the costs of the Incoterms CPT rule and, in addition, an insurance covering the risks of the goods in relation to their transport (risks borne by the buyer since the delivery of the goods at the place of origin).

10. With regard to the insurance governed by the Incoterms CIP rule:

a) The sum insured must cover at least 100% of the purchase price and must be in the same currency as the contract of sale.
b) The minimum insurance cover must correspond to the coverage of the ICC "A" clause of the Institute of Insurers of London.
c) It is an indispensable condition that the seller can claim directly from the insurer.
d) With regard to the insured route, it must be exclusively the one corresponding to the domestic routes to be traveled in the buyer's country.

11. In accordance with the Incoterms DPU rule:

a) The seller is obliged to take out insurance to cover the risks of the goods in transit (which are borne by the buyer since the goods are delivered at the place of origin).
b) The seller must contract and pay for transportation to the place specified in the rule, but delivers the goods for the purpose of transferring the risk to the buyer when it places the goods at the disposal of the carrier it has contracted.
c) The seller must arrange and pay for the transportation, assuming the risk, until it delivers the goods, unloaded from the means of transportation of arrival, at the agreed place of destination.
d) The buyer controls the logistic chain and offers a high level of service.

12. In accordance with the Incoterms DPU rule:

a) The buyer controls the logistics chain and provides a high level of service.
b) Neither party is obliged to take out transport insurance, although in any case it would be in the seller's interest to take out insurance covering the risks up to the place of delivery (named place of destination), including unloading there.

c) For the purpose of risk transfer, the seller delivers to the buyer at its premises located at the origin of the transport.
d) It is usually very suitable to be combined with documentary credits (like all those in Group D).

13. With the Incoterms DAP rule:

a) The seller must pay all the costs and bear the risk of transport until the goods are placed on the transport vehicle at the place of destination at the time of their arrival (at which moment, usually at the buyer's warehouse, the risk is transferred to the buyer).
b) The seller must order and pay for the transport to the place specified in the rule but delivers the goods for the purpose of transferring the risk to the buyer when it places the goods at the disposal of the carrier company it has contracted.
c) The buyer controls the logistic chain and offers a high level of service.
d) The seller is obliged to take out transport insurance to cover the risks borne by the buyer.

14. In accordance with the Incoterms DAP rule:

a) The buyer controls the logistics chain and provides a high level of service.
b) The seller dispatches the export and import if the operation requires it.
c) Both the seller and the buyer are obliged to take out transport insurance to cover the risks that each of them bears.
d) The seller delivers when the goods are placed at the disposal of the buyer on the means of transport without unloading at the named place of destination.

15. In accordance with the Incoterms DDP rule:

a) The buyer clears the import.
b) It implies for the seller the same obligations and costs as DAP, but in addition it must manage and pay the import clearance and its taxes (customs and other).

c) The buyer controls the logistics chain and provides a high level of service.

d) The seller must contract and pay for the transport to the place specified in the rule, but delivers the goods, for the purpose of transferring the risk to the buyer, when the goods are made available to the carrier hired by it.

Choose the correct answer (or the incorrect answer, if specified) from the options presented in each of the following questions.

1. The Incoterms rules for maritime transport are:

   a) EXW, FCA, CPT, CIP, DAP, DPU, and DDP.
   b) FAS, FOB, CFR, and CIF.
   c) EXW, FOB, CFR, and CIF.
   d) FCA, FOB, CFR, and CIF.

2. One factor against the use of maritime Incoterms rules with containerized shipping is:

   a) The inertia of habitual use.
   b) It clarifies the allocation of costs between seller and buyer.
   c) The complexity of risk allocation in case of damage.
   d) Freight forwarders' quotations are usually offered in maritime terms.

3. A factor in favor of the use of maritime Incoterms rules in container shipping is:

   a) Greater control over the costs that the seller may end up incurring.
   b) Greater risk of failure to meet delivery date.
   c) Complexity of risk allocation in the event of a claim.
   d) Freight forwarders' quotations are usually offered in maritime terms.

4. With the Incoterms FAS rule:

   a) The seller must deliver the goods, cleared for export, alongside the vessel contracted by the buyer (on the quay under the crane that will load the goods) at the named port of shipment (in the seller's country) where they are delivered at the seller's risk and expense.

b) The seller must deliver the goods, cleared for export, on board the vessel contracted by the buyer at the named port of shipment (usually in the seller's country). At that time, delivery is made and the risk (of damage to the goods in transit) passes to the buyer.

c) The seller must deliver the goods cleared for export on board the vessel (same as FOB) and arrange and pay for their transportation to the named port of destination.

d) The seller must deliver the goods cleared for export on board the vessel (same as FOB) and contract for and pay the cost of transportation to the named port of destination (same as CFR), but must also take out transportation insurance to cover the risks borne by the buyer in the terms indicated in the Incoterms rule.

5. In accordance with the Incoterms FAS rule:

a) Seller shall clear the goods for export and import, if necessary.

b) Seller shall pay the cost of loading the goods on board the vessel at the port of shipment.

c) The seller pays the cost of ocean transportation between the port of shipment and the port of discharge.

d) This arrangement is rarely used, and when it is used, it is usually for bulk and non-containerized goods.

6. In accordance with the Incoterms FAS rule:

a) The buyer clears for export and import, if necessary.

b) If combined with freight forwarding it would be convenient to use LIFO or regular line as shipping terms (in both cases the freight paid to the shipping company already includes the loading operation at origin).

c) The seller must pay the cost of unloading the goods at the port of destination.

d) Both parties (seller and buyer) are obliged to take out transport insurance, each one to cover the transport risks borne by the other.

7. With the Incoterms FOB rule:

   a) The seller must deliver the goods, cleared for export, alongside the vessel chartered by the buyer (at the quay under the crane that will load the goods) at the named port of shipment (in the seller's country) where they are delivered at the seller's risk and expense.
   b) The seller must deliver the goods, cleared for export, on board the vessel chartered by the buyer at the named port of shipment (usually in the seller's country). At that time, delivery is made and the risk (of damage to the goods in transit) passes to the buyer.
   c) The seller must deliver the goods cleared for export on board the vessel (same as FOB) and arrange and pay for their transportation to the named port of destination.
   d) The seller must deliver the goods cleared for export on board the vessel (same as FOB) and contract for and pay the cost of transportation to the named port of destination (same as CFR) but must also take out transportation insurance to cover the risks borne by the buyer in the terms indicated in the Incoterms rule.

8. In accordance with the Incoterms FOB rule:

   a) Buyer shall clear the goods for export and import, if necessary.
   b) The Seller shall pay the costs of loading the goods on board the vessel at the port of shipment and delivery after loading.
   c) The Seller shall pay the cost of sea transport between the ports of shipment and discharge.
   d) The seller is obliged to take out insurance to cover the risks of sea transport borne by the buyer.

9. In accordance with the Incoterms FOB rule:

   a) The buyer pays for the loading of the goods on board the vessel at the port of shipment.
   b) The seller ships for export and the buyer ships for import.
   c) The seller pays for ocean transportation between ports.
   d) The seller receives a BL with prepaid transportation at the port of origin.

10. With the Incoterms CIF rule:

   a) The seller must deliver the goods, cleared for export, alongside the vessel chartered by the buyer (at the quay under the crane that will load the goods) at the named port of shipment (in the seller's country) where they are delivered at the seller's risk and expense.
   b) The seller must deliver the goods, cleared for export, on board the vessel chartered by the buyer at the named port of shipment (usually in the seller's country). At that time, delivery is made and the risk (of damage to the goods in transit) passes to the buyer.
   c) The seller must deliver the goods, cleared for export, on board the vessel (same as FOB) and arrange and pay for their transportation to the named port of destination.
   d) The seller must deliver the goods cleared for export on board the vessel (same as FOB) and arrange for and pay the cost of transportation to the named port of destination (same as CFR) but must also take out transportation insurance to cover the risks borne by the buyer in the terms indicated in the Incoterms.

11. In accordance with the Incoterms CFR rule:

   a) The buyer must arrange and pay for ocean transportation between ports.
   b) The seller pays the cost of ocean transportation but assumes the same risks as in the FOB rule, until the goods are on board the vessel at the port of shipment.
   c) The seller assumes the risks of transportation between the port of origin and the port of destination as he pays the ocean freight there.
   d) The seller is obliged to take out insurance to cover the risks of maritime transport borne by the buyer.

12. In accordance with the Incoterms CFR rule:

   a) The buyer is obliged to take out insurance to cover the risks of maritime transport.
   b) The seller will obtain a BL with collect at the port of origin.
   c) The seller assumes the risks of transportation until the goods are on board the vessel at the port of destination.
   d) The seller obtains a prepaid BL at the port of origin.

13. With the Incoterms CIF rule:

   a) The seller must deliver the goods, cleared for export, alongside the vessel chartered by the buyer (at the quay under the crane that will load the goods) at the named port of shipment (in the seller's country), where they are delivered at cost and risk.
   b) The seller must deliver the goods, cleared for export, on board the vessel chartered by the buyer at the named port of shipment (usually in the seller's country).
   c) The seller must deliver the goods cleared for export on board the vessel (same as FOB) and arrange for and pay the cost of their transportation to the named port of destination.
   d) The seller must deliver the goods cleared for export on board the vessel (same as FOB) and arrange for and pay the cost of transportation to the named port of destination (same as CFR) but must also take out transportation insurance to cover the risks borne by the buyer under the terms of the Incoterms.

14. In accordance with the Incoterms CIF rule:

   a) Neither party is required by this rule to take out transport insurance.
   b) The seller pays the cost of ocean freight (and insurance to cover the risks thereof, which are borne by the buyer) but assumes the same risks as under the FOB rule until the goods are on board the vessel at the port of shipment.
   c) The seller must take out an insurance policy with a sum insured of at least 100% of the purchase price and in the same currency as the contract of sale.
   d) The minimum insurance cover must be in accordance with the ICC "A" clause of the Institute of London Underwriters (LMA/IUA).

15. In accordance with the insurance regulated by the rule of Incoterms CIF:

   a) As regards the insured transport route, it must cover the risks of the goods during transport from the geographical point where delivery takes place (in the case of CIF, when the goods are delivered to the first carrier at the seller's warehouse) to at least the designated port of destination.

b) The sum of the insured value or sum insured must cover at least 120% of the purchase price and be contracted in the same currency as the purchase contract.
c) It is an indispensable condition of the insurance to be contracted that the Seller may make a direct claim against the insurer.
d) The minimum insurance coverage must correspond to the coverage of the ICC "C" clause of the Institute of London Underwriters (LMA/IUA).

Test 4
Related to chapters 6 and 7 of this manual:
• Criteria for choosing the optimal Incoterms rule
and applying it to the contract of sale
• Case studies

Choose the correct answer (or the incorrect answer, if specified) from the options presented in each of the following questions.

1. The use of an Incoterms rule appropriate to the means of transport and its operation would mean in accordance with the recommendations of the International Chamber of Commerce:

   a) Use CFR instead of FOB for containerized ocean shipments.
   b) Use FCA instead of FOB for containerized ocean shipments.
   c) Use CIF instead of FOB for containerized ocean shipments.
   d) Use FAS instead of FOB for containerized ocean shipments.

2. The use of an Incoterms rule appropriate to the means of transport and its operation would mean in accordance with the recommendations of the International Chamber of Commerce:

   a) Use of CFR with door-to-door road transportation.
   b) Use of FOB for door-to-door road transportation.
   c) No use of Incoterms for sea transport (FAS, FOB, CFR and CIF) with door-to-door road transport.
   d) Use of FAS for door-to-door road transportation.

3. To clarify which party (seller or buyer) bears the risk of loss in container transport, we should use the following Incoterms:

   a) FOB, CFR, CIF, DAP, and DDP.
   b) FAS, FOB, CFR, CIF, DAP, and DDP.

    c) FCA, FOB, CFR, CIF, DAP, and DDP.
    d) FCA, CPT, CIP, DAP, and DDP.

4. In the case of particularly complex transactions involving new markets, new customers, new logistics service providers, high-risk goods, complex destination customs, etc., it is advisable for the seller to propose the use of:

    a) A short Incoterms rule, such as FCA or FOB.
    b) Group D Incoterms rules to better control the logistics chain.
    c) The buyer's warehouse DAP rule.
    d) The buyer's warehouse DDP rule.

5. If we consider customs and international taxation when choosing the ideal Incoterms rule:

    a) The most logical criterion is that each party clears customs in its own country, so we could rule out both FCA and DDP.
    b) The most logical criterion is that each party clears customs in its own country, so we could rule out both EXW and DAP.
    c) The most logical criterion is that each party clears customs in its own country, so we could rule out both EXW and DDP.
    d) The most logical criterion is that the seller clears both export and import (to control the coordination of customs documentation), so the recommended rule is DDP.

6. Regarding the relationship between the Incoterms rules and the means of payment, we can point out that:

    a) To the extent that a documentary means of payment has been agreed and it requires certain documentation to be provided by the seller, such documentation should be that which evidences the seller's delivery and other obligations under the Incoterms rule.
    b) There is no relationship between the two.
    c) The Incoterms rules refer to the means of payment only when it is non-documentary, as in the case of advance payment.
    d) The Incoterms rules indicate in one of their ten obligations the means of payment to be used and the documentation to be presented in each case.

7. If the factor of minimizing the transportation risk is considered when choosing the ideal Incoterms rule, we can indicate that:

    a) A selling company will prefer to agree on DAP port of destination rather than CPT port of destination.
    b) A selling company will prefer to agree on DAP port of destination rather than CFR port of destination.
    c) A selling company will prefer to agree on DAP buyer's warehouse rather than CPT buyer's warehouse.
    d) A selling company will prefer to agree on CPT port of destination rather than DAP port of destination.

8. Taking into account the factor of greater control over the supply chain and higher service levels...

    a) A selling company will prefer to agree to the FCA warehouse of the seller rather than the DAP warehouse of the buyer.
    b) A selling company will prefer to agree to the buyer's DAP warehouse rather than the seller's FCA warehouse.
    c) A selling company will prefer to agree to FCA seller's warehouse rather than CIF port of destination.
    d) A selling company will prefer to agree to FCA seller's warehouse than to DAP destination terminal.

9. If the factor of choosing the Incoterms rule that minimizes the total cost is considered:

    a) If the seller could contract and pay the cost of the logistics chain at a lower price than the buyer, the ideal would be to agree on the seller's FCA warehouse as opposed to the buyer's DAP warehouse.
    b) In the event that the buyer can contract and pay the cost of the logistics chain at a lower price than the seller, the ideal would be to agree on the buyer's WTP warehouse, as opposed to the seller's WTP warehouse.
    c) In the event that the buyer can contract and pay the cost of the logistics chain at a lower price than the seller, the ideal would be to agree on the DAP port of destination, versus the FCA warehouse of the seller.

    d) In the event that the seller can contract and pay the cost of the logistics chain at a lower price than the buyer, the ideal would be to agree on DAP buyer's warehouse, versus FCA seller's warehouse.

10. If the selling company is much larger and more international than the buyer, we can say:

    a) DAP at the buyer's warehouse would be preferable to FCA at the seller's warehouse.
    b) FCA at the seller's warehouse would be preferable to DAP at the buyer's warehouse. C
    c) FOB port of shipment would be preferable to DAP buyer's warehouse.
    d) FCA at seller's warehouse would be preferable to DAP at port of destination.

11. The criterion for the choice of Incoterms refers to the greater bargaining power of the seller or the buyer:

    a) The greater or lesser difficulty of customs clearance for each operation.
    b) More or less control over the entire logistics chain.
    c) The minimization of the risk of transportation of the goods.
    d) That one of the parties (seller or buyer) can impose on the other the Incoterms rule to be used in the sale.

12. Completing the Incoterms rule to obtain a complete sales contract implies that:

    a) It does not make sense because the Incoterms rules govern all aspects of a sale and purchase.
    b) In addition to the Incoterms rule, it is necessary to specify exclusively the means of payment to be used.
    c) Considering that there are aspects that are not covered by the Incoterms, it is very important that the parties expressly agree on them and that they are reflected in the sales contract.
    d) In addition to the Incoterms, it is necessary to specify exclusively the law applicable to the contract and the competent jurisdiction for any disputes.

13. Not to use variants of the Incoterms rules implies that:

    a) These variants should not be used (examples: FOT, CPT unloaded, EXW loaded, etc.) as they are not regulated and create legal uncertainty as to the obligations of the parties.
    b) The Incoterms rule should always be specified with the place where the seller's warehouse is located.
    c) The Incoterms rule should always refer to the 2000 version.
    d) The parties may not specify more aspects of the sales contract than those regulated by the Incoterms.

14. The correct wording of the Incoterms rule implies that:

    a) It must be written in English.
    b) The Incoterms rule must always be indicated with the place where the seller's warehouse is located.
    c) The letters of the rule must be indicated first, followed by the geographical location as accurately as possible, and finally the version of the rule. For example, «FOB Terminal de Servicios Portuarios Patagonia Norte, Puerto San Antonio Este, Argentina. Incoterms 2020".
    d) The geographical location should be indicated as accurately as possible, followed by the letters of the Incoterms rule and then the version of the rule. For example, «Terminal de Servicios Portuarios Patagonia Norte, Puerto San Antonio Este, Argentina. FOB. Incoterms 2010".

15. Coordinating sales and transport contracts implies that:

    a) This coordination is not necessary because the Incoterms rule applies to both the sales contract and the transportation contract.
    b) The Incoterms rule applies to the transportation contract, but not to the sale and purchase contract.
    c) The sale and purchase price is the same as the price payable under the transportation contract.
    d) It is convenient to inform the carrier of the agreed Incoterms rule and check whether the costs and obligations of the transportation contract are in accordance with it.

Test solutions

The solutions are presented below.

Test 1:

1d	2d	3b	4a	5c
6c	7b	8a	9d	10b
11c	12b	13d	14c	15c.

Test 2:

1b	2d	3a	4b	5d
6a	7b	8a	9d	10b
11c	12b	13a	14d	15b.

Test 3:

1b	2c	3d	4a	5d
6b	7b	8b	9b	10c
11b	12d	13d	14b	15d.

Test 4:

1b	2c	3d	4a	5c
6a	7d	8b	9d	10a
11d	12c	13a	14c	15d.

Web resources

Self-assessment test

Improve your knowledge of the Incoterms 2020 rules.

Learn how to apply them correctly from any device or browser.

Go to **www.margebooks.com** and take the self-assessment tests.

**Lean Manufacturing.
Step by step**

Luis Socconini

**Lean Six Sigma.
Management System
for Leaders**

Luis Socconini, Carlo Reato

**Practical guide to the
Incoterms 2020 rules**

David Soler

**Sales and operations
planning.
S&OP in 14 steps**

Cristina Peña Andrés

**5S Practical guide to improve
quality and productivity**

Marco Barrantes, Luis Socconini

**Shipping & Commercial Case
Law**

Albert Badia

Tel. +34-931 429 486 – marge@margebooks.com – www.margebooks.com